CW01645221

# Radical Figures

# Painting in the New Millennium

Michael A
Cecily Brown
Nicole Eisenman
Sanya Kantarovsky
Tala Madani
Ryan Mosley
Christina Quarles
Daniel Richter
Dana Schutz
Tschabalala Self

Gavin Smart

## **Wonders and Anxieties** Iwona Blazwick

'I'm like a developer building twelve-storey high-rise condos on the ruins of art history.'
Nicole Eisenman

A sequence of *mises-en-scène* unfolds – unruly bodies roil in sexual congress, gigantic heads split apart to reveal multi-dimensional universes, acts of violence unleash spirals of colour and trees metamorphose into spirits. These hallucinogenic images, by turns sensual and disturbing, characterise a generation of painters who span the late twentieth and early twenty-first centuries. They look back to modern art history and outwards across social and political landscapes to devise highly subjective visual vocabularies in which to express the zeitgeist.

Over the last century figurative painting has proved remarkably resilient in withstanding all that could relegate it to oblivion: the ascent of the camera; Modernism's drive to abstraction and fragmentation; the use of the artist's body itself as subject and object; and the queasy embrace of reactionary ideologues and of the market. But it has not been impervious. Having absorbed or countered these ruptures within its aesthetic register, figurative painting today also carries the aftershock of two seismic moments in its modern trajectory.

In 1905 Ernst Ludwig Kirchner and Karl Schmidt-Rottluff, members of a new Expressionist movement, Die Brücke, proclaimed it as 'a product of surging fermentation, a cry for freedom from boundaries'.[1] Meanwhile, in their 1912 *Almanac of the Blue Rider*, artists Wassily Kandinsky and Franz Marc announced: 'We are standing at the threshold of … the epoch of Great Spirituality. In the nineteenth century … when … the "great victory" of the material seemed most intense, the first "new" elements of a spiritual atmosphere were formed'.[2]

Like the artists featured in *Radical Figures*, these young European painters stood at the beginning of a century. Reacting to an era shaped by industrialisation, materialism and the spoils of empire, and inspired by the legacy of the Fauves and by African and Pacific sculpture expropriated for Western museums, the German Expressionists lifted 'the veil of appearance' to depict an inner world that was both atavistic and spiritual.[3] Their fluid renditions of the figure pulsate with sinuous line and – released from the job of tonal modelling – vivid colour. Bodies appear synthesised with rural and urban environments, utterly immersed in their cultural and social present. These young artists also sought political and existential freedom. Their rejection of mimesis and perspective, their dense compositions and unbounded sensuality were a provocation that ultimately led to the show trial of the Nazis' *Degenerate Art* exhibition in 1937. These and other pioneers of Expressionism such as James Ensor, Gustav Klimt, Edvard Munch or Egon Schiele prefigure a generation of painters who have emerged around the turn of the twenty-first century.

The second episode in recent art history that reverberates through twenty-first-century figurative painting erupted in the 1980s after a decade of Conceptual and Minimalist art. The new spirit in painting reclaimed the possibilities of figuration in pursuit of narrative and allegory. In Europe, the return to figuration signalled disillusionment with the modernist avant-gardes and with revolutionary ideologies that had distilled into totalitarianism. In the United States, New Image Painting artists turned to irony and appropriation to comment on a culture shaped by neoliberal economics and the mass media. The so-called Neo-Expressionism found local definition in Germany as Neue Wilden, and in Italy as the Transavanguardia. The self-reflexive incorporation of historic movements modified by terms such as 'trans' and 'neo', as well as the wider term 'Postmodernism', acknowledged the impossibility of originality without precedent. The paintings of artists such as Georg Baselitz, Jörg Immendorff and Anselm Kiefer in Germany; Sandro Chia, Francesco Clemente and Mimmo Paladino in Italy; and David Salle and Julian Schnabel in America put art-historical referents into play with contemporary imagery to create allegorical scenarios.

Executed on an epic scale, these modern history paintings might draw from antiquity or folklore, cite philosophical and literary references while also embracing pop culture, as they reflect on the evolution of Western capitalist culture. The surface of the canvas itself becomes a carrier for material fragments that have ranged from dead flowers and metal, to velvet and broken crockery. The human figure may appear upside down or trapped between other images. The twentieth century, with all its disgraces and confusions, crowds onto the canvas.

*Radical Figures* brings together a group of artists whose work owes a debt to both the ecstatic forms of the early twentieth-century Expressionists and the knowing Postmodernism of a 1980s generation. They also recall, as precedent or inspiration, artists including George Condo, Peter Doig, Marlene Dumas, Philip Guston, Jacob Lawrence, Marisa Merz, Frida Kahlo, Maria Lassnig, Chris Ofili, Faith Ringgold and Dorothea Tanning.

What unites the work of the twenty-first-century expressionists assembled in this book and the exhibition it accompanies? They do not share an ideological or aesthetic programme, or even a locality. But they do share a political commitment to representing diversity in race and sexuality at a time when identity itself is becoming increasingly fluid, and lost or repressed histories are being excavated and reclaimed. There is also a dark undercurrent to this work that reminds us of the volatility and fragility of our hard-won liberties – of a world in which entire populations are being displaced by conflict and climate change, while we all inch nearer to environmental disaster.

The painters celebrated here – Michael Armitage, Cecily Brown, Nicole Eisenman, Sanya Kantarovsky, Tala Madani, Ryan Mosley, Christina Quarles, Daniel Richter, Dana Schutz and Tschabalala Self – are distinct from peers such as Lynette Yiadom-Boakye, Njideka Akunyili Crosby, Chantal Joffe or Amy Sherald, who have also dramatically revived figurative painting today. These artists have done so by co-opting the genre of portraiture – traditionally dedicated to immortalising the elites – to make visible those who are socially invisible.

Distinct from the portraitists, the artists here devise complex tableaux animated by multiple protagonists, within a foreshortened picture frame. A strong graphic style delineates dynamic bodies that are at once singular yet entwined in erotic, dialogic or violent encounters. They deploy brilliant, even fluorescent, colours that may serve to describe but can also spin off to evoke a cosmos of non-human phenomena. Political leitmotifs thread through all their paintings. Some make visible an identity, a way of being that, because of sexuality, race or class, has been absent or distorted within canonical representation. Others place historical events and current affairs on the same stage, insisting on the influence of the past – for example, of colonialism or patriarchy – in the present. A geopolitical panorama, filtered first through the media, and secondly through the subjective unconscious of the artist, generates images that flit through these canvases like ghosts. These beguiling pictures waver between the wonders of an exhilarating dream and the anxieties of nightmare, each revealing truths newly told.

**1** Friedrich Köhler-Haussen (c. 1908), quoted in Andreas Gabelmann, ed.; Claire Albiez, trans., *Ernst Ludwig Kirchner: ein Künstlerleben in Selbstzeugnissen* (Ostfildern, Germany, Hatje Cantz Verlag, 2010), p. 28.
**2** Wassily Kandinsky and Franz Marc, 'Preface' in *The Blaue Reiter Almanac* (1911) (London: Tate, 2006), p. 7.
**3** Franz Marc, 'Die neue Malerei' [The New Painting], *Pan*, 2, no. 16, 7 March 1912, p. 468.

# **Radical Figures: Painting in the New Millennium** Lydia Yee

Painting had its last hurrah in the 1980s, when the stock market boom fuelled the brash brushwork and swagger of Neo-Expressionism. A group of loosely aligned artists, primarily working in Germany, Italy and the United States, helped revive the fortunes of Expressionist painting with large canvases that featured figurative subject matter, seemingly spontaneous brush marks, bold colours and heavily textured surfaces.[1] Attracting attention for both their self-conscious painterly transgressions and their virile posturing, they exhibited together in prominent international exhibitions, including *A New Spirit in Painting* (1981) at the Royal Academy in London, *Zeitgeist* (1982) at Martin Gropius Bau in Berlin, and *Documenta 7* (1982) in Kassel, Germany. Their success, in turn, helped power the rapid expansion of the art market.

Leading critics were, however, quick to pronounce the death of painting in a spate of articles that appeared in leading art magazines and journals. The Neo-Expressionist revival of painting was declared to be morally bankrupt because it attempted to reinstate an outmoded notion of authorship that laid claim to the authenticity of the gesture; because it represented a conservative recuperation of style and art as commodity, and because it failed to sufficiently engage with representation as constructed or mediated.[2] Much of this criticism, which pitted photography against painting, was mounted by critics whose allegiance was to the Pictures generation artists, including Barbara Kruger, Sherrie Levine, Jack Goldstein, Robert Longo, Richard Prince, Cindy Sherman, using appropriation strategies rooted in film and photography to critique the ideology behind mass-media imagery.

*Radical Figures* highlights the renewed interest in expressive and experimental modes of figurative painting during the past two decades, particularly its aesthetic and social dimensions. A new generation of artists have been grappling with how to engage with issues around representation, identity politics and pressing social concerns at a time of unprecedented change in our relationship to information, technology and the environment. They echo the words of Philip Guston, who declared in an interview fifty years ago: 'I got sick and tired of all that Purity. I wanted to tell stories.' But why are they turning away from pixels and towards pigment to tell the stories of the twenty-first century? Perhaps it has to do with the ubiquity of the photograph (by some estimates more than 1.8 billion images are uploaded every day) and the speed at which we view them. The strength of painting lies in its slowness, in both its execution and its viewing. Its surface is heterogeneous, its subjects ambiguous; it is meant to be read; we cannot take it in all at once.

A protégé of the Jungen Wilden painters Werner Büttner and Albert Oehlen, Daniel Richter studied with the former at the University of the Fine Arts in Hamburg and worked for the latter as a studio assistant. Like other painters of his generation who followed in the Neo-Expressionist wake, Richter had a fraught relationship with representational painting. His early works from the 1990s are abstract exercises in mark making, a dense, psychedelic accumulation of brushstrokes, lines, patterns, doodles and self-conscious drips, deriving from graffiti, decals, illustration and even figurative elements. These canvases are as indebted to Richter's work as a graphic designer as they are to Oehlen's 'post-non-objective' paintings.[3] Richter's hallucinatory lines

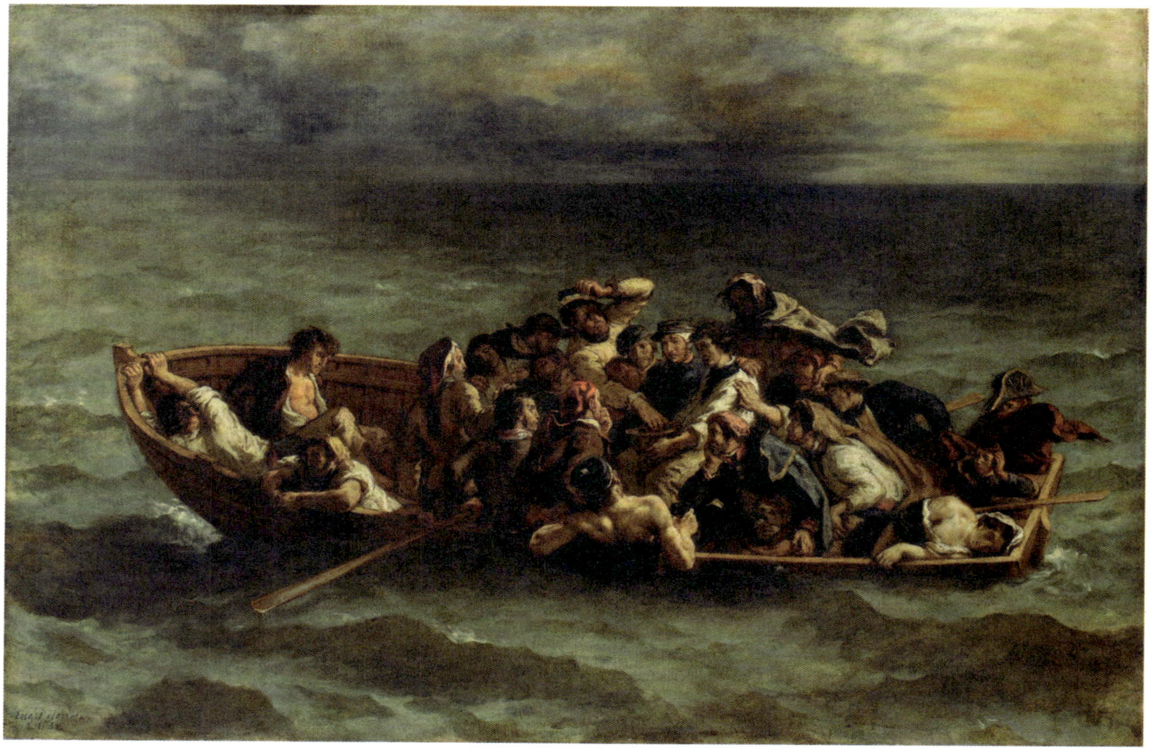

Eugène Delacroix, *The Shipwreck of Don Juan*, 1840, oil on canvas, 135 × 196 cm

reappear later in paintings such as *"HEY JOE"* (2011) [pl. 31], where they outline the topography of the mountains. They suggest latent seismic activity as well as the instability of masculinity, as represented by the two 'heroic' loners – a Taliban fighter and the Marlboro man – having a smoke together. The painting evokes the Romantic landscape tradition, particularly that of Caspar David Friedrich, whose figures are seen from behind, contemplating the sublime of awe-inspiring landscapes. The work is titled after the Jimi Hendrix song in which one man confesses his homicidal intentions to another.

Richter oscillates between the poles of abstraction and figuration. In the early 2000s, he began a series of paintings based on current events. *Tarifa* (2001) [pl. 29], for example, is inspired by a photograph from a news story in summer 2000 about African migrants trying to reach the southernmost tip of Spain in a small boat. *Tarifa* can be understood as a contemporary history painting – evoking the long lineage of shipwrecks and other maritime disasters in European art, from Turner's *The Shipwreck* (1805), to Géricault's *The Raft of the Medusa* (1818–19) and Delacroix's *The Shipwreck of Don Juan* (1840) – but one that also deals with painting's relationship to photography. Upon first seeing a daguerreotype in 1839, the French history painter Paul Delaroche proclaimed: 'From today, painting is dead!' Although Richter's source was a photograph taken in daylight, he reimagines the scene of an orange raft, straining under the weight of its occupants, as if it were captured at night by an infrared or thermal-imaging camera. What look like abstract patterns on the figures and their clothing can also be read as heat maps of bodies. Although the painting is large in scale, its vertical format is unusual for a history painting or a seascape. Moreover, Richter eschews a classical composition by cropping off the raft at the left edge of the painting, thereby emphasising its photographic origins. But *Tarifa* also includes abstract passages, most notably the blue and white squiggles and speckles against an inky expanse, to convey the choppy motion of the sea.

Seascapes, shipwrecks and beach scenes are ostensibly the subjects of a recent body of work by Cecily Brown. The London-born artist, who has lived in New York since 1994, brings together references to nineteenth-century maritime painting with the gestural abstraction of the New York School. 'It is absurd to paint a figure', Brown says, 'when everything has already been done, but I still want a presence and am not that interested by abstract painting.'[4] In her paintings, tension is an important pictorial device, between abstraction and figuration, between matter and motion, between art-historical references and pornographic sources. The rollicking surfaces of Brown's canvases congeal into figures before dissolving back into water, atmosphere and ultimately painterly marks. Oil paint is an apt medium to mimic the movement of water and the way in which light plays off its surface and reflects the colours above and below.[5] By layering paint, Brown is able to build up a complex surface of colour, luminosity, movement and texture.

The title of Brown's painting *Oinops* (2016–17) [pl. 6] refers to the ancient Greek for 'wine-faced' or 'wine-like', which is used by Homer to describe the sea in both *The Iliad and The Odyssey*. Here, 'oinops' could refer to the dark colour of the sea or suggest the precariousness of the boat. Broad strokes of blue and black around the edge of the canvas surround a vortex of activity at the centre – slashes of pink, red and white with patches of black, brown and grey. It is difficult to discern human figures from the boat and the water: the one emerges from and merges with the others. *The Last Shipwreck* (2018) [pl. 8] is even more unstable: bodies, boat and water blend together and are overlaid with the ominous outlines of birds, waiting to pick the flesh off the bones of the disaster victims. The scene is a mash-up of Brown's Shipwreck drawings (2017) after paintings by Delacroix and Géricault and her Bestiary drawings (2012) based on a nineteenth-century illustrated compendium of beasts. Turning to art history was a way for Brown to address the difficult subject of the sea and the beach as highly contested sites today, where issues of national identity, ethnicity, gender and religious beliefs intersect.[6]

The push and pull of paint and of bodies on canvas have been at the heart of Brown's work. She recalls that she wanted 'the paint to embody the same sensations that bodies would. Oil paint very easily suggests bodily fluids and flesh.'[7] Her words recall those of the Dutch American painter Willem de Kooning who famously said: 'Flesh is the reason oil paint was invented.'

The work of the Kenyan-born painter Michael Armitage reflects on attitudes towards sexuality and gender in East Africa in paintings such as *Mangroves Dip* (2015) [pl. 4] and *Kampala Suburb* (2014) [pl. 2] In the latter, he depicts two men kissing in a domestic setting, an intimate act of resistance to the Ugandan Anti-Homosexuality Act of 2014. The death penalty was initially prescribed for 'the offence of homosexuality', before the punishment was amended to life imprisonment. Armitage paints on his signature lubugo bark cloth from Uganda, which is traditionally used to make burial cloths and garments for ceremonial use. These canvases are assembled from multiple pieces of the bark cloth, and Armitage must apply layers of paint in small strokes because of the roughly textured surface. Seams and stitches show through the paint like scars on the skin, and it is fitting that Armitage paints bodies on this cloth, which is used to wrap real bodies.

A nude based on Velázquez's *The Toilet of Venus* (1647–51), also known as the Rokeby Venus, reclines in a lush and colourful landscape in *#mydressmychoice* (2015) [pl. 3]. Aligned along the top edge of the painting and facing the brown-skinned female figure is a group of men, represented only by dark trousers and shoes. While the style of the painting is classical, the title is taken from a social-media hashtag. It refers to a video that circulated online in 2014 of a female food trader in Nairobi who was stripped and assaulted by several men because she was wearing a miniskirt. #MyDressMyChoice was started by a coalition of mothers to protest this incident and support the rights of women to dress as they wish. While the subject matter and canvas are closely associated with East Africa, where Armitage was raised, the style and palette resembles that of Gauguin's Tahitian paintings. Armitage deliberately takes on the French Post-Impressionist painter's exoticising gaze, problematising this position and, at the same time, examining his own culture with other eyes. 'I've never had the weight of feeling like western art history is my own,' Armitage reveals. 'I always feel like I'm looking in.'[8]

Tala Madani moved with her mother from Tehran to the small town of Monmouth, Oregon, as a teenager and started drawing by default. The public library was a refuge, but she found reading English challenging, so she began to copy images from art books, comics and other sources. Since graduating from the Yale University School of Art in 2006, Madani has been painting darkly humorous, cartoon-like scenes populated almost exclusively by stout, middle-aged men with stereotypically Middle Eastern features, who pray, bond, and take part in bizarre, often humiliating, self-destructive or sexualised rituals. Madani recalls observing groups of men when she accompanied her uncle on errands during her childhood in Tehran and later seeing Turkish men in tea houses in Berlin, and wondering what they did together in the café, gymnasium or mosque, spaces that were not accessible to women. *Light Balance* (2012) [pl. 20], for example, appears to depict some sort of inexplicable acrobatics in which each man, dressed only in underwear, stands or sits on the shoulders of another man, and those on the left shine a torch on the face or crotch of the ones on the right. Madani's men oscillate between those who are apparently pure, as in *Sitting in White* (2008) [pl. 18], and those covered in or playing with blood, excrement or semen, who seem to be impure or dirty. These works satirise masculinity as infantile, but the artist also views this childish lack of inhibition as creative and liberating. Working quickly on modestly scaled canvases, Madani tries to paint at the speed at which she thinks, seeing painting as a record of her thinking process.

In a recent series, *Shit Moms*, Madani reflects on her own predicament as an artist and a mother. A trio of pink babies play with an abject female figure formed from a pile of brown matter in *Shit Mom (Deluxe)* (2019) [pl. 21]. Not only does the artist feel like a shit mom for dedicating too much time to her studio, but she has produced 'shit' paintings when the colours have mixed and turned into a sludgy brown mass. 'Humour and satire are certainly effective forms of approaching difficult subjects', she explains. 'I'm also very interested in the physical sense of release that humour can give us.'[9]

Humour is also key to the work of Sanya Kantarovsky, albeit a darker, wry wit. 'Humour is central to my work', he says. 'Art has never been about morality or about the pure and clean and correct. It's always been about the grime and pain and totally unfair contradictions of being alive – and humour, very much so, is a kind of pressure valve.'[10] Born in Moscow, Kantarovsky emigrated to Rhode Island with his family at the age of ten. Drawing on a wide range of influences, including Russian literature, folktales, illustrations, comics and children's books, as well as modern art, he paints figures in ambiguous relationships. *Feeder* (2016) [pl. 13], for example, features two characters rendered in quick, loosely defined washes of oil and pastel, one in a ruffled collar and large hat reminiscent of Pierrot, who administers a mysterious green liquid, possibly medicine or poison, to a smaller, sickly pet-like figure. A stock character from the *commedia dell'arte* tradition, Pierrot, the sad clown, became an alter ego for the alienated artist in the late nineteenth and early twentieth century and is the subject of works by Picasso, Ensor, Beckmann and Chagall, artists who have been an influence on Kantarovsky. After graduating from the Rhode Island School of Design, he worked briefly as an illustrator before attending the MFA program at UCLA. While illustration needs to communicate quickly, Kantarovsky explains: 'A painting is the opposite: it's an open-ended proposition which unravels in the moment that it's regarded in the flesh and continues working for as long as it's looked at.'[11]

Kantarovsky's recent work relates to the existential and emotional dilemmas of parenthood. *Letdown* (2017) [pl. 14] depicts a strong bond between the mother and the child she carries on her back, but this is not a conventional painting representing maternal tenderness. The mother is hunched and blue with scraped knees and elbows, struggling to bear the weight of her child as she trudges through a lugubrious landscape. The title has a double meaning, referring both to the release of breast milk, a source of nourishment placed at the centre of the canvas, and to disappointment, which is in keeping with the dismal scene.

The Sheffield-based painter Ryan Mosley trades on the ambiguity of images rather than language. His work often makes use of the theatre stage, in which the perspectival space between audience, performers and background are flattened, a formal device he learned from the pre-Renaissance paintings that he observed in the National Gallery, where he worked as a guard. In *Cave Inn* (2011) [pl. 23], the audience watches a couple dancing in lock step across a stage. Mosley creates an optical illusion, with the negative space reading as a skull, delineated by the dark silhouettes of parasols, botanical elements and bearded figures. Similarly, *Wearing Another's Head on Your Jacket* (2014) [pl. 25] is a double portrait: a figure seen in profile wears a coat that is decorated with another face. Mosley wants his paintings to 'embody their own contradictions and do something very interesting with both fact and imagination'.[12]

Another painting that relates to Mosley's ongoing interest in the world of theatre is *Duchess of Oils* (2014) [pl. 24] which grew out of an idea of painting an actor who simultaneously manifests all the roles he or she has ever performed. The sexually ambiguous figure of the duchess has grown several additional faces, with different eyes, noses, lips and facial hair.

Dana Schutz gives visual form to hypothetical or even impossible scenarios. For a series of early paintings, she began by imagining a body eating itself. Goya's *Saturn* (1820–23) [p. 137], in which the god devours his own son, offered one art-historical precedent. Rendered with similarly broad brushstrokes and thick impasto, her *Man Eating His Chest* (2005) [pl. 34] presents a figure gorging himself on his own torso, creating a gaping hole and revealing the sea behind him. Painting begets painting. For Schutz, these self-eaters relate to the creative process of digesting influence and experience to produce something new. This work can also be seen as a way of contending with the self-referential formalism of American post-war painting, as articulated by the critic Clement Greenberg, who championed the essential flatness of the picture plane as a surface for colour and disavowed any reference to the world beyond.[13] Schutz humorously sends up this logic by creating self-generating artworks. In *New Legs* (2003) [pl. 33], an androgynous artist sculpts two forms, which the painting's title reveals are a new pair of legs, or perhaps the artist has sacrificed her legs to the act of creation. She literally uses paint squeezed from the tube and daubed onto the canvas to sculpt her figures. 'I thought they could be abstract paintings', she muses, 'because they were so self-involved, very structural.'[14]

In a more recent work by Schutz, *Suspicious Minds* (2019) [pl. 36], abstraction meets grotesque figuration. The strong vertical and horizontal stripes of the sun umbrella and the bathers' costumes evoke the abstractions of Bridget Riley and Daniel Buren, while the monstrous, anthropomorphic bird-like creatures bring to mind works by Bosch, Picasso, Ernst and Beckmann. Where does the suspicion, distrust or paranoia reside? In the painting, the artist or the viewer?

The artist's daily life and creative process are recurring themes in the work of New York-based artist Nicole Eisenman. In *Brooklyn Biergarten II* (2008) [pl. 11], she captures the social scene of artists and creative types in T-shirts and trucker caps, as well as a few men in suits, smoking and drowning their sorrows in pints of beer, while in the background the figure of Death looks on. Made at the time of the recent financial crisis, it recalls the *fin de siècle* paintings of Ensor and Munch. The beer garden is, for Eisenman, 'where we go to socialize, to commiserate about how the world is a fucked-up place and about our culture's obsession with happiness'.[15] *Sleeper* (2016) [pl. 12] is a more serene painting, a heavily impastoed work focusing on the head of the figure in repose. For artists from Picasso to Guston, sleeping and dreaming are important activities that fuel the imagination and creativity.

Eisenman's enormous diptych *Progress: Real and Imagined* (2006) [pls. 9–10] is an allegory of the creative act. In the left panel, the artist is at work in a confined studio – filled with paint and other artistic supplies, reference material, work in progress, an uneaten sandwich and a broken light bulb – aboard a houseboat. She is at sea, trying to maintain focus as drawings and pieces of paper swirl around her in a maelstrom, and the crew struggle to maintain an even keel in the rough waters. The right panel features a cycle of life and creativity in a society dominated by women, who hunt, bathe, give birth and produce art. A severed head and leg are the only evidence of a male presence. Responding to a question about the hyper-masculine Neo-Expressionist painting of the 1980s, Eisemnan declared: 'To me, it's radical, and it felt radical when I saw it for the first time ... My feeling about painting and gender is that whatever any dude feels entitled to, I feel like: "Fuck I'm entitled to that too."'[16]

Christina Quarles also aims to embody the painterly gesture and to broaden the lineage of a style long associated with canonical Eurocentric male painters. Using fluid brushwork, she works in acrylic on canvases that are scaled to her body. Her polymorphous subjects are equally fluid in terms of gender and sexuality; their sinuous and fragmented bodies drip, embrace, intertwine, and merge with other bodies. As a queer artist of colour Quarles writes, 'I hope to make work that is more about what it is like to live in a body looking out at the world, rather than the experience of looking onto a body ... [R]ather than making paintings of what a racially multiple body looks like, I hope to make paintings that explore what living in a racially multiple body feels like.'[17] Her words

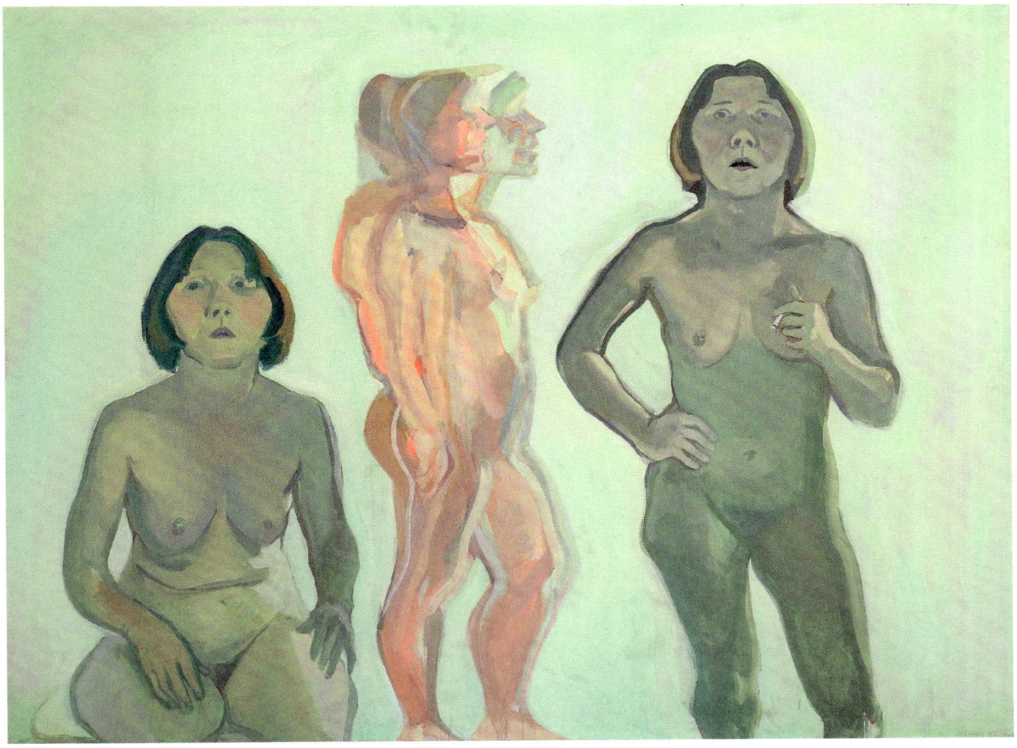

Maria Lassnig, *Dreifaches Selbstporträt / New Self* [Triple self-portrait / New Self], 1972, oil on canvas, 173 × 230 cm

resonate with Maria Lassnig's notion of body awareness painting: 'When, in my painting, I became tired of analytically depicting nature, I searched for a reality that was more fully in my possession than the exterior world, and I found it waiting for me in the body house in which I dwell, the most real and clearest reality.'[18]

Quarles draws from life, not to make preparatory drawings for her paintings, but rather to physically prepare to work on canvas. Like a dancer who rehearses movement, she develops a muscle memory of what it is like to draw a body. In order to replicate the sensation and texture of hair, she runs a comb through wet paint. Having worked as a graphic designer, Quarles also uses digital tools to work on her compositions, importing images of work in progress into Adobe Illustrator to further develop the composition and making digital patterns that she outputs as vinyl stencils. Such stencils are used to create the looping green hedge in *Casually Cruel* (2018) [pl. 26] and the red and white checked table cloth in *Sun Bleached* (2018) [pl. 27].

Tschabalala Self's paintings are heterogeneous in their materiality, and paint is one element among others, including fabric, printed and collage elements. Her process is a mix of painting, sewing and quilting techniques, in which she constructs the figure from various piece of fabric and sews these to canvas with colourfully painted or printed backgrounds. While stitching is also used to hold the fabric in place, and also to create lines, paint may be employed to give further definition to the face of her figures. Self's vignettes are inspired by her Harlem neighbourhood, where she was raised and where she continues to live. Named after Self's sister, *Koco at the Bodega* (2017) [pl.37] is from a series of works exploring the local corner store as a neighbourhood gathering place for commercial and social exchange.

Taking an inventive approach to working with materials and what they signify, Self uses a hand-printed brick pattern across multiple works. It forms the torso and legs of the female figure in *Lenox* (2017) [pl.38], evoking The Commodore's song 'Brick House', which describes a curvaceous woman's body. The same pattern reappears in *Fade* (2019) [pl.40] as vertical stripes on a sleeveless T-shirt and again as a brick facade in in *NYPD* (2019) [pl.39]. Recently, Self has been combining wall-painting and sculptural elements alongside her canvases, building on the two-dimensional assemblage and taking it into three-dimensional space.

As a seemingly outmoded medium in a digital era, painting finds itself at a complex juncture in the twenty-first century, particularly when it comes to representing bodies. The slow, laborious process of painting the figure is at odds with our instantaneous culture of taking, editing and sharing images. Rather than the illusion of perfection perpetuated by social media, many painters today expand and destabilise fixed motions of identity by fragmenting, exaggerating and morphing the figure. Painting, unlike the seamless surface of the photograph, is highly subjective, an accretion of tactile layers of pigment, form and reference, creating bodies and narratives that are open to ambiguity, impurity and, ultimately, to invention. And if we look carefully at its construction, its facture is apparent.

**1** In Germany, Georg Baselitz, Jörg Immendorf, Anselm Kiefer and Markus Lüpertz were among those associated with the Junge Wilden or Neue Wilden (Young Wild Ones or New Fauves); in Italy, Francesco Clemente, Enzo Cucchi and Sandro Chia were part of the Transavanguardia, and in the United States, Jean-Michel Basquiat and Julian Schnabel were part of the Neo-Expressionist circles.
**2** See Benjamin Buchloh, 'Figures of Authority, Cuphers of Regression', *October* (Spring 1981); Douglas Crimp, 'The End of Painting'; *October* (Spring 1981) Thomas Lawson, 'Last Exit: Painting', *Artforum* (October 1981); Hal Foster, 'The Expressive Fallacy', *Art in America* (January 1983).
**3** Prior to attending art school, Richter worked as a designer on graphics for flyers, posters and record covers for punk bands.
**4** 'Cecily Brown', Alain Elkann Interviews, 24 February 2019, www.alainelkanninterviews.com/cecily-brown/ (accessed December 2019).
**5** When oil paint is exposed to oxygen, it slowly hardens through a polymerisation reaction, forming a glossy semi-transparent plastic film. See Mark Miodownik, *Liquid: The Delightful and Dangerous Substances That Flow Through Our Lives* (London: Penguin, 2019), pp. 91–92.
**6** Brown's painting *Where, When, How Often and with Whom* (2017) is based, in part, on photographs of French police confronting a woman wearing a burkini on a beach in Nice in 2016. See Lærke Rydal Jørgensen and Anders Kold, eds., *Cecily Brown: Where, When, How Often and with Whom* (Humlebæk, Louisiana Museum of Modern Art, 2018).
**7** Brown, quoted in Gaby Wood, 'I Like it Cheap and Nasty', *The Guardian*, 12 June 2005, www.theguardian.com/artanddesign/2005/jun/12/art1 (accessed December 2019).
**8** Armitage, quoted in Laura Allsop, 'The Disturbing Dreams of Michael Armitage', *Apollo*, 2 June 2017, www.apollo-magazine.com/i-alwa feel-like-im-looking-in-michael-armitage/ (accessed December 2019).
**9** Madani, quoted in, 'Tala Madani: Exhibition Notes', Nottingham Contemporary, Nottingham 2014, reproduced at www.nottinghamcontemporary.org/sites/default/files/MadaniExhibitionNotes.pdf (accessed December 2019).
**10** Kantarovsky, quoted in Dodie Kazanjian, 'The Darkly Comic Art of Sanya Kantarovsky', *Vogue*, 15 May 2019. www.vogue.com/article sanya-kantarovsky-luhring-augusti (accessed December 2019).
**11** Ibid. pp. 88–90.
**12** Mosley, quoted in Jennifer Higgie, 'Carnival Theory', *Frieze*, 19 March 2015, https://frieze.com/article/carnival-theory (accessed December 2019).
**13** See Clement Greenberg, '"American-Type" Painting' (1955), in John O'Brian and Clement Greenberg, eds., *Collected Essays and Criticism* (Chicago, University of Chicago Press, 1993).
**14** Schutz in 'Dana Schutz by Mel Chin', *Bomb*, 1 April 2006. https://bombmagazine.org/articles/dana-schutz/ (accessed December 2019
**15** Nicole Eisenman interview with Brian Sholis, artforum.com, 6 September 2008, www.artforum.com/interviews/nicole-eisenman-discusses-her-new-exhibition-in-berlin-21064 (accessed December 2019).
**16** Eisenman, quoted in Barry Schwabsky, 'Nicole Eisenman's Pat to Genius,' *The Nation*, 14 July 201 (accessed December 2019).
**17** Quarles, quoted in 'Christina Quarles: Casually Cruel', Tate website: www.tate.org.uk/art/artworks/quarles-casually-cruel-t15219 (accessed December 2019).
**18** Lassnig, quoted in 'Maria Lassnig: Ways of Being', Stedelijk website: www.stedelijk.nl/en/news/maria-lassnig-2 (accessed December 2019).

# What Does It Mean to Inhabit a Body in the Twenty-first Century? Daniel Culpan

As we cede ever more physical space to the digital, the distinction between the 'real world' and online is becoming increasingly blurred. When moving ceaselessly between forms – web chat, dating apps, 'IRL' interaction – consciousness itself is smeared like ectoplasm across various platforms, while our physicality is increasingly transferred onto the glowing pixels of multiple screens. Our every move seems haunted by a kind of ephemerality, as we leave post-humous footprints on cached browsers; shadows in the afterglow of a closed tab.

We live uneasily with these doubles of ourselves, both flesh and not. Our restless attention is marked by a free-floating anxiety that something better – and perhaps more 'real' – is happening elsewhere. As a result, the collective psyche is caught between the scattered present – this granular, collapsible moment shrunk to the size of a smartphone screen – and some warm, analogue past.

Moreover, our online lives mean we increasingly exist as monetisable units of productivity, whose peaks and troughs can be mapped to various metrics of 'success': likes, re-tweets, right swipes. It's a vision of the future – flattened, over-determined, grossly manipulated – that was bleakly conjured by Michel Houellebecq in his 2005 novel, *The Possibility of an Island*. A member of a cult that believes in neo-human cloning creates an art installation that evokes a virtual hyper-reality:

> 'I had the impression of moving inside a milky, isotropic space, which sometimes condensed, suddenly, into granular micro-formations – on moving closer I could make out mountains, valleys and whole landscapes, which became rapidly more complex, then disappeared almost immediately, and the decor fell back into a vague homogeneity, criss-crossed by oscillating potentialities.'[1]

In our endlessly mediatised world, we've largely become representations of ourselves – online avatars, filtered profile images, Snapchat simulations. As a result, we've become hooked on the narcissism of being at the centre of our own endlessly curated universe. Yet the fact of our physical being cannot so easily be altered. Our incoherent, shattered present has, in turn, produced dissonant bodies: glitchy, isolated, drifting through the timelessness of a permanent 'now'.

The current discourse around identity politics – the drawing of lines around who we are – begins to look more and more like a defensive reaction-formation at a time when our very humanness, and the material fact of our being, is interfacing with new technological possibilities. (Ray Kurzweil's concept of the Singularity, prophesying the human-machine matrix, now seems prescient rather than bonkers.)[2] Sex and art remain perhaps the last available modes of possible transcendence. And despite developments in virtual reality and AI, it's arguably a more classical mode of figuration – oil paint on canvas – that has best anticipated, and now responds to, the body as a site of evolution: social, political and physical.

In our digital metamorphosis, who is documenting our evolving human shape? Though the photograph – exhaustive, omnipresent – may be the medium of our age, it might yet be the anachronism of paint that tells the truth about how we see now. Regarding the body rendered in paint, we're able to remove ourselves from the pre-interpreted world of social media, to temporarily tune out of the digital noise.

In our over-stimulated field of vision, figurative painting becomes a place of refuge: for meditation, sustained attention, self-analysis. Whereas screens are mirrors for our own self-regard, the canvas offers a reflection of our deepest, most complex selves.

In an era of sincere shallowness, our fears about authenticity – and the anxieties around the loss of a private, innermost self – are played out, paradoxically, in 'public': on Instagram profiles and the performativity of Twitter. In our search for 'realness', we embrace the superficial, both distancing us from – and melding us closer to – our avatars: filters, contouring, the normalisation of cosmetic procedures that lend the same homogeneous look of internet-ready blankness. We're advertisements for ourselves: a 24/7 personality branding exercise dispersed across various media.

While these images have the effect of junk food – spiking our attention before leaving us depleted and empty – paint literally *sinks in*, an antidote to the tripped fuse of our attention span. Cecily Brown's turn towards abstraction is emblematic of the kind of hypnotic incoherence that has become the hallmark of the twenty-first century. Her figures dissolve and reconfigure themselves in tornadoes of paint. As far as 'realism' exists in her oeuvre, it can be seen in the breakdown of forms: the desiccated energy; the way in which the eye is overwhelmed by an avalanche of sensory information. In *The Last Shipwreck* (2018) [pl. 8], we see an analogue of our own febrile moment: a scramble of bodies, their human lineaments fast losing all intelligibility, set against the infinity of blue sky meeting the sea.

In a crucial sense, we've achieved the vision outlined by French philosopher Jean Baudrillard: that of the total simulacrum, in which the original is entirely replaced by its synthetic representation. A world of true counterfeits. Living under the influence of market-driven virtuality (dividing us all into 'influencer' and 'influenced'), we've internalised the logic of late capitalism. We've become 'optimised': endorsements for products, click bait and the endless recycling of brand names. To update William Burroughs' junkie logic, the internet is the ideal product, in which no sales talk is necessary. Rather than the buyer, we're the bought. We *are* the product.

We can see this kind of digital uncanny in the kinds of bodies that have become most emblematic of – and have most ferociously capitalised on – these new forms of technology. The Kardashians, with their strange malleability and potent blankness, the lack of affect that seems to stand in for personality, have become the poster family for this skin-deep aesthetic. Walking billboards for their own product lines, they have ensured that their social media feeds are revenue streams for their eerily absent omnipresence. (In a move both characteristically irony-free, and totally of the zetigeist, Kim's book of selfies was called *Selfish*.) It's unsurprising that this new template for the physical has, in turn, produced new anxieties about the relationship between body and image. Meanwhile, our post-truth era has found its apotheosis in the 'deep fake': CGI humanoids that can't be differentiated from real-life human beings by the naked eye.

As with Freud's concept of the return of the repressed, the further we stray from the materiality of the body, the more it becomes inescapable. In our age of the selfie, figurative painting offers an unmediated, direct way of seeing: through another human being's eyes, rather than the cold gaze of a machine. In its embodiedness, and bold feeling, figuration removes us from the disassociative realm of algorithms and data, granting us an object that lives.

What's perhaps most disturbing about phenomena such as the Kardashians and deep fakes (not to mention robots that increasingly mimic and even out-perform humans) is how they foreshadow a kind

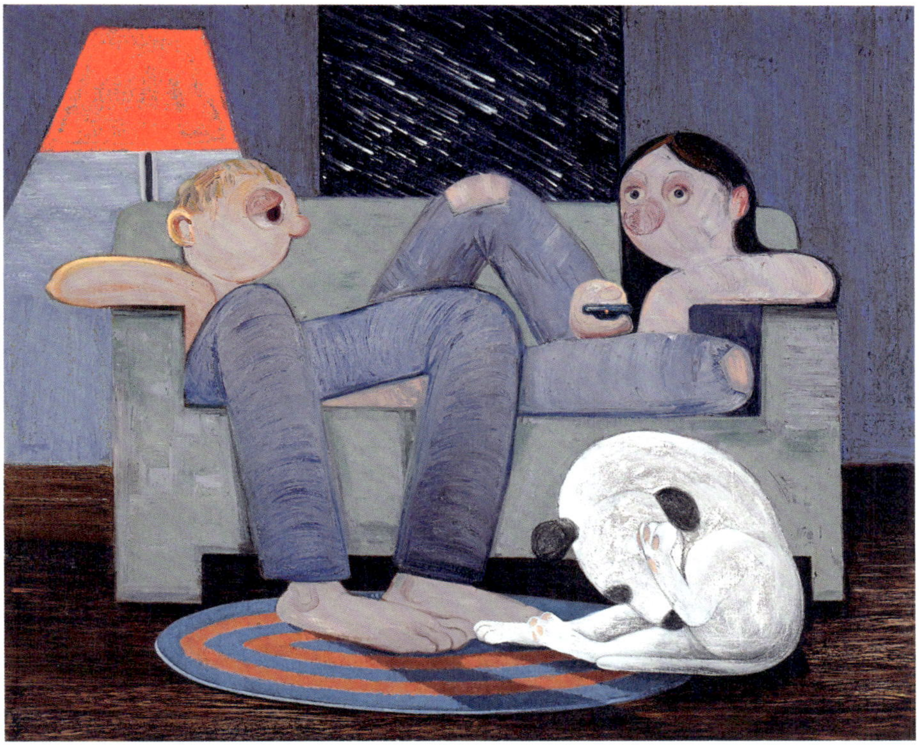

Nicole Eisenman, *Watchers*, 2016, oil on canvas, 111.8 × 134.6 cm

of perfectability at the cost of the very qualities that make us human. They inhabit a recognisable form while emptying it of all meaning: floating bodies that don't properly signify, devoid of empathy, true feeling and – increasingly – any kind of intelligence beyond the artificial.

Fusing the comic zeal of Philip Guston with Hogarthian satire, many of Nicole Eisenman's figures skewer modern selfhood in all its contradictions. With their blocky limbs and giant needy eyes, they resemble human puppets: pseudo-adults dumbstruck by their own physicality. Eisenman is alert to the infantilising turn in modern society; how the injunction to 'enjoy!' becomes its own kind of routine. We've morphed into button-pressing attention junkies, estranged in our own skins, constantly chasing – and thwarting – the meaningful connection for which we constantly yearn.

Moreover, Eisenman's work chronicles a very modern kind of urban isolation: a post-millennium version of social life in which we frequently find ourselves together, alone. In *Watchers* (2016), a couple lounge on a sofa. One looks blankly down, possibly at a phone; the other stares at the tv, remote in hand. A dog licks itself in the foreground. In its rigorous proportions, everything has its place here: a kind of communal stasis, in which its subjects connect but remain curiously disassociated.

One of the enduring fantasies of the internet is its ability to eliminate everything we most fear and despise about having a body: ageing, imperfection, weakness, even desire itself. Through our online doppelgangers, we can crop or delete the parts we find most troubling, or enhance the best bits with the right light or perfect filter. All the while, the gulf between who we actually are and what we long to be yawns ever wider. And within that space grows a yearning for an accurate portrayal, a truthful rendering, beyond mere representation. At the dawn of the millennium, one of the recurring fears about the internet was how nothing would stick; how entire forms of digital life could be erased in a click. Now, we struggle with a different reality: how everything we do online leaves a permanent trace, and how often that trace is a deception.

This sense of a true likeness – meaningful permanence – is answered (at least in part) by figurative painting. Whereas a generation of millennials is wise to the smoke and mirrors of a life lived online – manipulating its possibilities while simultaneously disdaining its effects – figure painting tears away these veils, becoming seeing that we can actually believe in. (Think of Lucian Freud, his sitters stripped bare and scrutinised, spared nothing: each bruise and wrinkle, every blemish and imperfection. The opposite of online airbrushing.)

Jenny Saville uses paint to depict similarly unruly, 'unconventional' bodies. In *Matrix* (1999), we see a trans man reclining on a table, his ostensible masculinity (shaved head, moustache) juxtaposed with breasts, his vagina thrust into the foreground of the canvas. As with much of Saville's work, this is flesh as provocation, but also as bold admission. In some sense, we're all bodies undergoing 'transition', editable units moving from screen to app, before contracting back into the lineaments of reality. We're amorphous beings: more mutable and porous than we think. Our bodies figure as both boundaries and the vehicles for crossing them.

What is the future of figuration in art? Does oil painting risk becoming a rarefied mode that can only speak to the past? In our conditions of extreme instability, there's a seduction to declaring the 'death' of a medium at the very moment that it's in unprecedented flux. And yet, with a cerebral, ideas-heavy conceptualism largely driving contemporary art, it's self-evident how unfashionable figure painting has become. Whereas the form demands attentiveness, reflection and depth of vision, the market is hungry for loudly megaphoned ideas that telegraph glib emotion.

Technology has become something of a fetish in an art world obsessed with novelty. Galleries are awash with screening rooms and headsets, transporting the viewer into an immersive gallery-without-walls. Will the conservative practice of oil painting, by confronting the modern condition while refusing to play the game of modernity, find a new vitality – or even move into the position of the radical outlaw?

As technology increasingly becomes an extension of our own bodies, figuration in art may yet become both a space of escapism – a refuge from the drifting, eternal present of the screen – and resistance. The practice of sustained, rigorous, deep looking will not only have the potential to alter our perception, but to reimagine the possibilities of the self altogether.

**1** Michel Houellebecq, *The Possibility of an Island* (London: George Weidenfeld and Nicholson Ltd., 2005).

**2** Ray Kurzweil, *The Singularity Is Near: When Humans Transcend Biology* (New York: Viking, 2005).

plates 1–4 Michael Armitage

plates 5–8 Cecily Brown

plates 9–12 Nicole Eisenman

plates 13–16 Sanya Kantarovsky

plates 17–21 Tala Madani

plates 22–25 Ryan Mosley

plates 26–28 Christina Quarles

plates 29–32 Daniel Richter

plates 33–36 Dana Schutz

plates 37–40 Tschabalala Self

1
**Michael Armitage**
*Peace Coma*
2012
Oil on lubugo bark cloth
110 × 75 cm

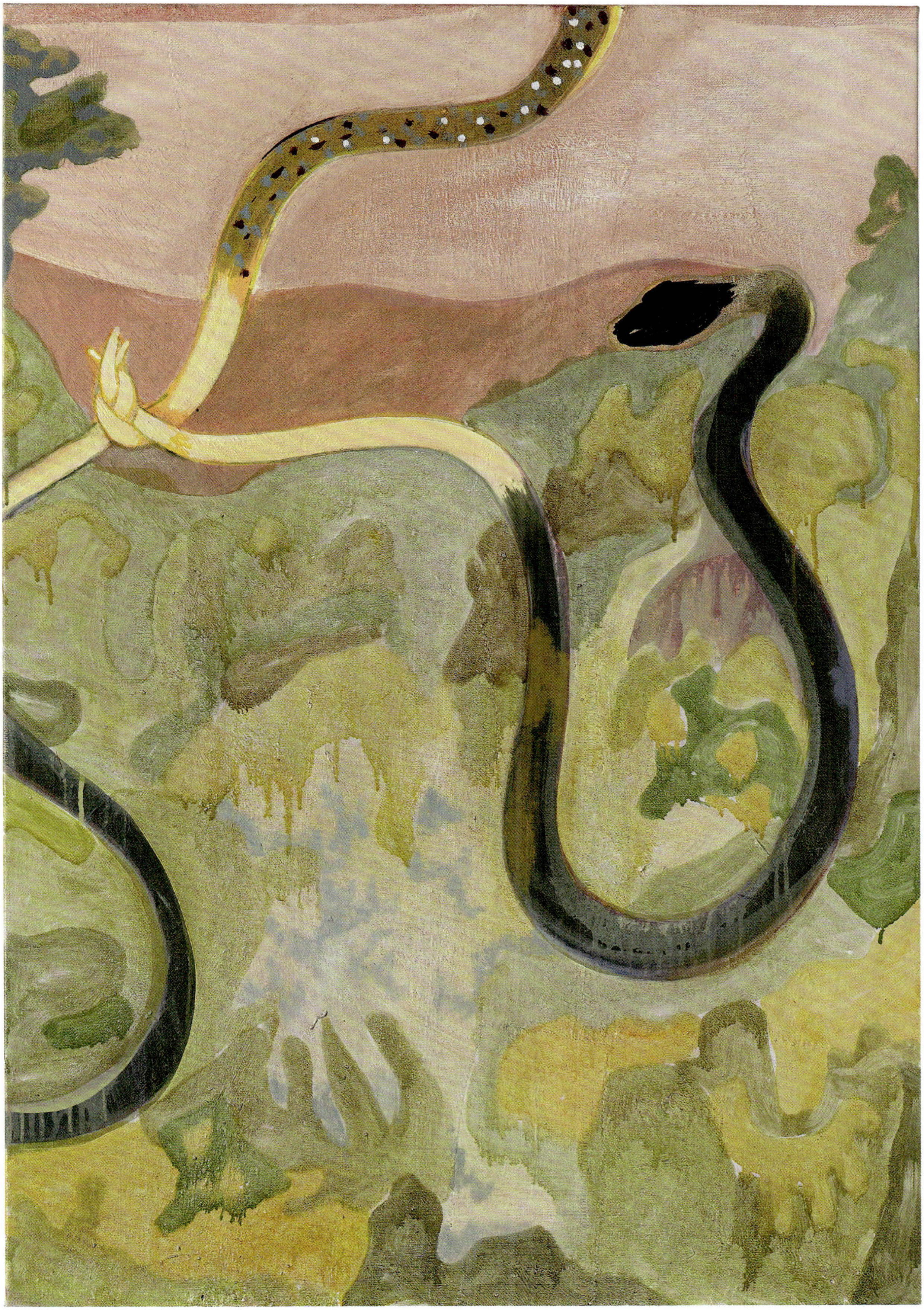

2
**Michael Armitage**
*Kampala Suburb*
2014
Oil on lubugo bark cloth
196 × 150 cm

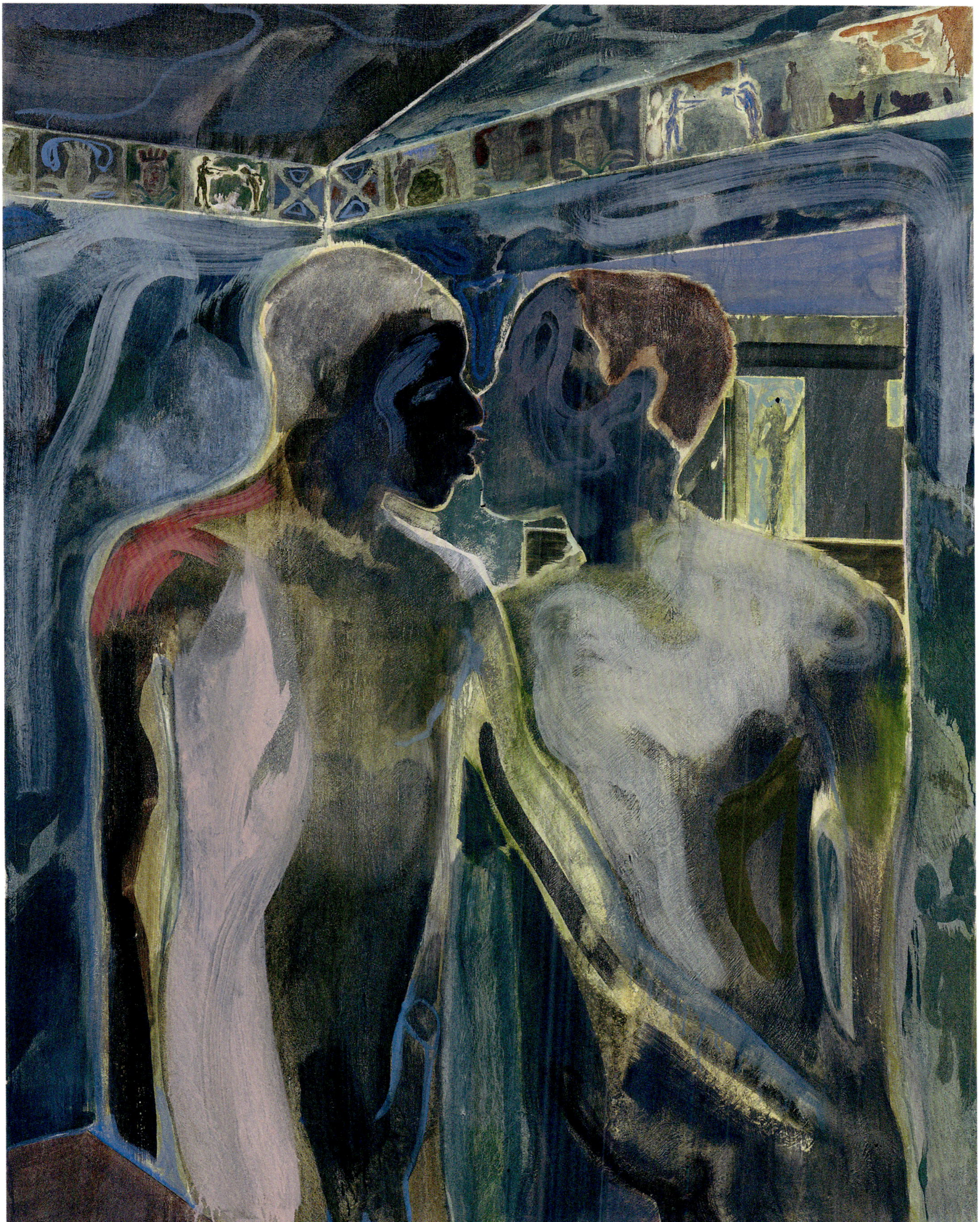

3

**Michael Armitage**

*#mydressmychoice*

2014

Oil on lubugo bark cloth

149.9 × 195.6 cm

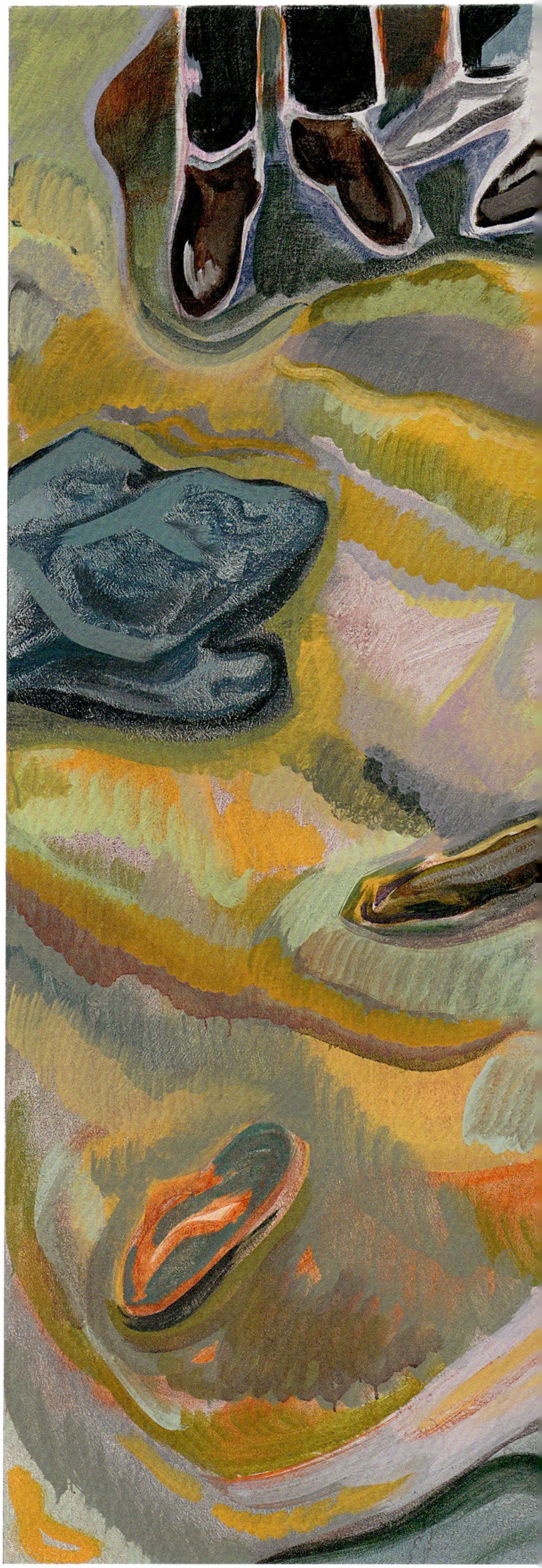

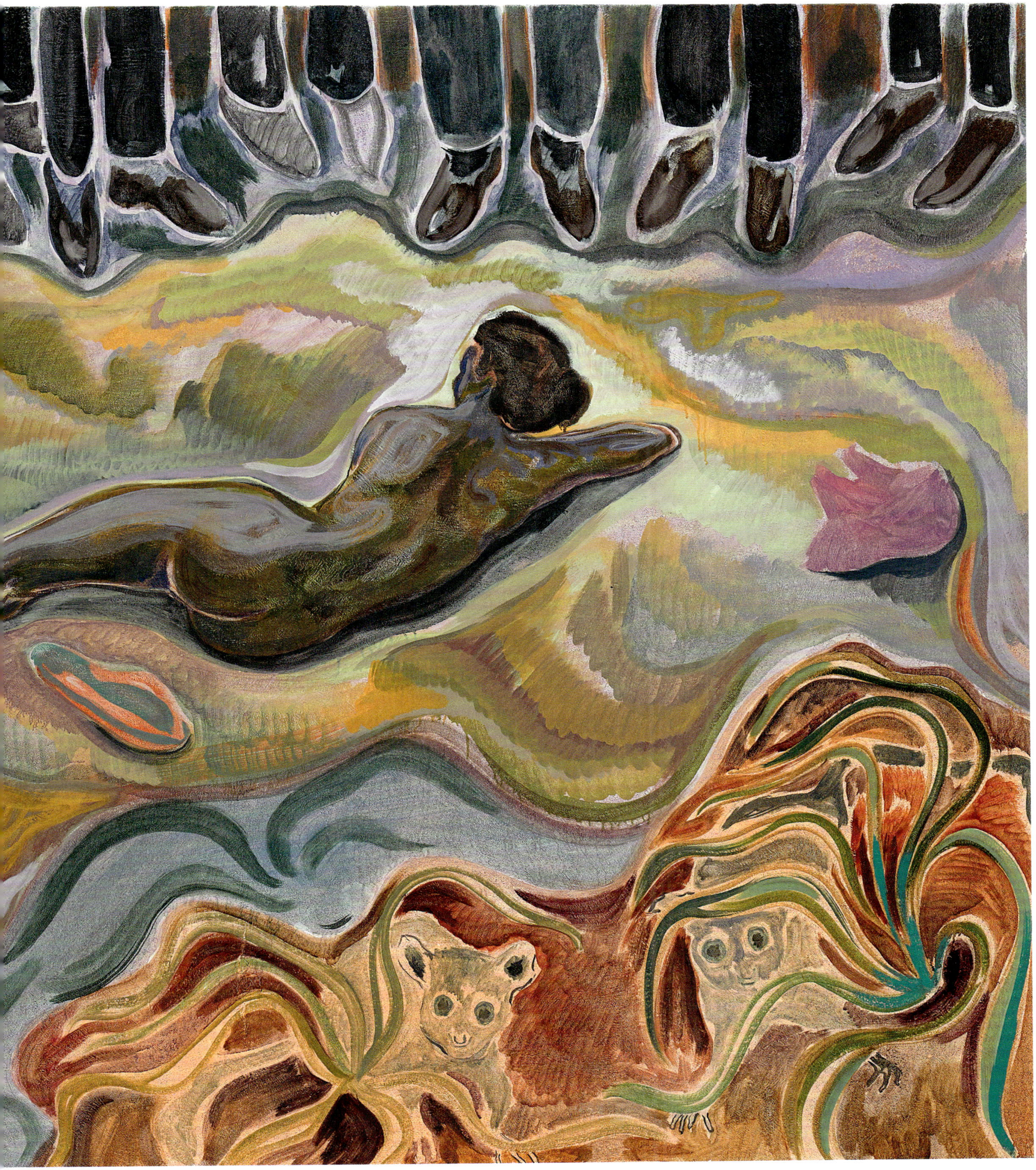

4

**Michael Armitage**

*Mangroves Dip*

2015

Oil on lubugo bark cloth

221 × 170.2 cm

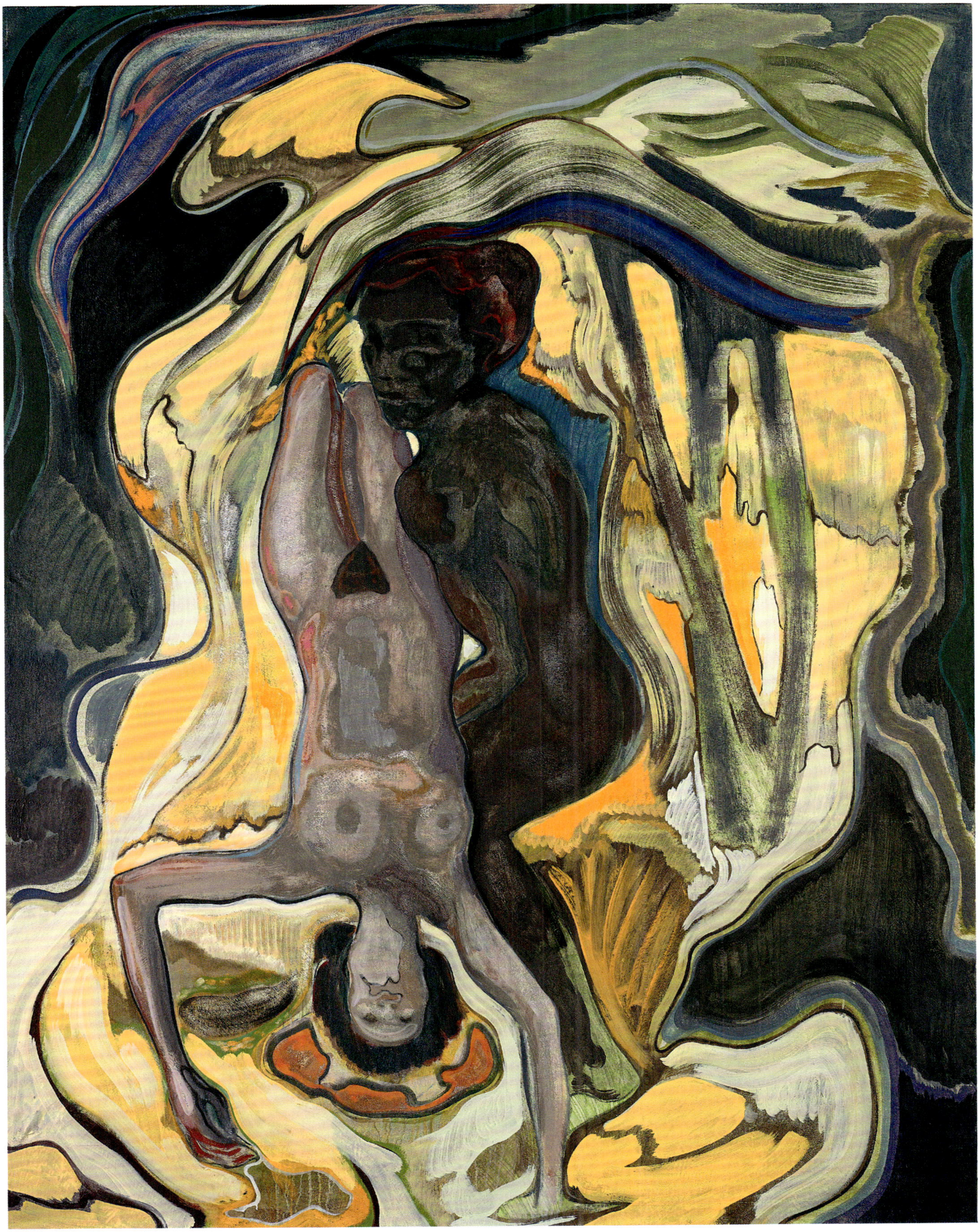

5
**Cecily Brown**
*Maid's Day Off*
2005
Oil on linen
200.7 × 198.1 cm

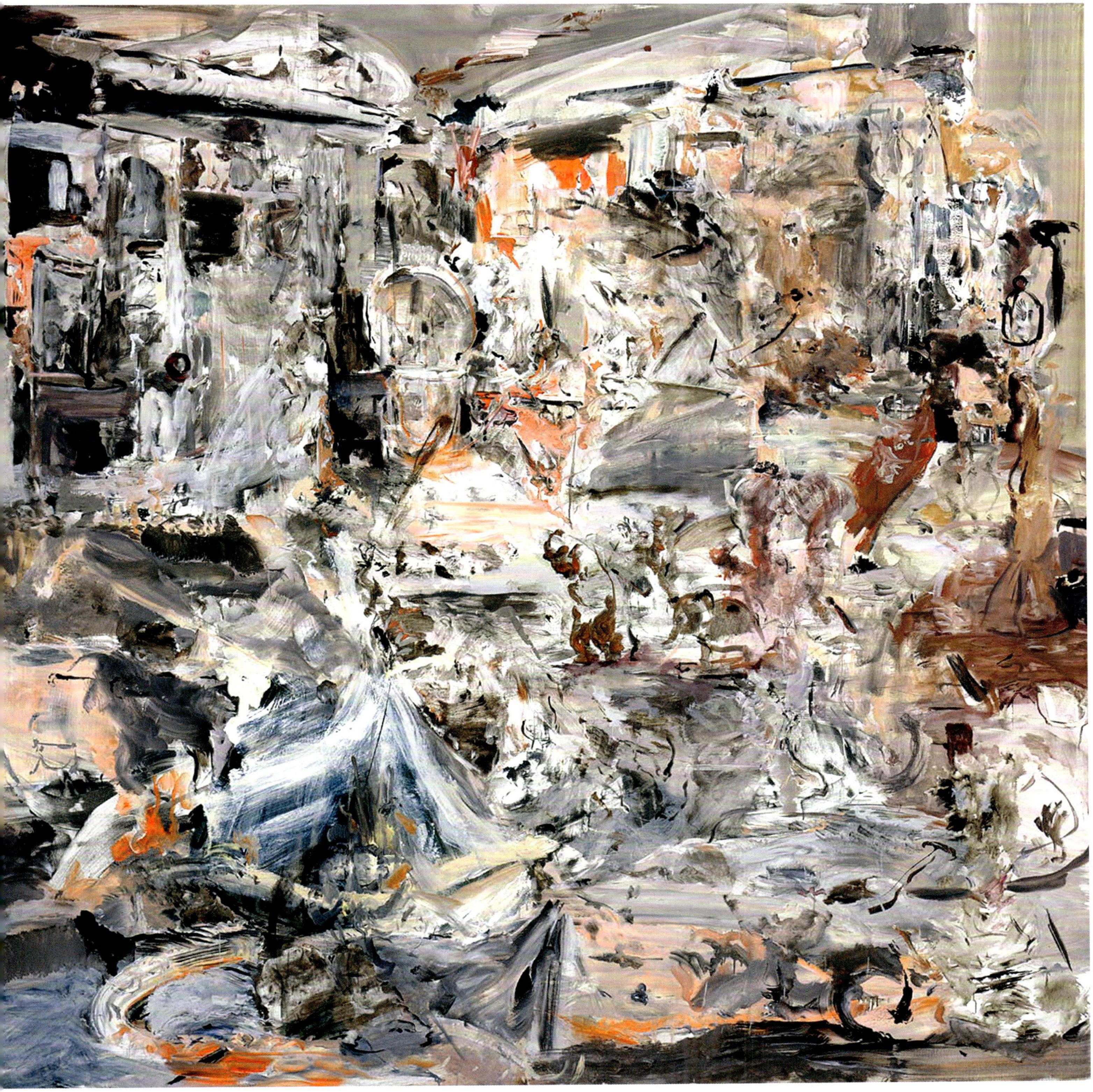

6

**Cecily Brown**

*Oinops*

2016–17

Oil on linen

154.9 × 180.3 cm

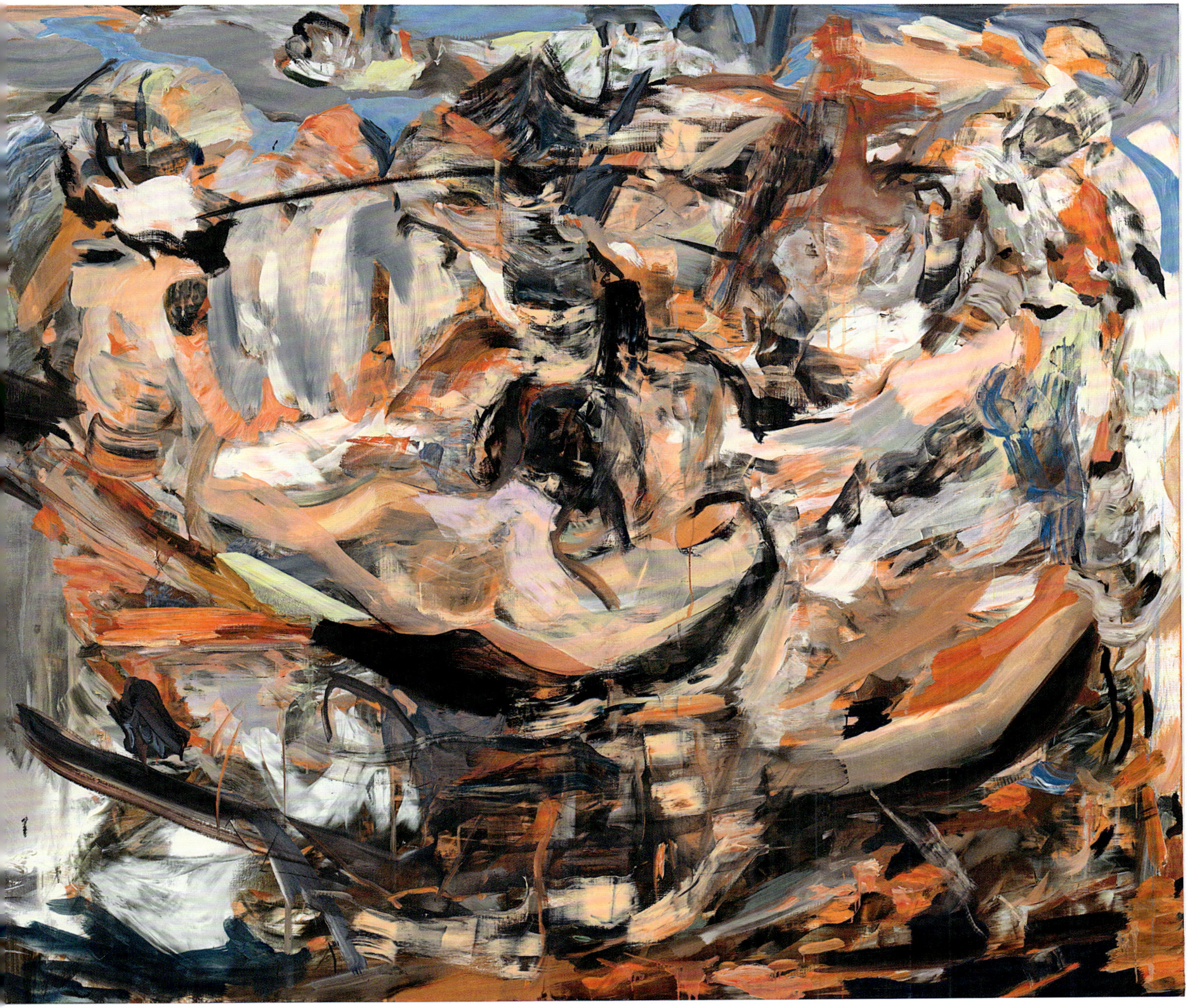

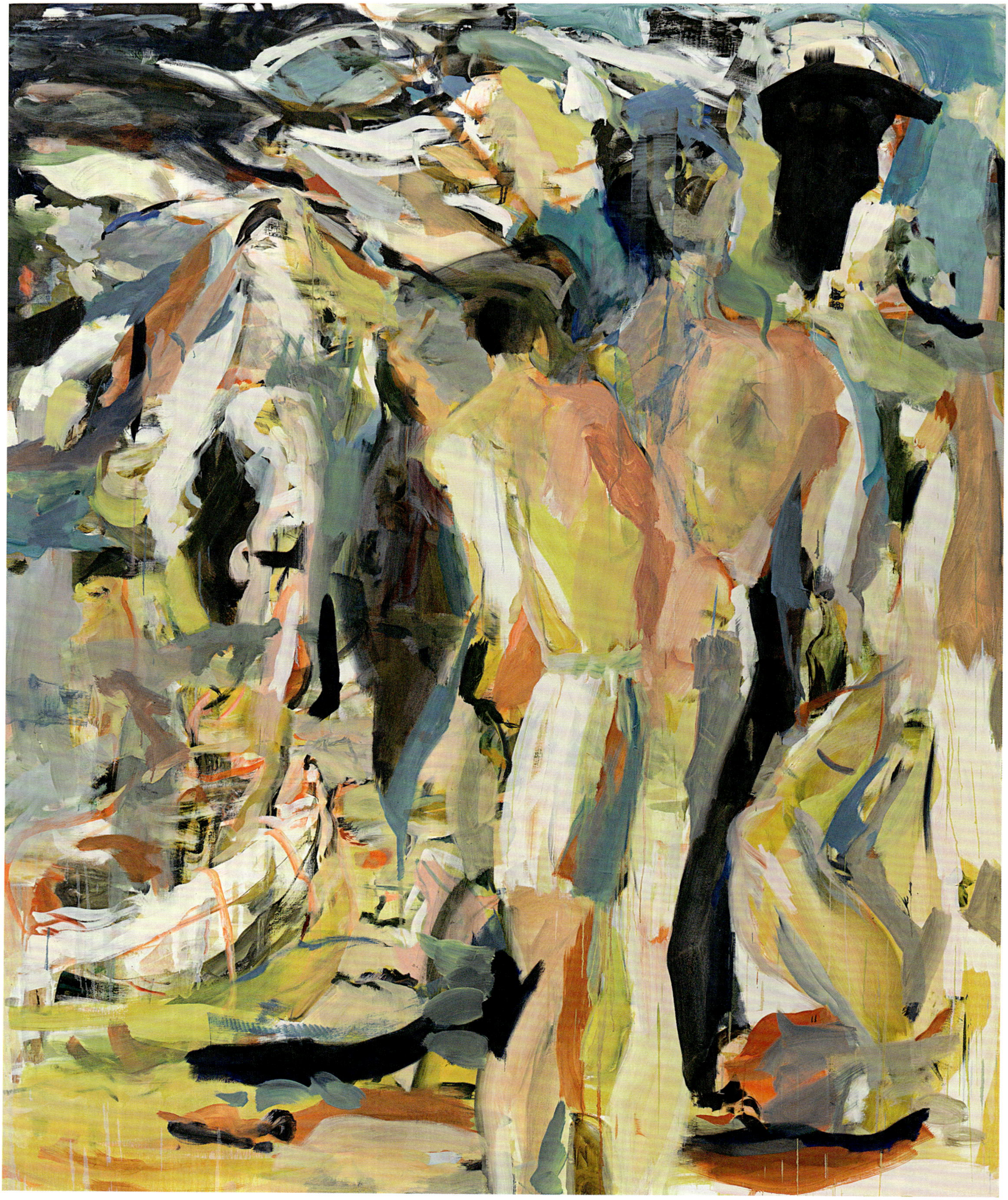

7
**Cecily Brown**
*Lucky Beach*
2017
Oil on linen
210.8 × 170.2 cm

8

**Cecily Brown**

*The Last Shipwreck*

2018

Oil on linen

210.8 × 200.7 cm

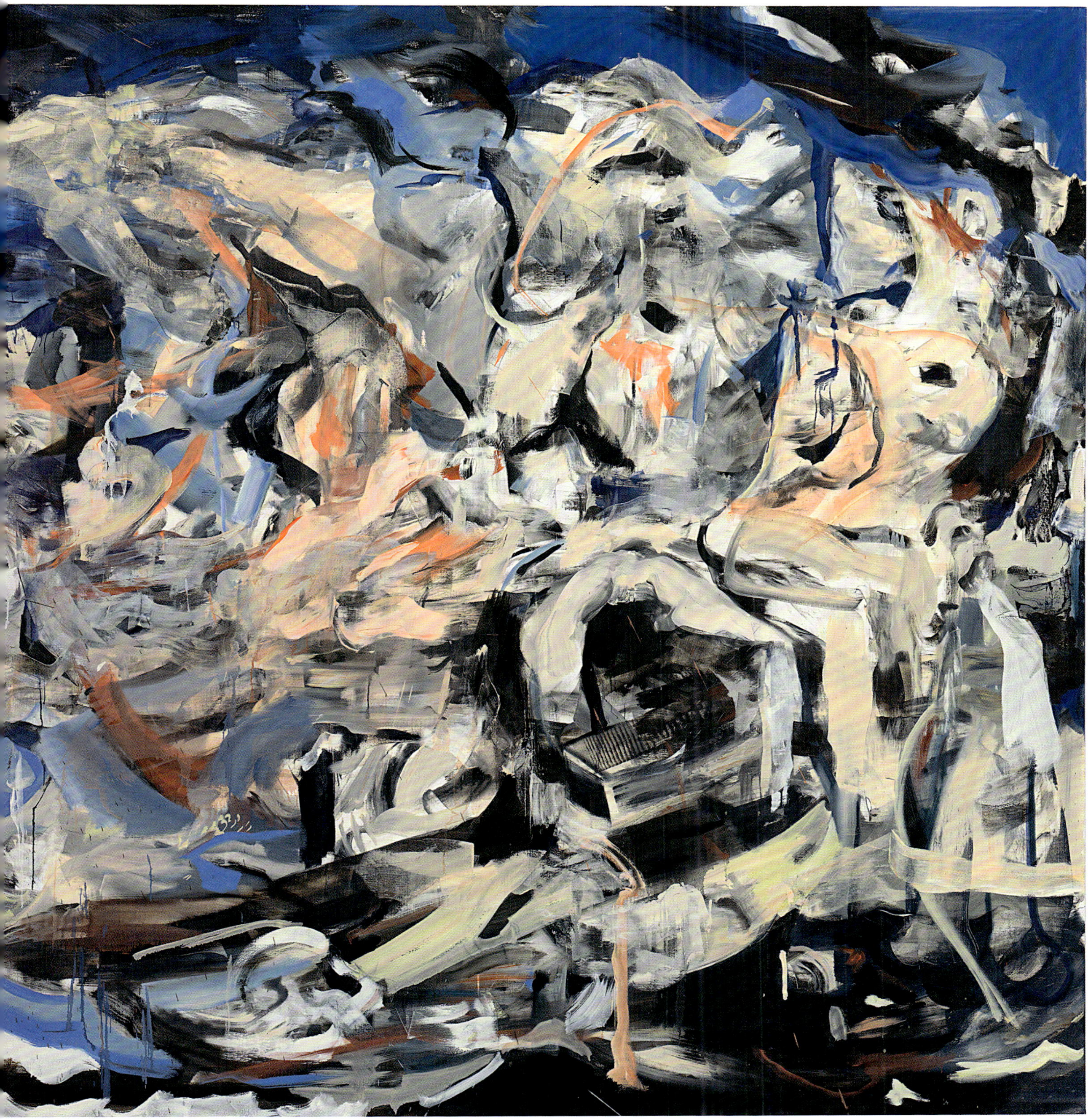

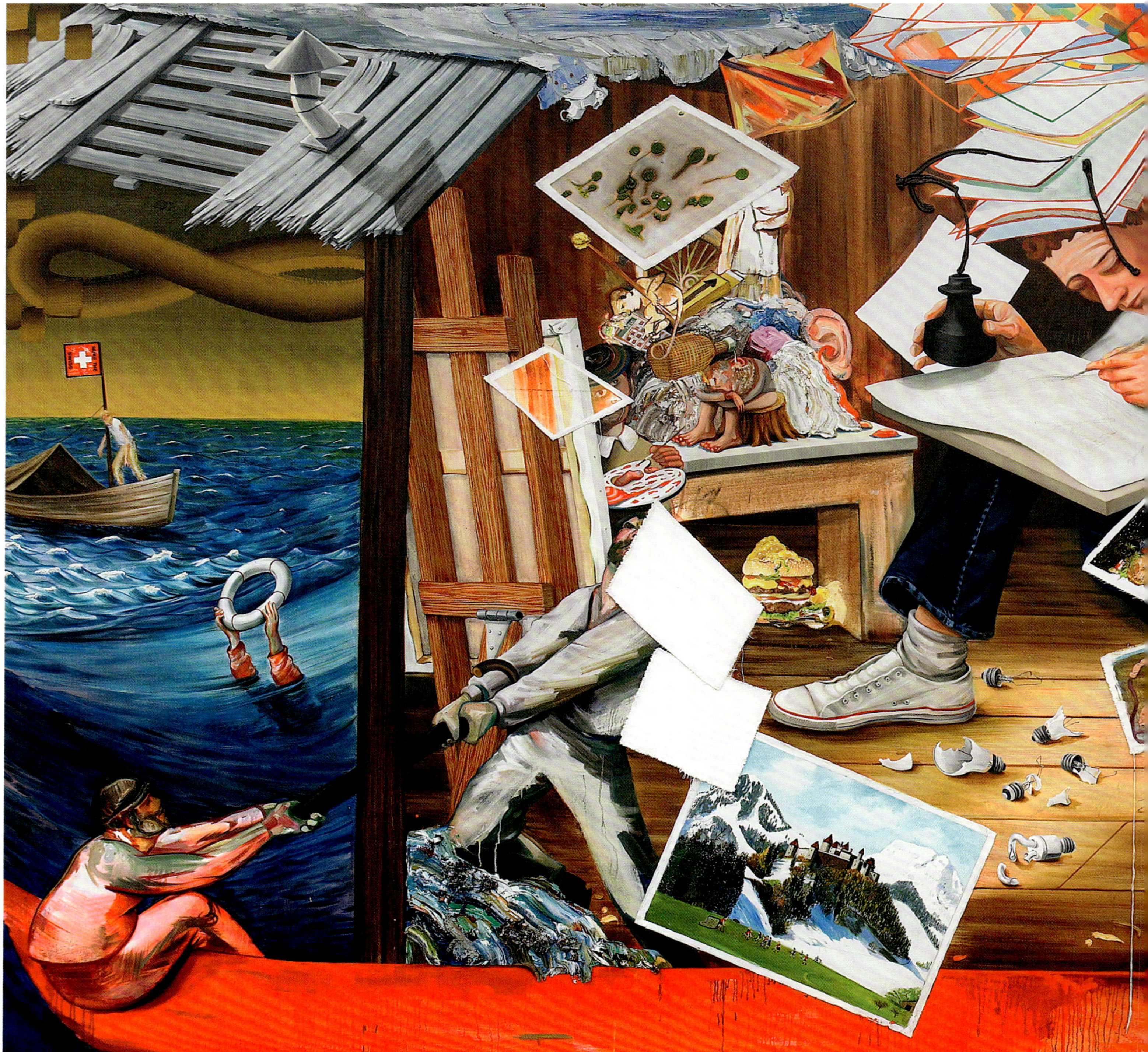

9
**Nicole Eisenman**
*Progress: Real and Imagined* [left panel]
2006
Oil on canvas
234.5 × 481 cm

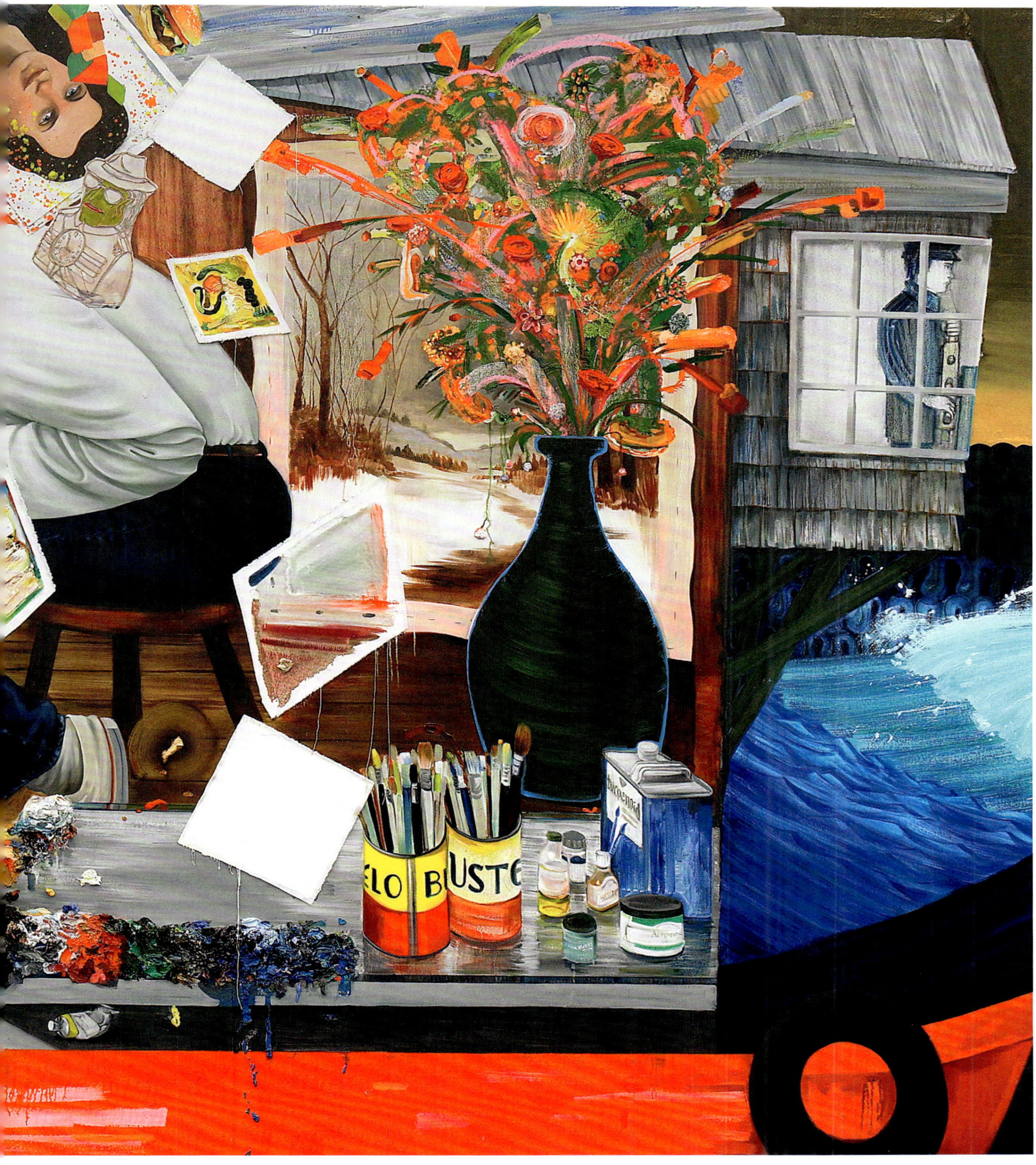

10
**Nicole Eisenman**
*Progress: Real and Imagined* [right panel]
2006
Oil on canvas
234.5 × 491 cm

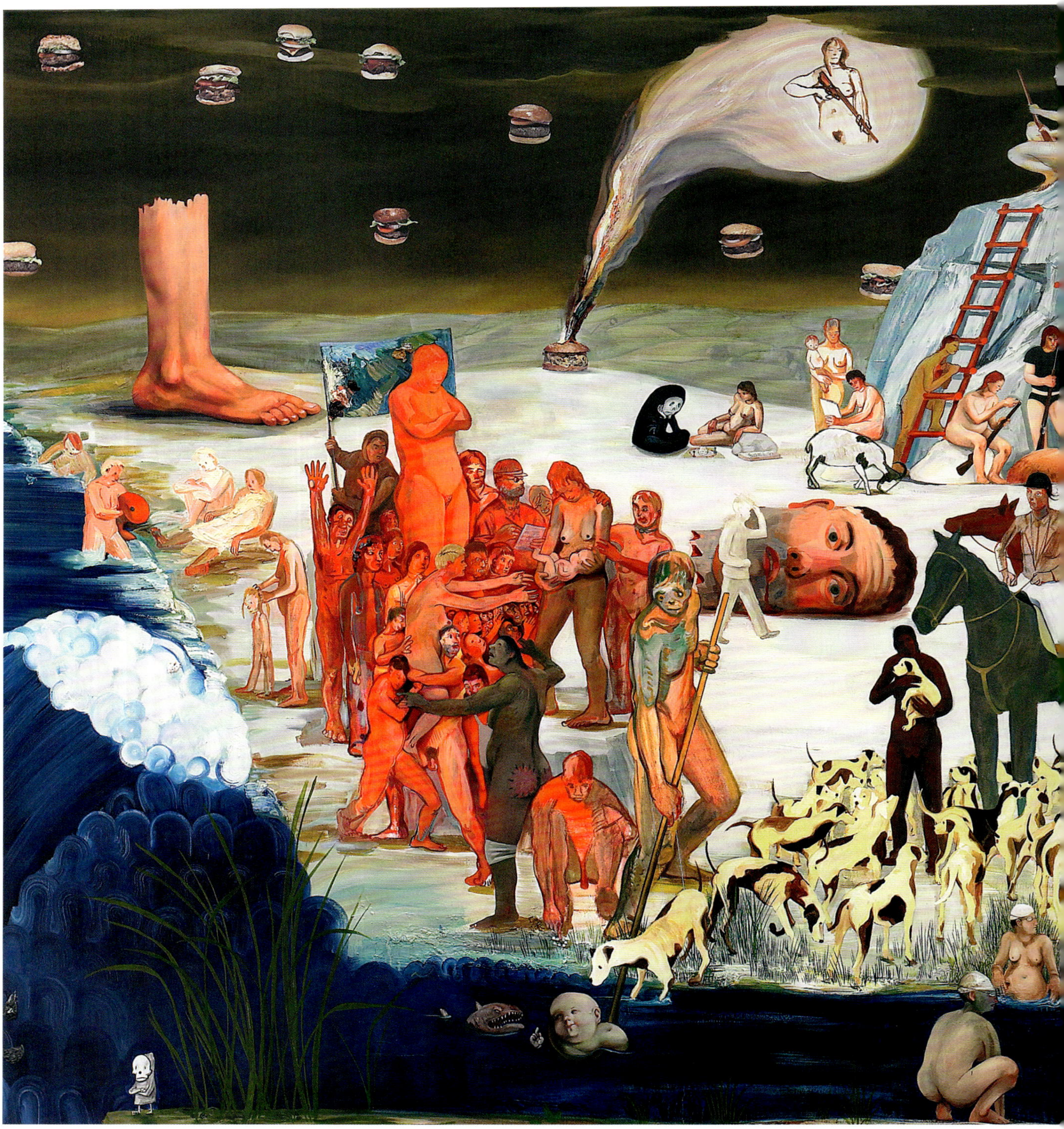

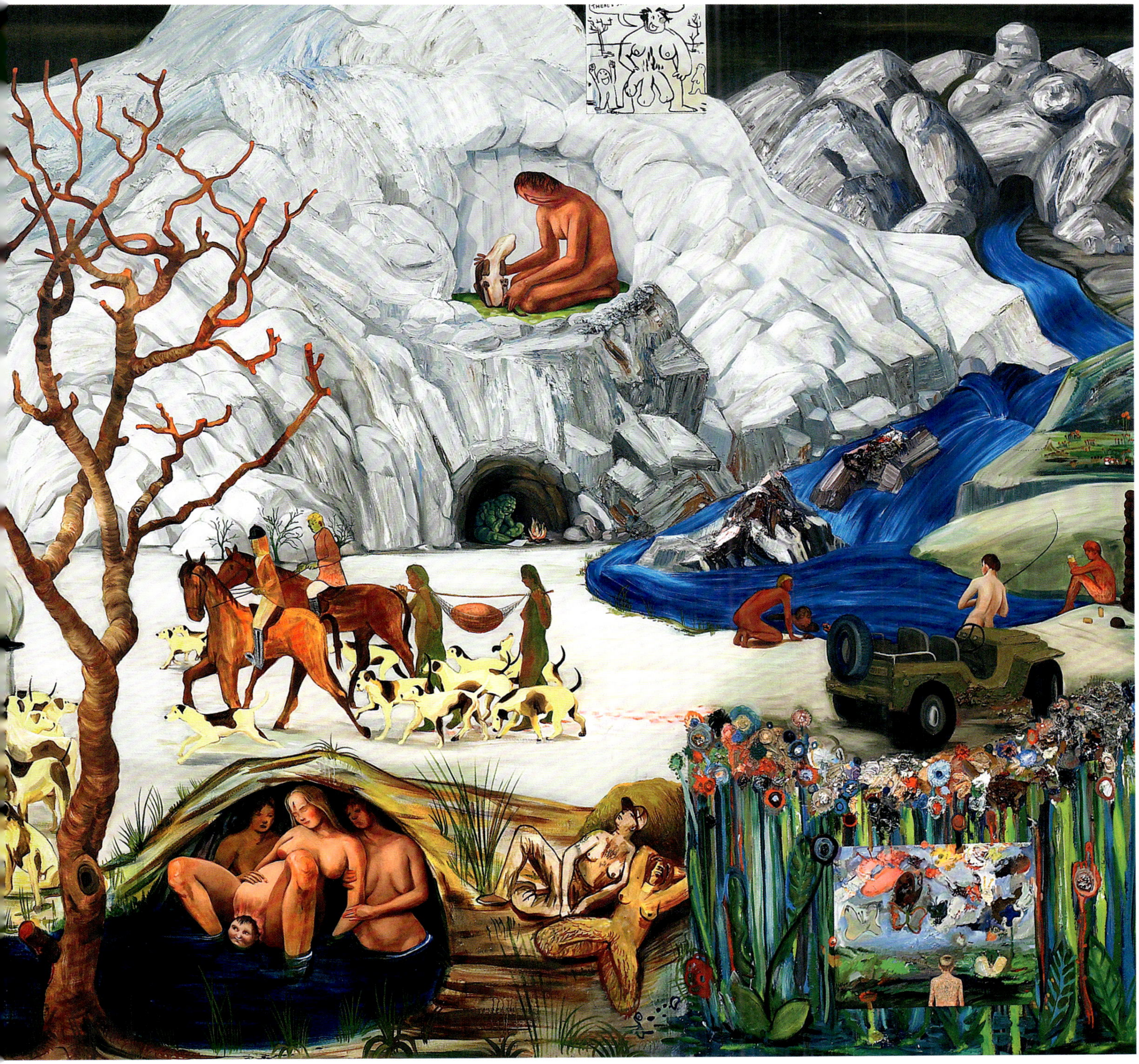

11
**Nicole Eisenman**
*Brooklyn Biergarten II*
2008
Oil on canvas
165.1 × 208.3 cm

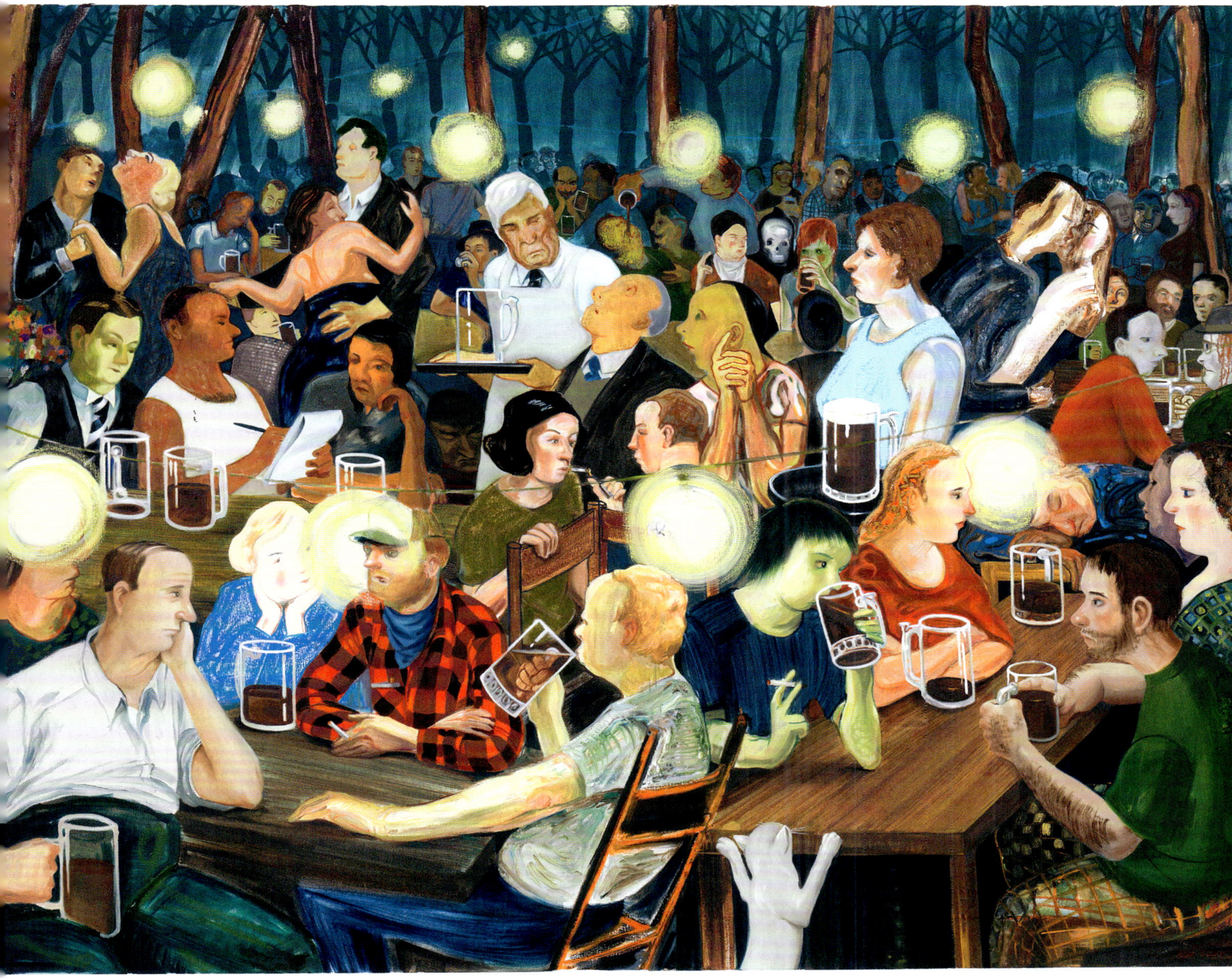

12
**Nicole Eisenman**
*Sleeper*
2016
Oil on canvas
45.7 × 60.9 cm

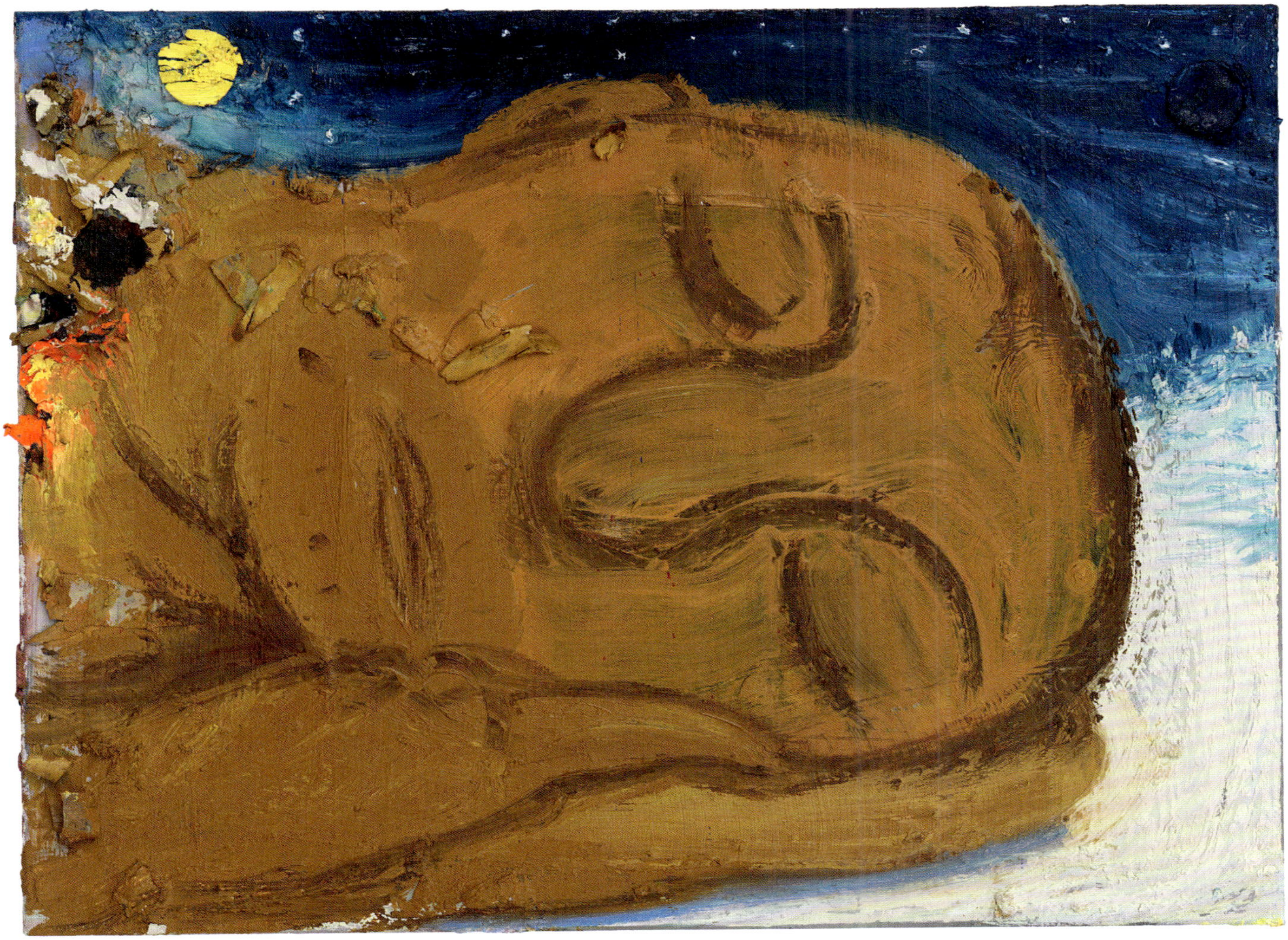

13
**Sanya Kantarovsky**
*Feeder*
2016
Oil and oil pastel on canvas
190.7 × 140 cm

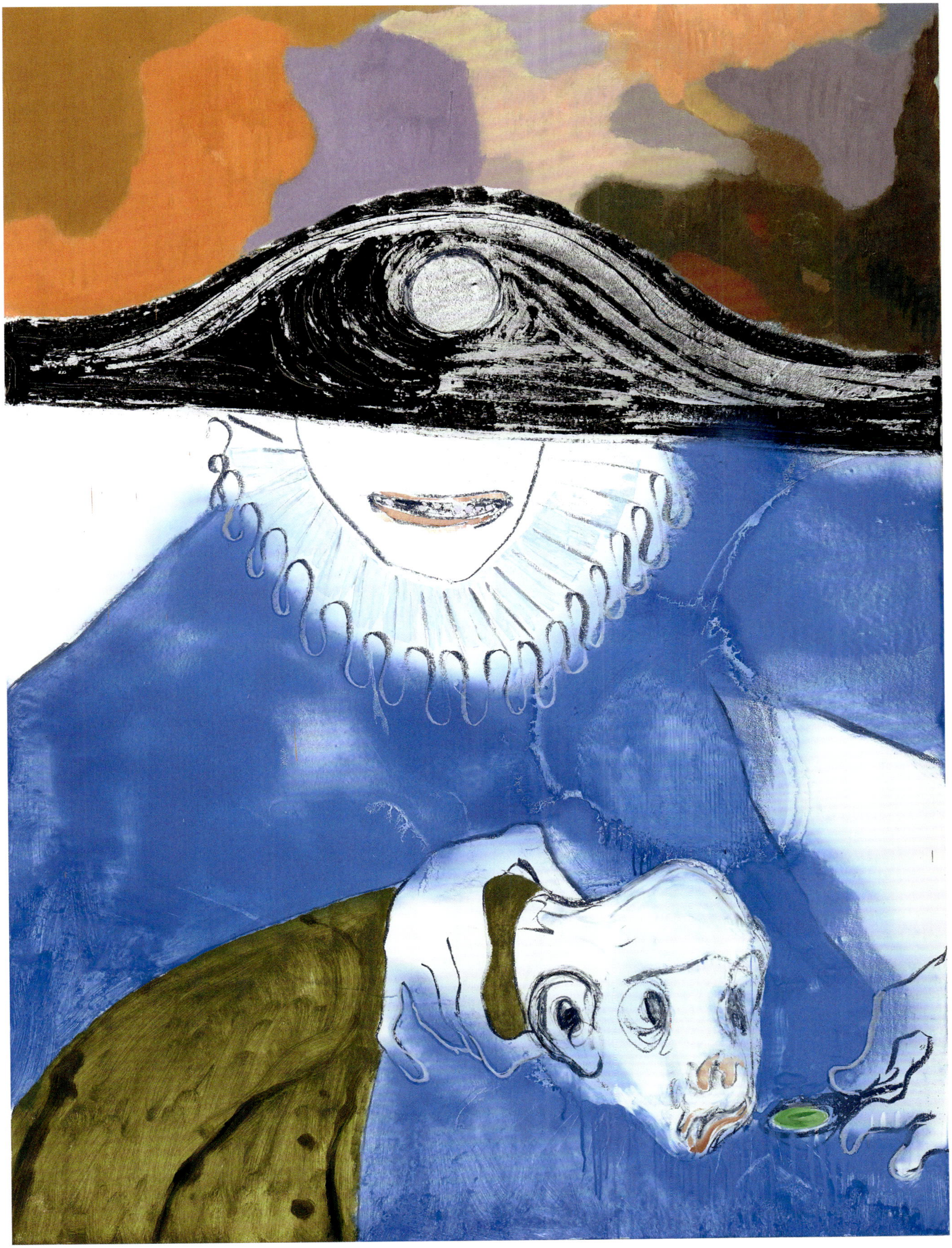

14
**Sanya Kantarovsky**
*Letdown*
2017
Oil, watercolour and pastel on canvas
215.9 × 165.1 cm

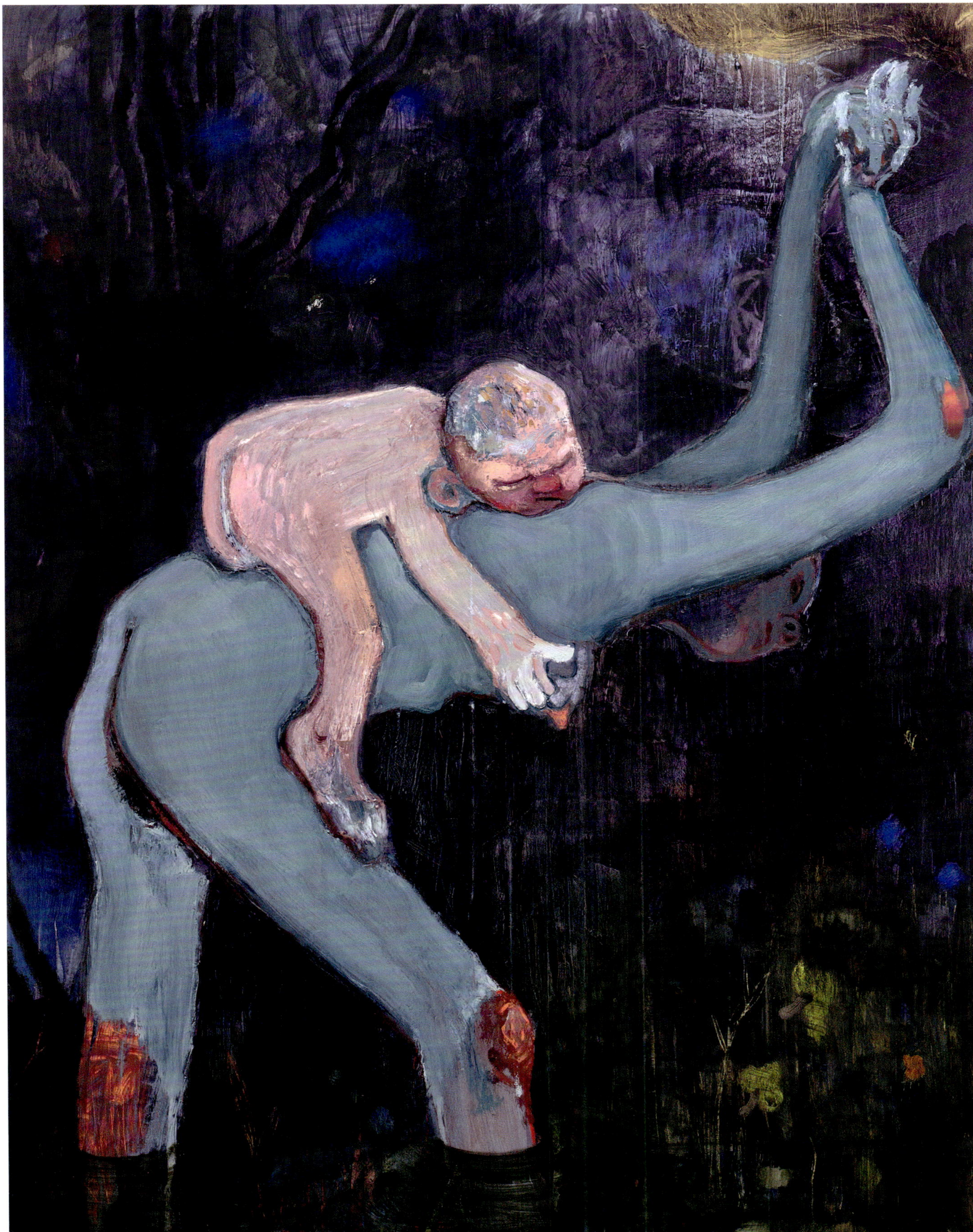

15
**Sanya Kantarovsky**
*Deprivation*
2018
Oil, watercolour and pastel on canvas
215.9 × 165.1 cm

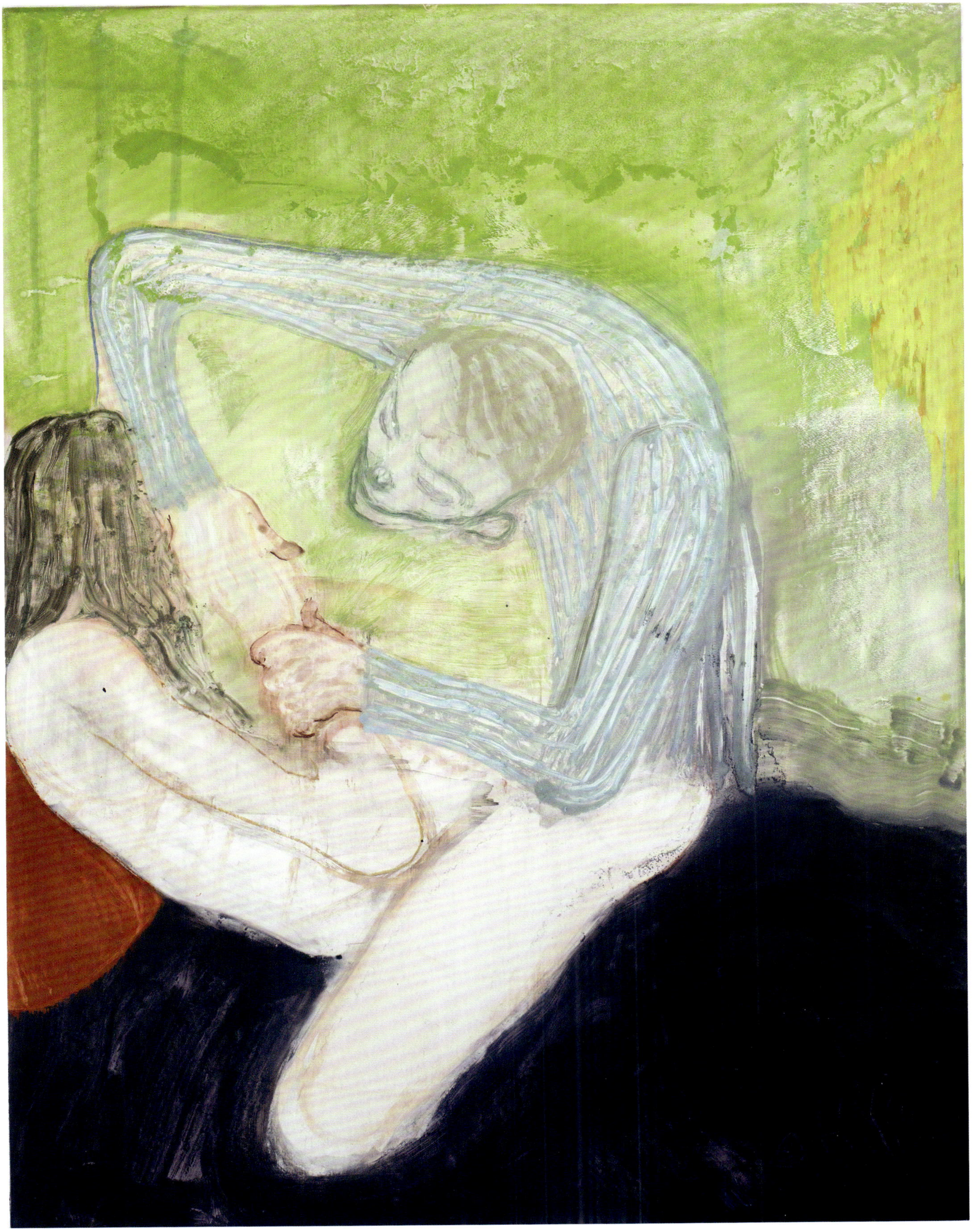

16
**Sanya Kantarovsky**
*Друг [Friend]*
2018
Oil and watercolour on canvas
215.9 × 165.1 cm

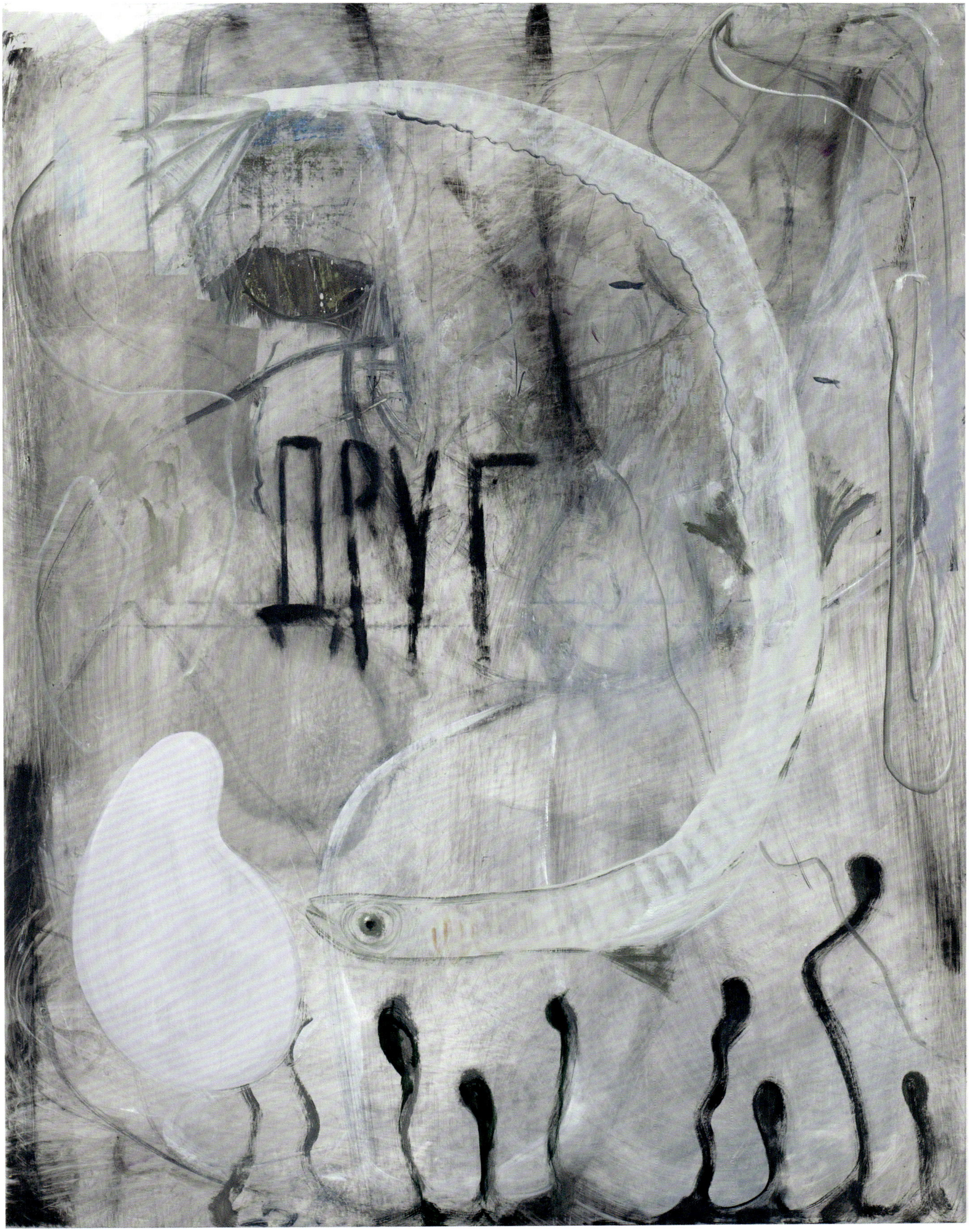
ДРУГ

17
**Tala Madani**
*Dirty Stars*
2008
Oil on wood
30 × 40 cm

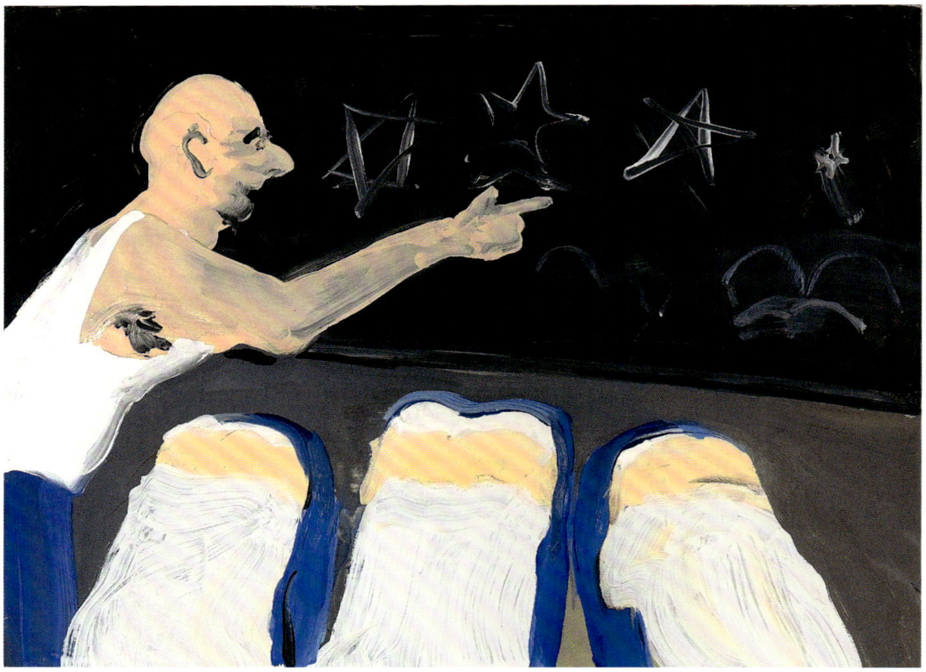

18
**Tala Madani**
*Sitting in White*
2008
Oil on linen
40 × 40 cm

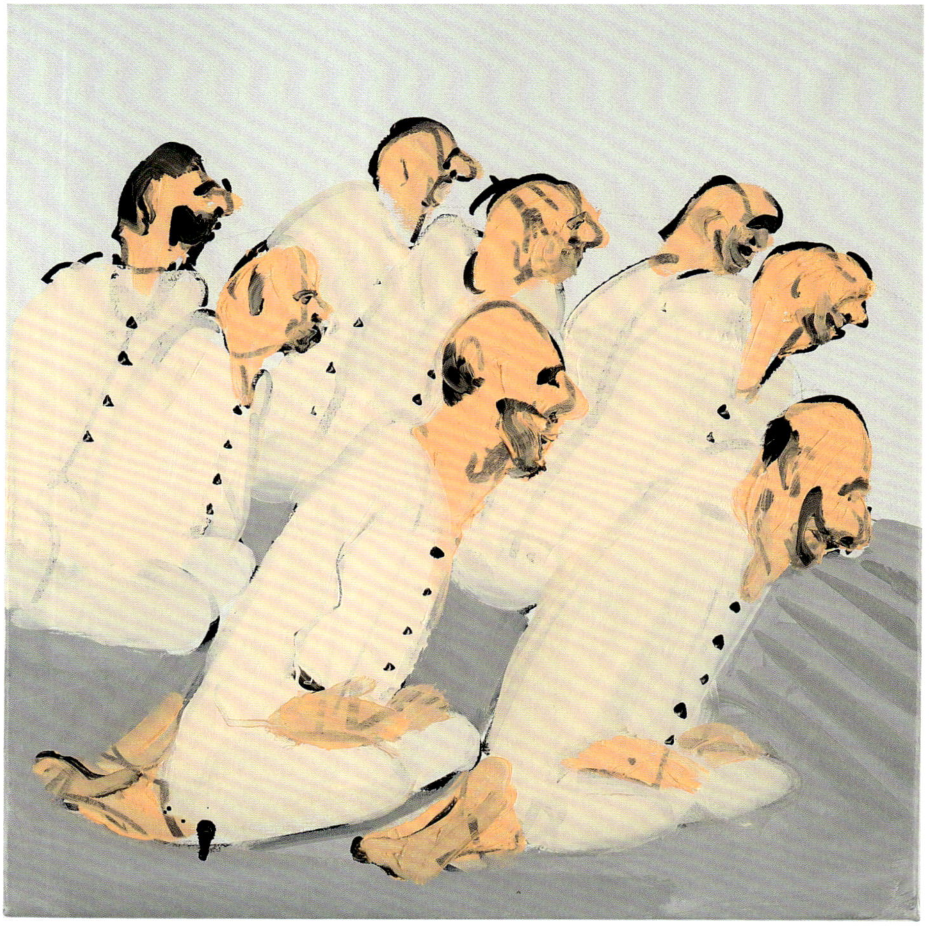

19

**Tala Madani**

*Campfire*

2011

Oil on linen

61 × 45.7 cm

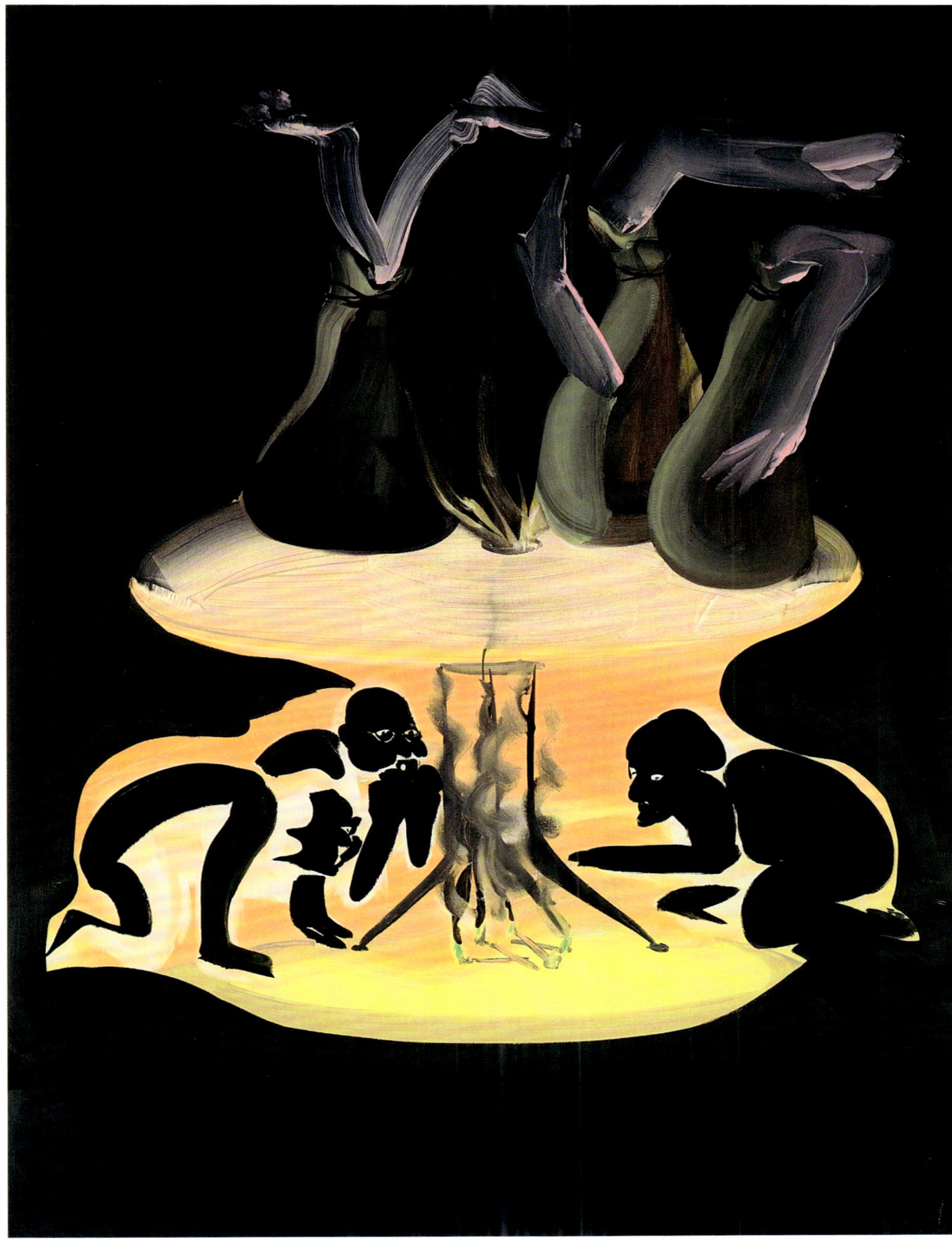

20

**Tala Madani**

*Light Balance*

2012

Oil on linen

50.8 × 40.6 cm

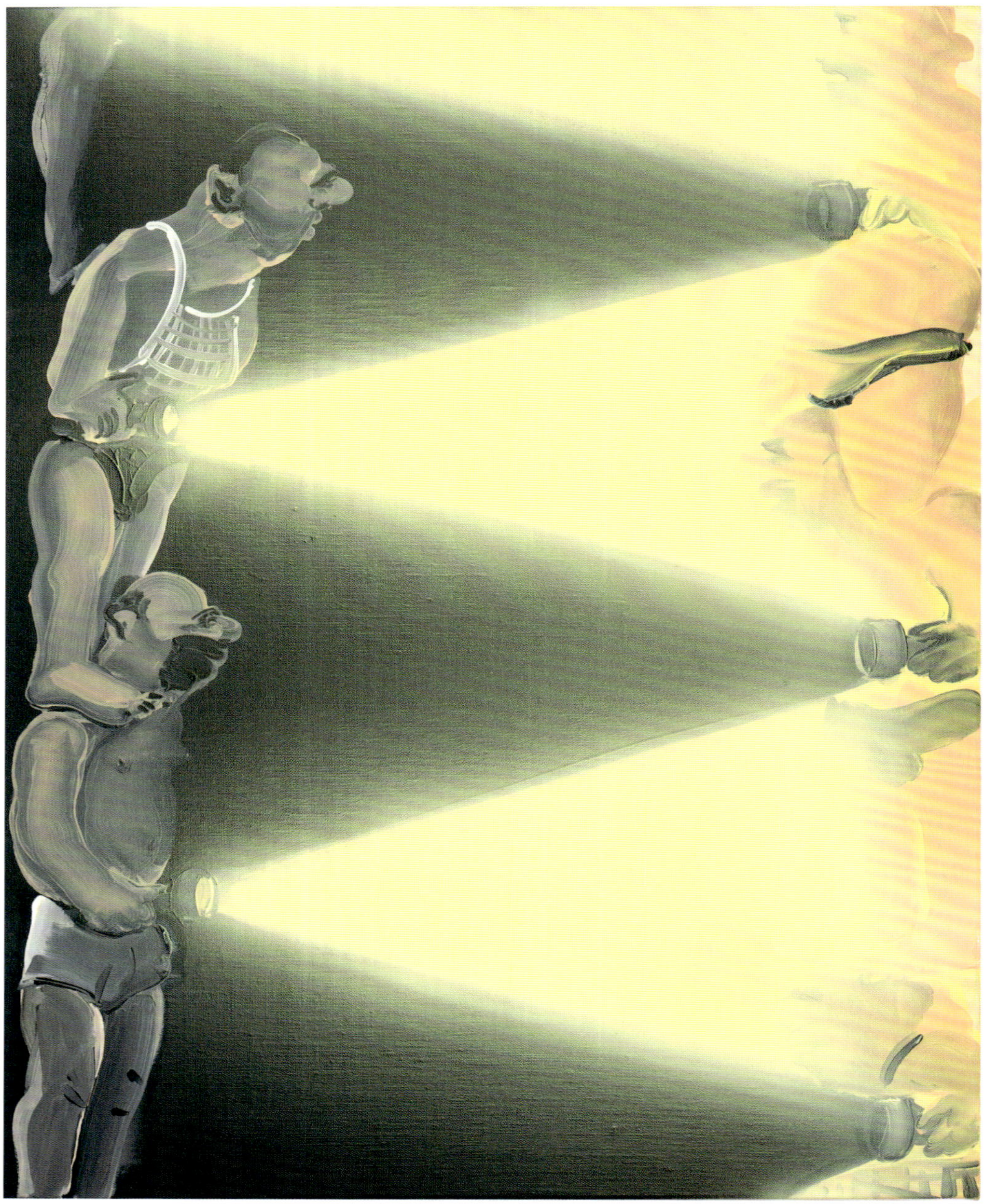

21
**Tala Madani**
*Shit Mom (Deluxe)*
2019
Oil on linen
50.8 × 61 cm

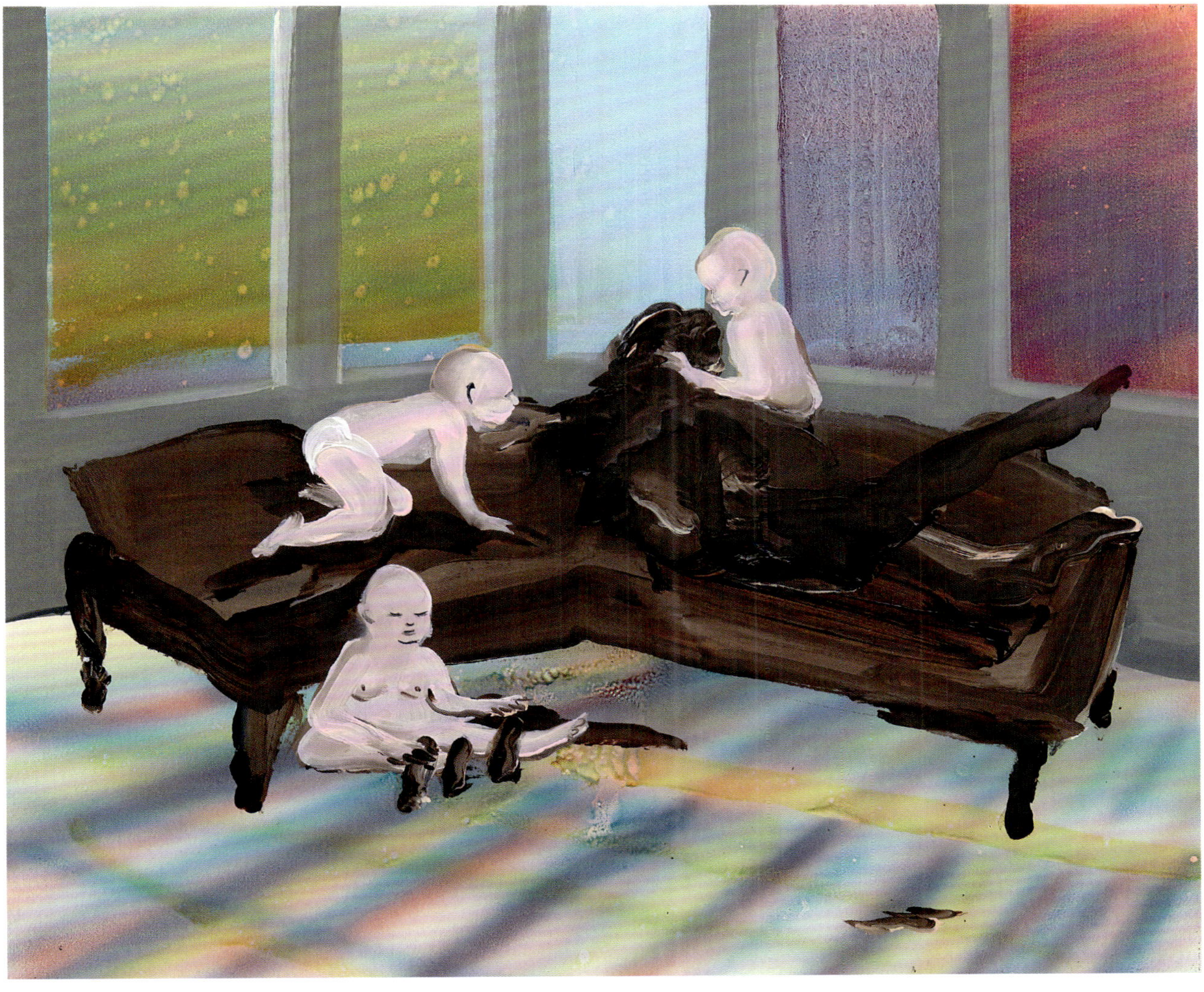

22
**Ryan Mosley**
*Teaching Snakes to be Snakes*
2008
Oil on canvas on aluminium
170 × 190 cm

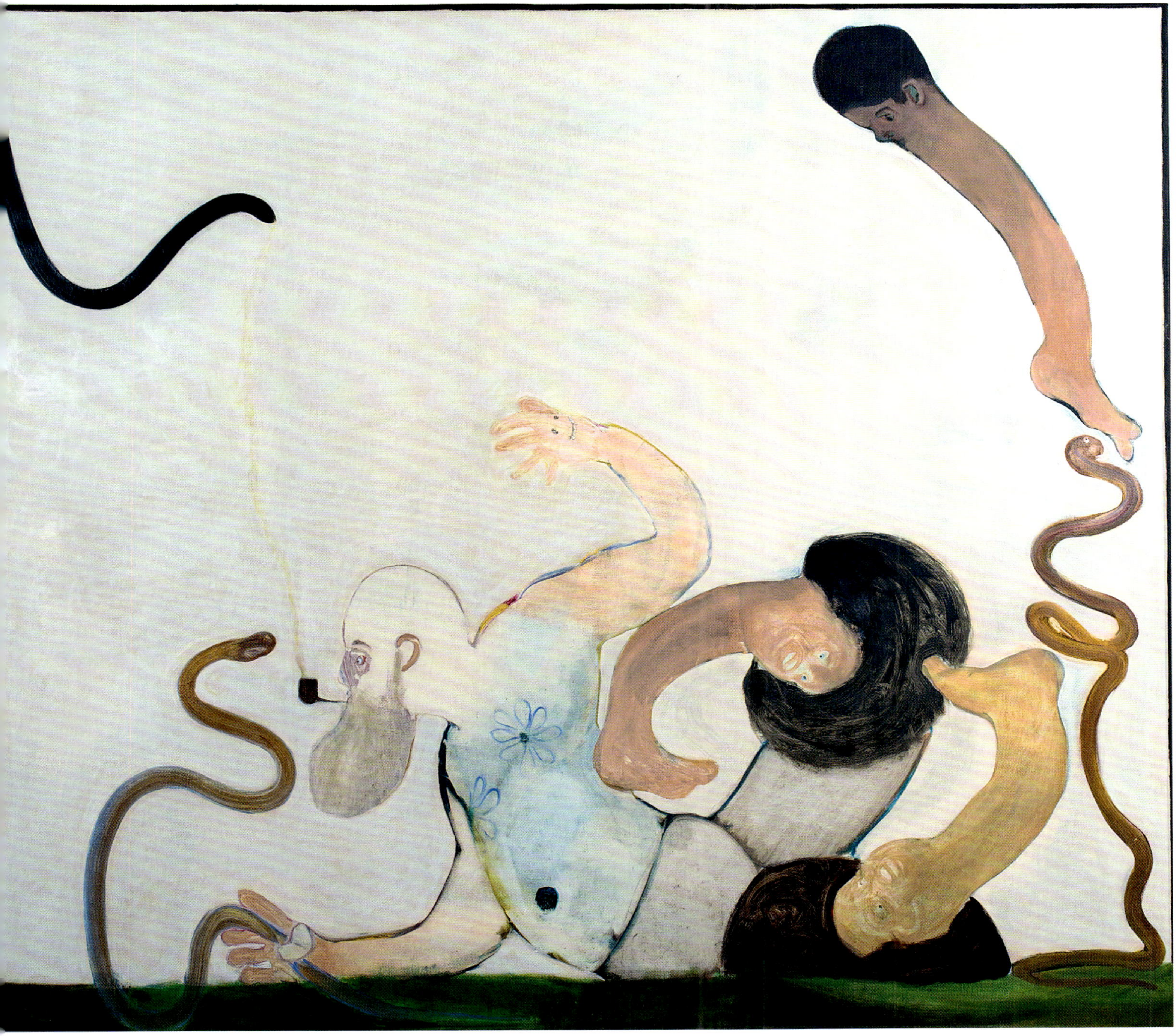

23
**Ryan Mosley**
*Cave Inn*
2011
Oil on linen
214 × 180 cm

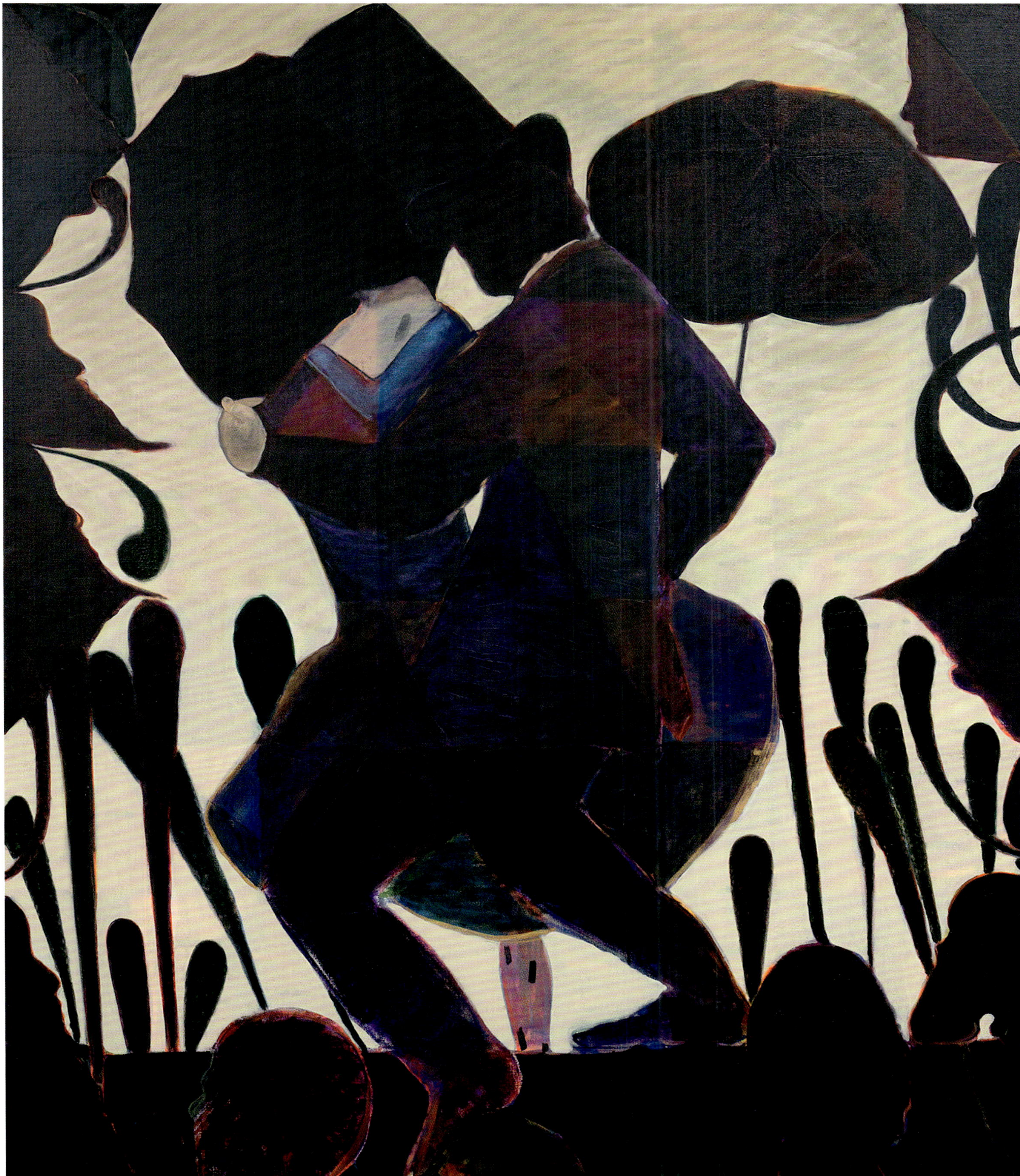

24
**Ryan Mosley**
*Duchess of Oils*
2014
Oil on linen on board
65 × 55 cm

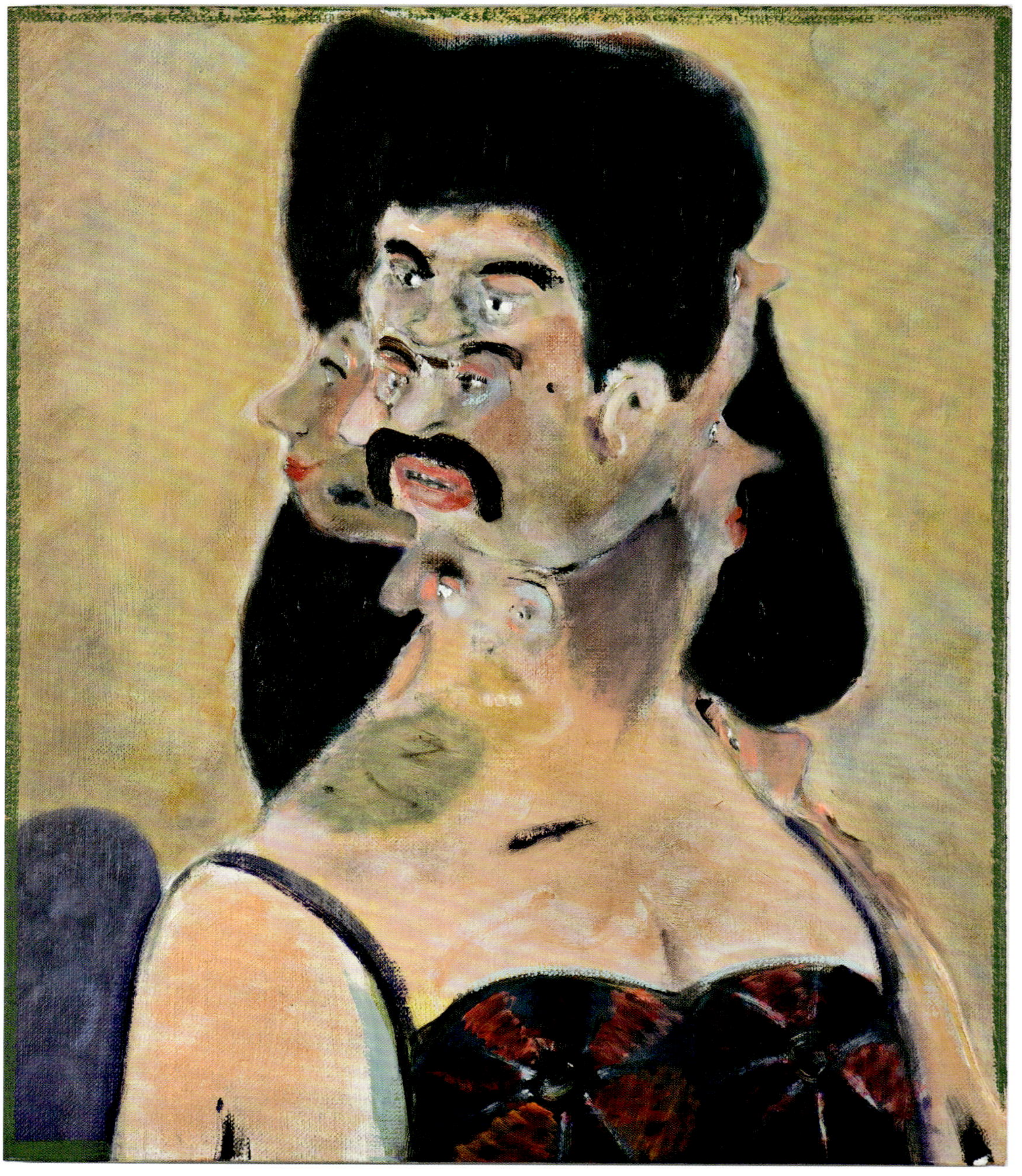

25
**Ryan Mosley**
*Wearing Another's Head on Your Jacket*
2014
Oil on linen on board
65 × 55 cm

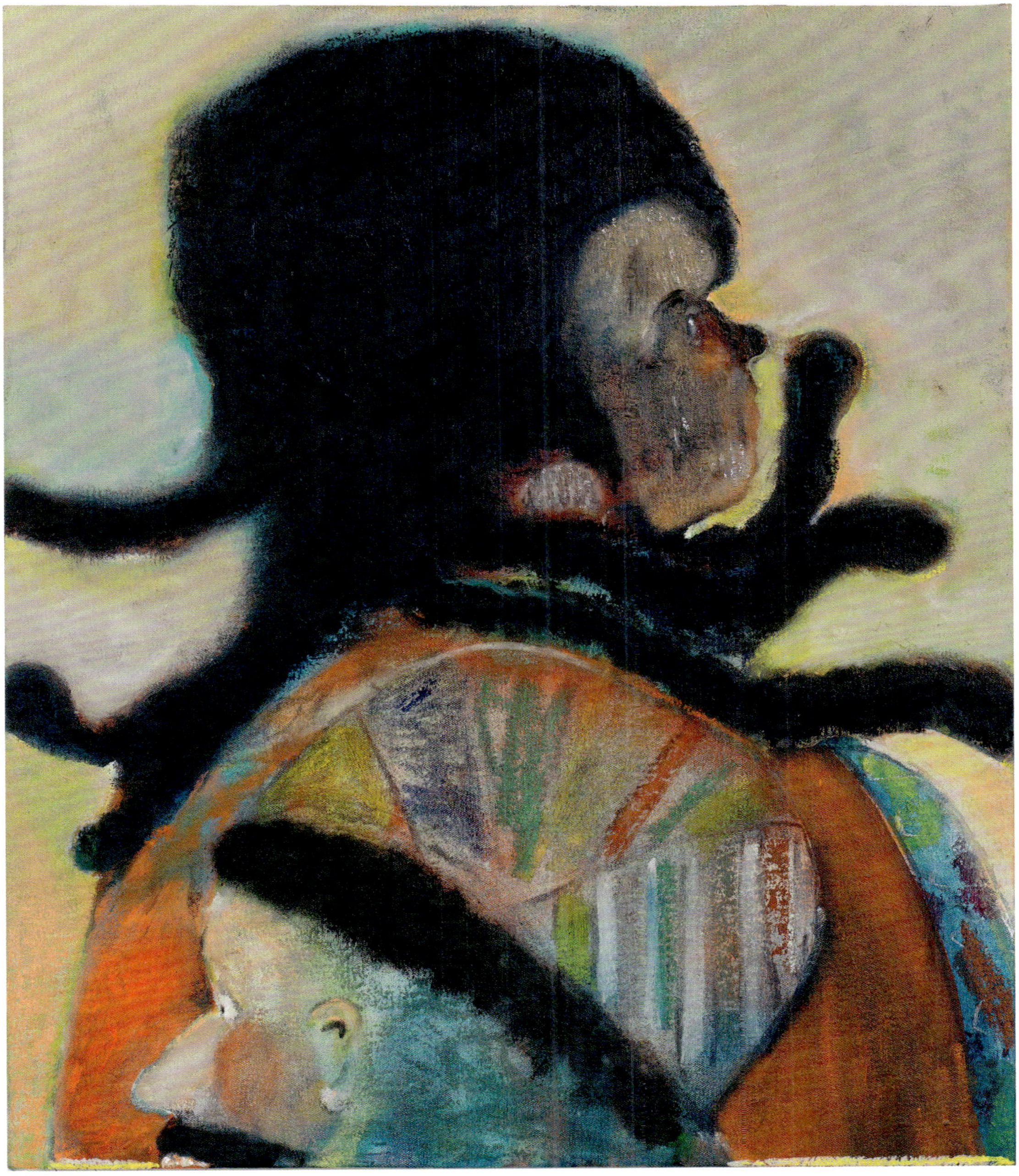

26
**Christina Quarles**
*Casually Cruel*
2018
Acrylic on canvas
196 × 244.3 cm

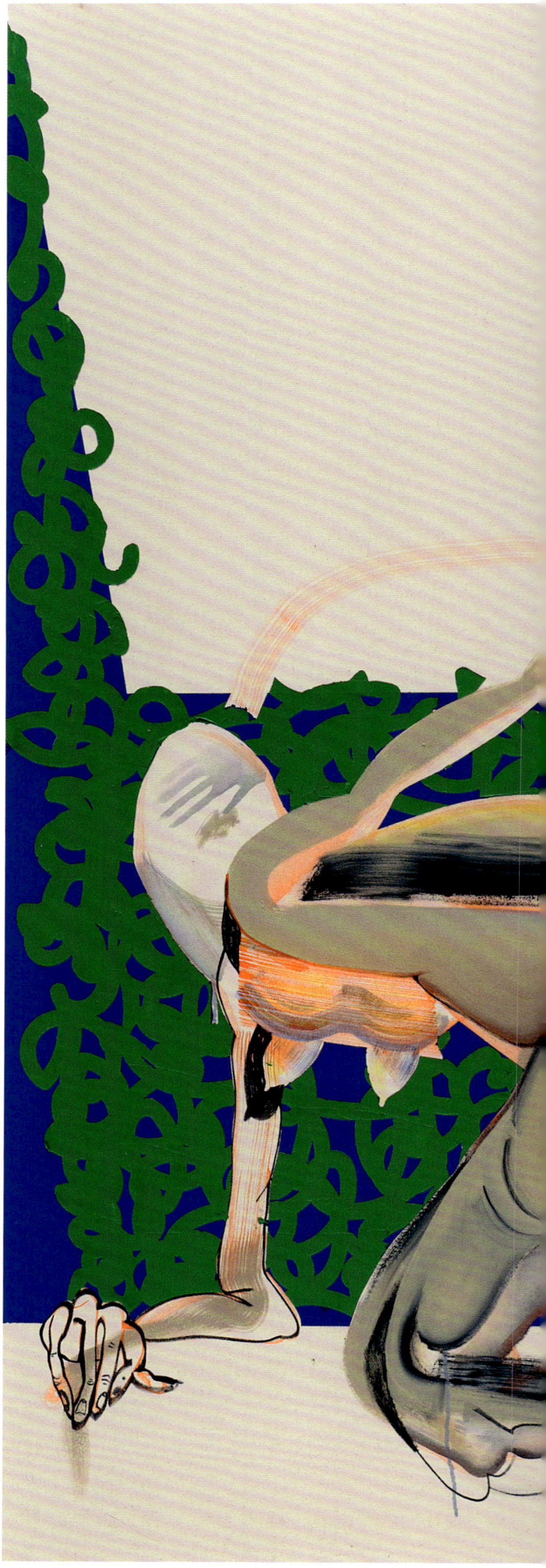

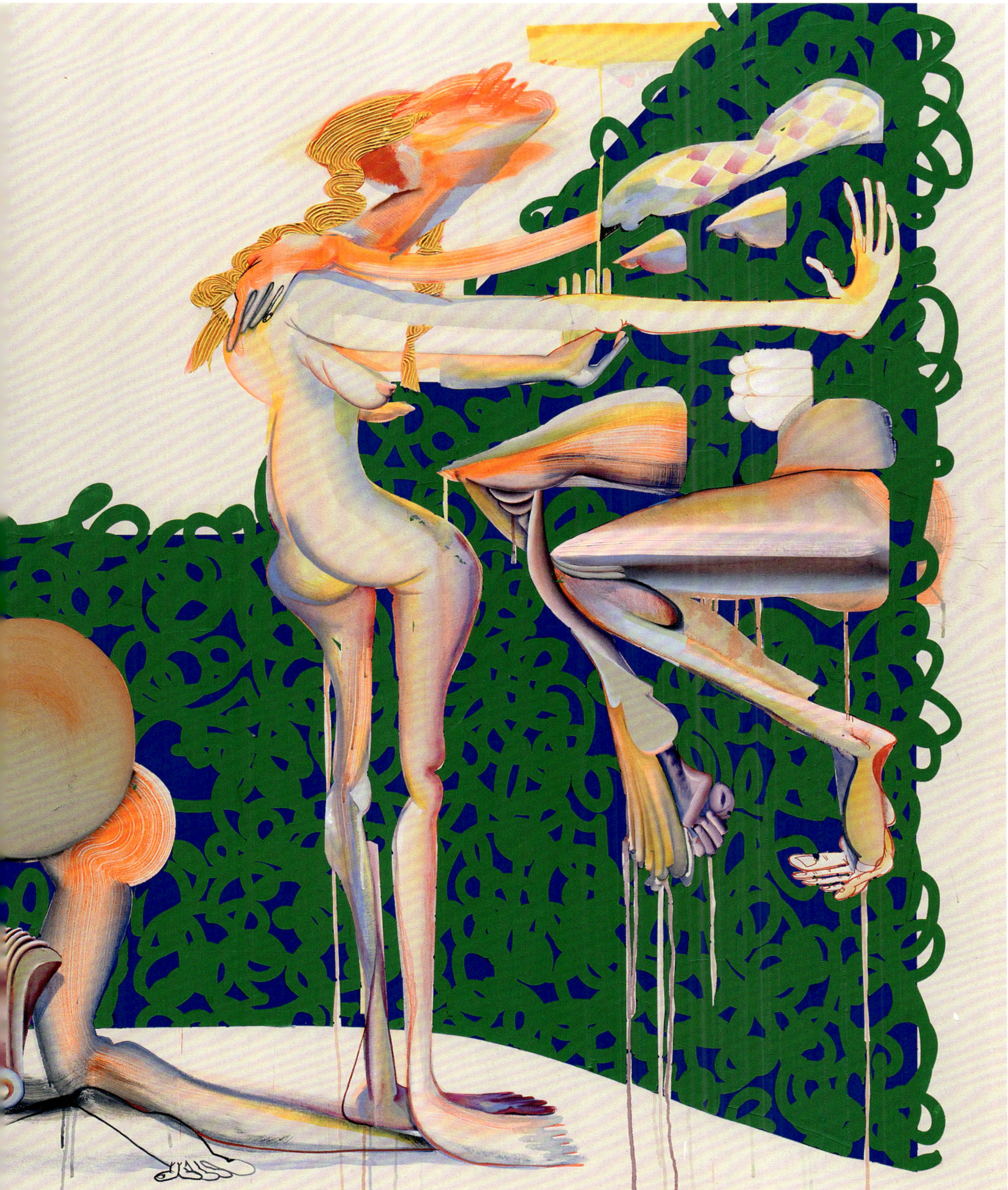

27
**Christina Quarles**
*Sun Bleached*
2018
Acrylic on canvas
152.4 × 182.9 cm

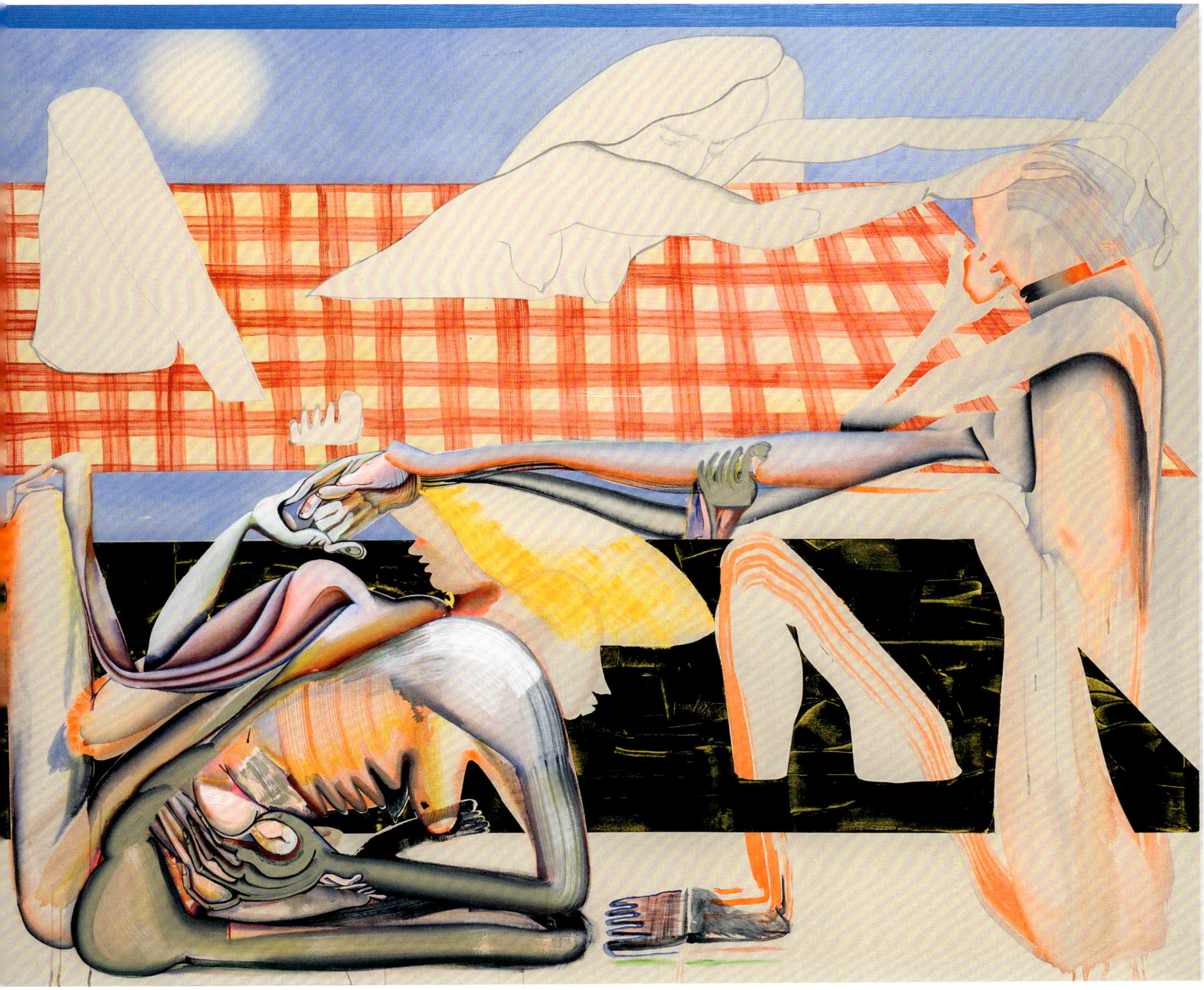

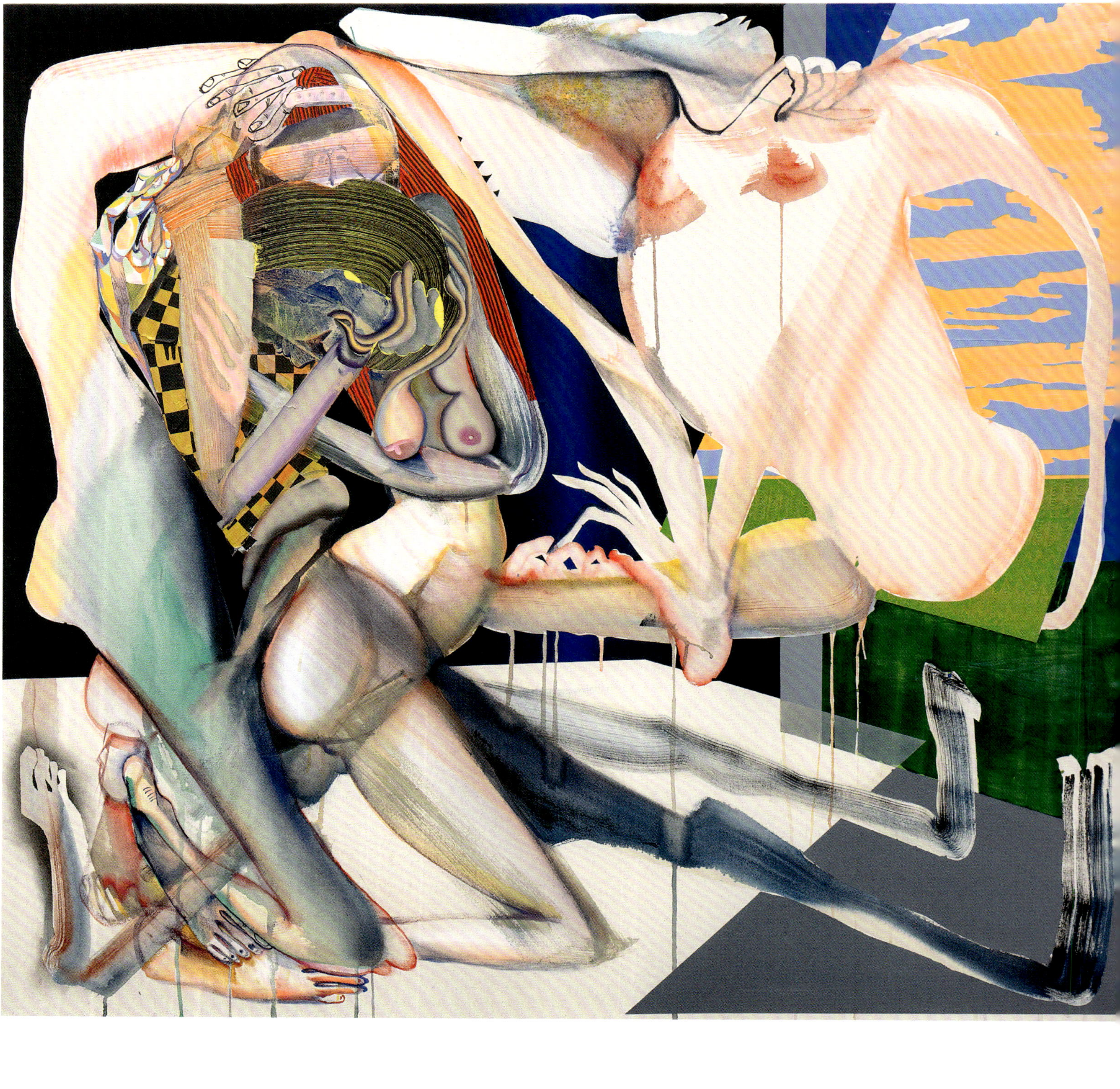

28
**Christina Quarles**
*For Whom Tha Sunsets Free*
2019
Acrylic on canvas
142.2 × 152.4 cm

29
**Daniel Richter**
*Tarifa*
2001
Oil on canvas
350 × 280 cm

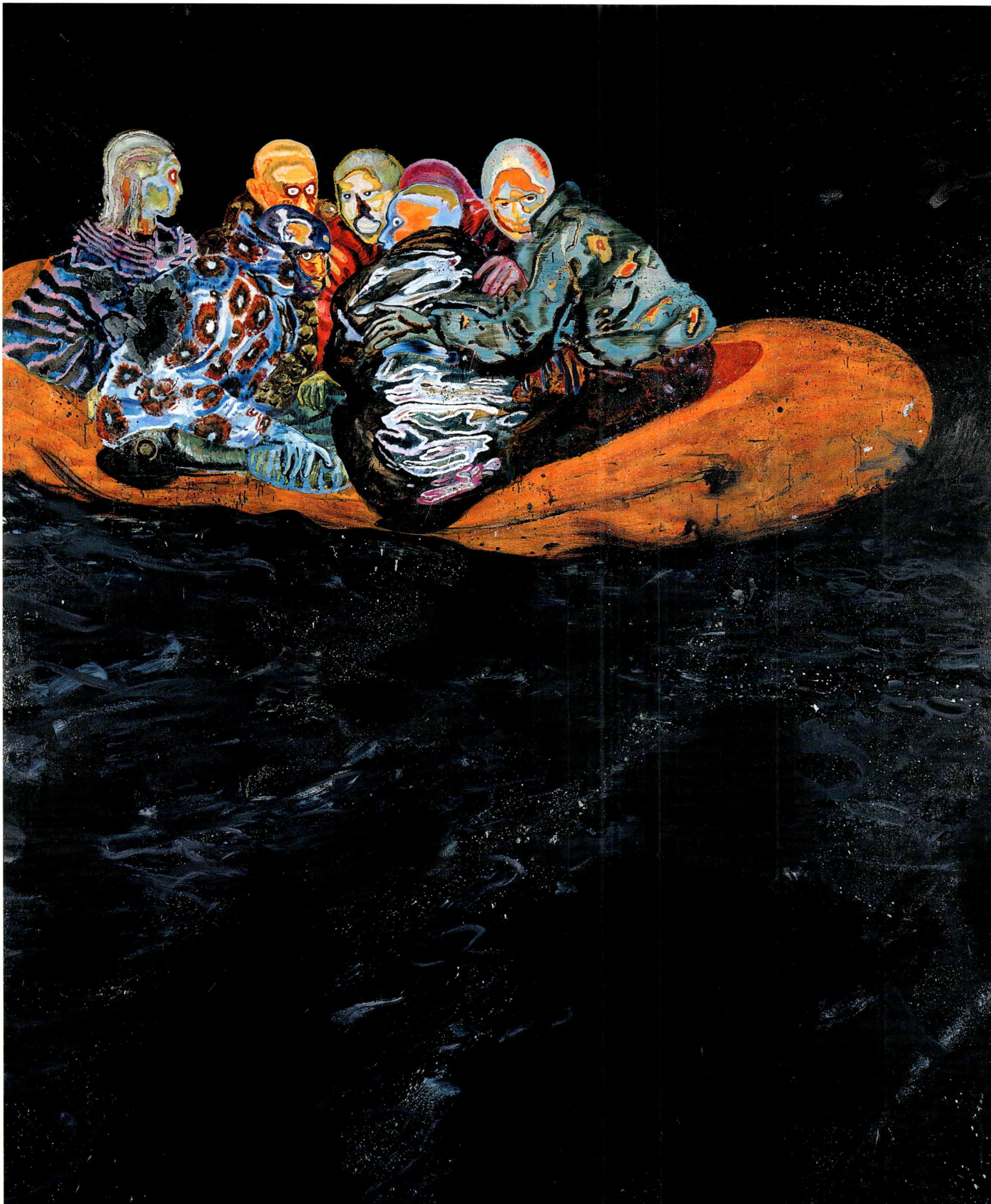

30

**Daniel Richter**

*Das erstaunliche Comeback des Dr. Freud*

2004

Oil on canvas

212 × 260 cm

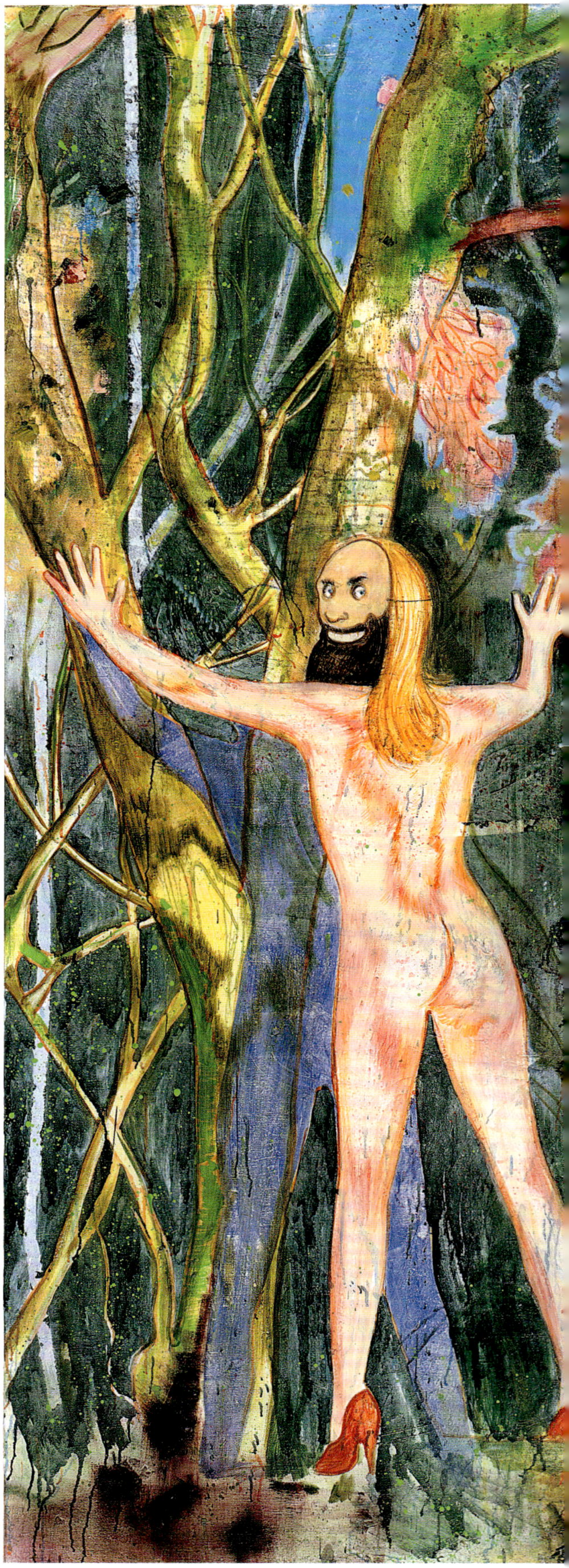

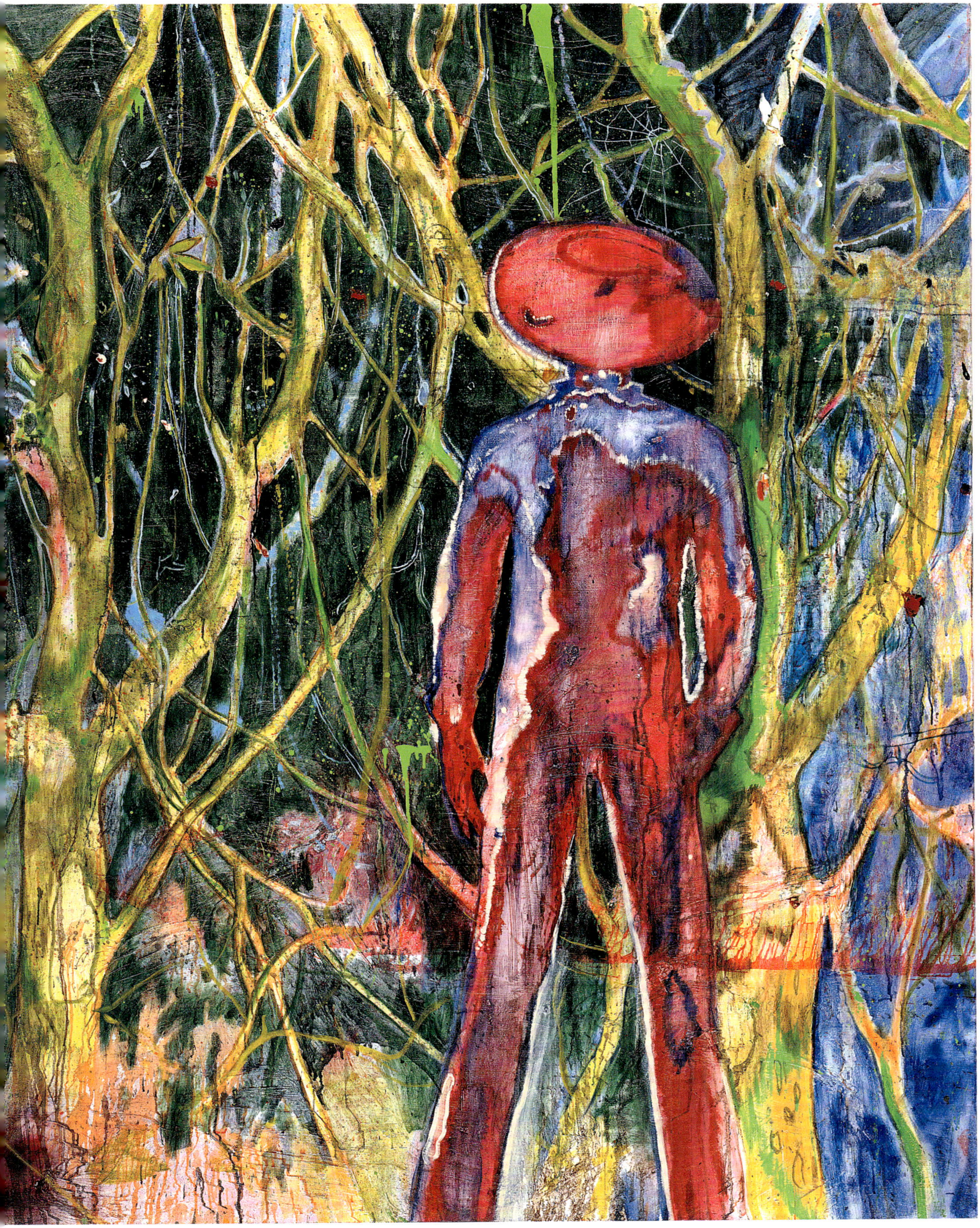

31
**Daniel Richter**
*"HEY JOE"*
2011
Oil on canvas
240 × 180 cm

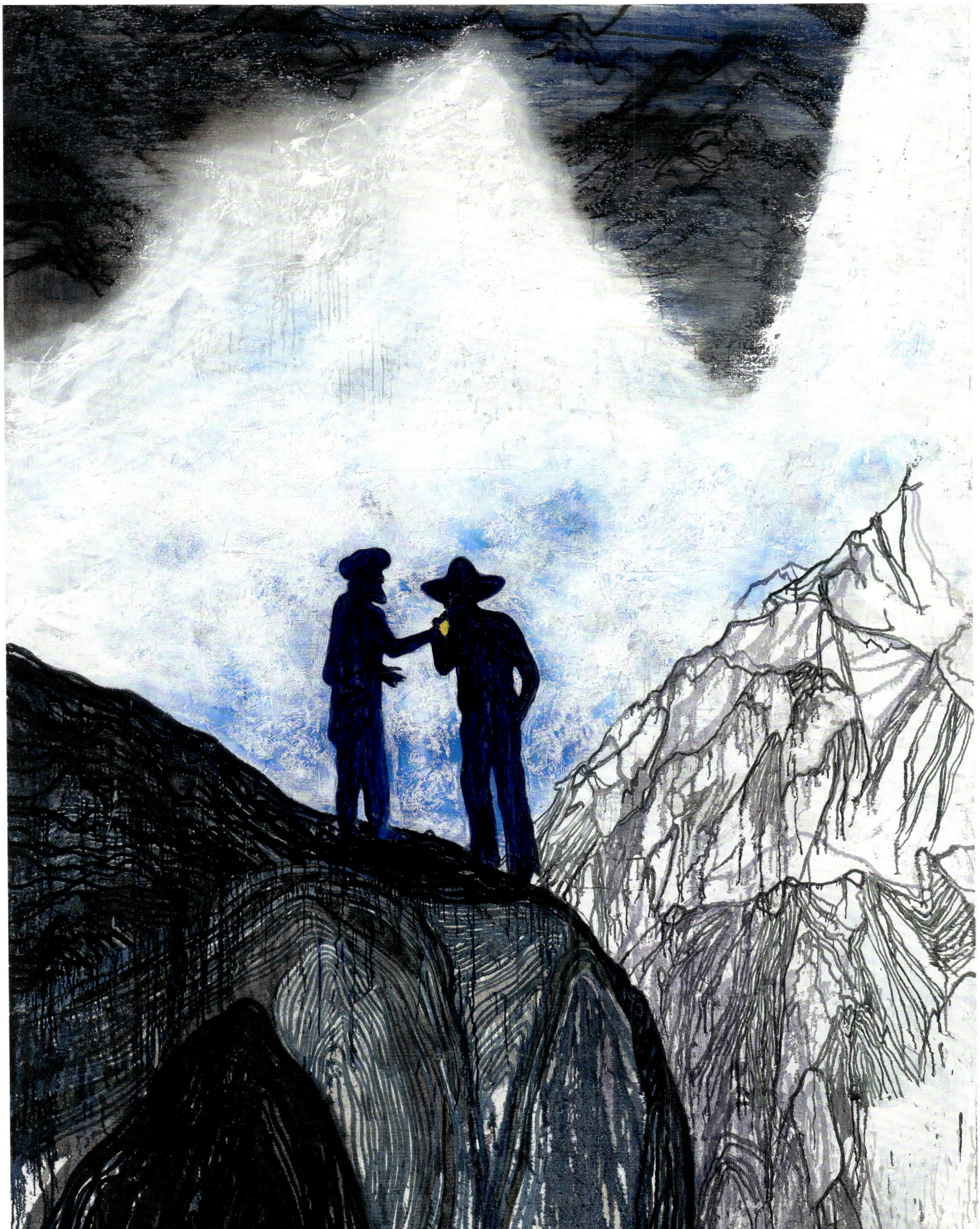

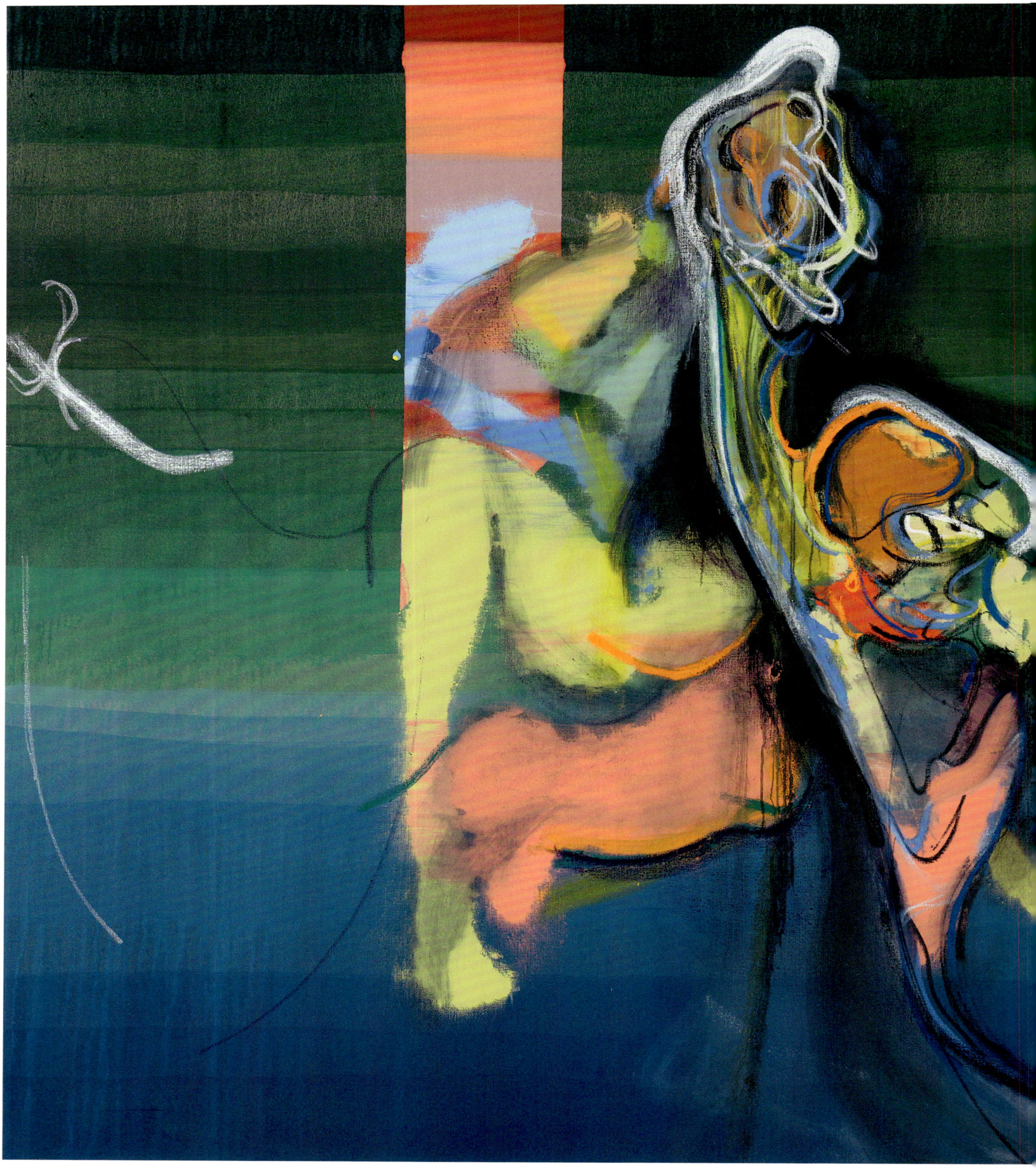

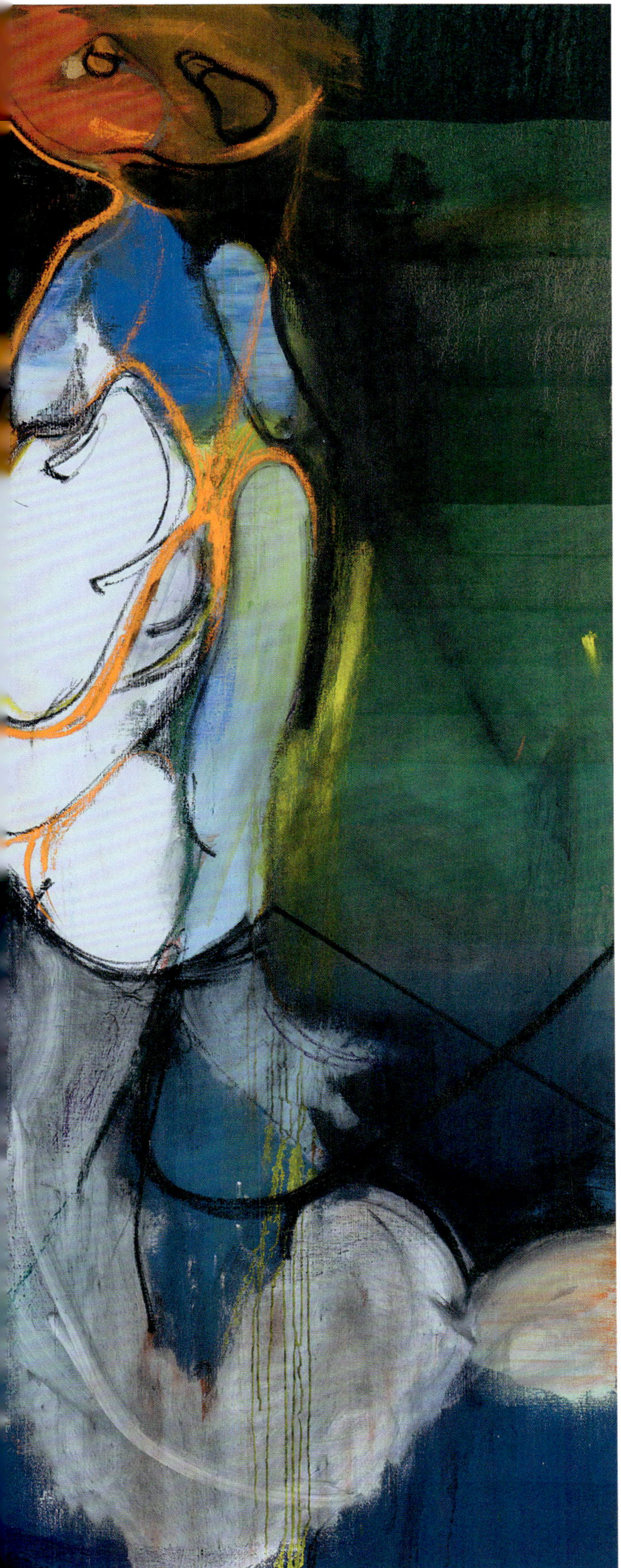

32
**Daniel Richter**
*Asger, Bill und Mark*
2015
Oil on canvas
200 × 270 cm

33

**Dana Schutz**

*New Legs*

2003

Oil on canvas

152.4 × 167.6 cm

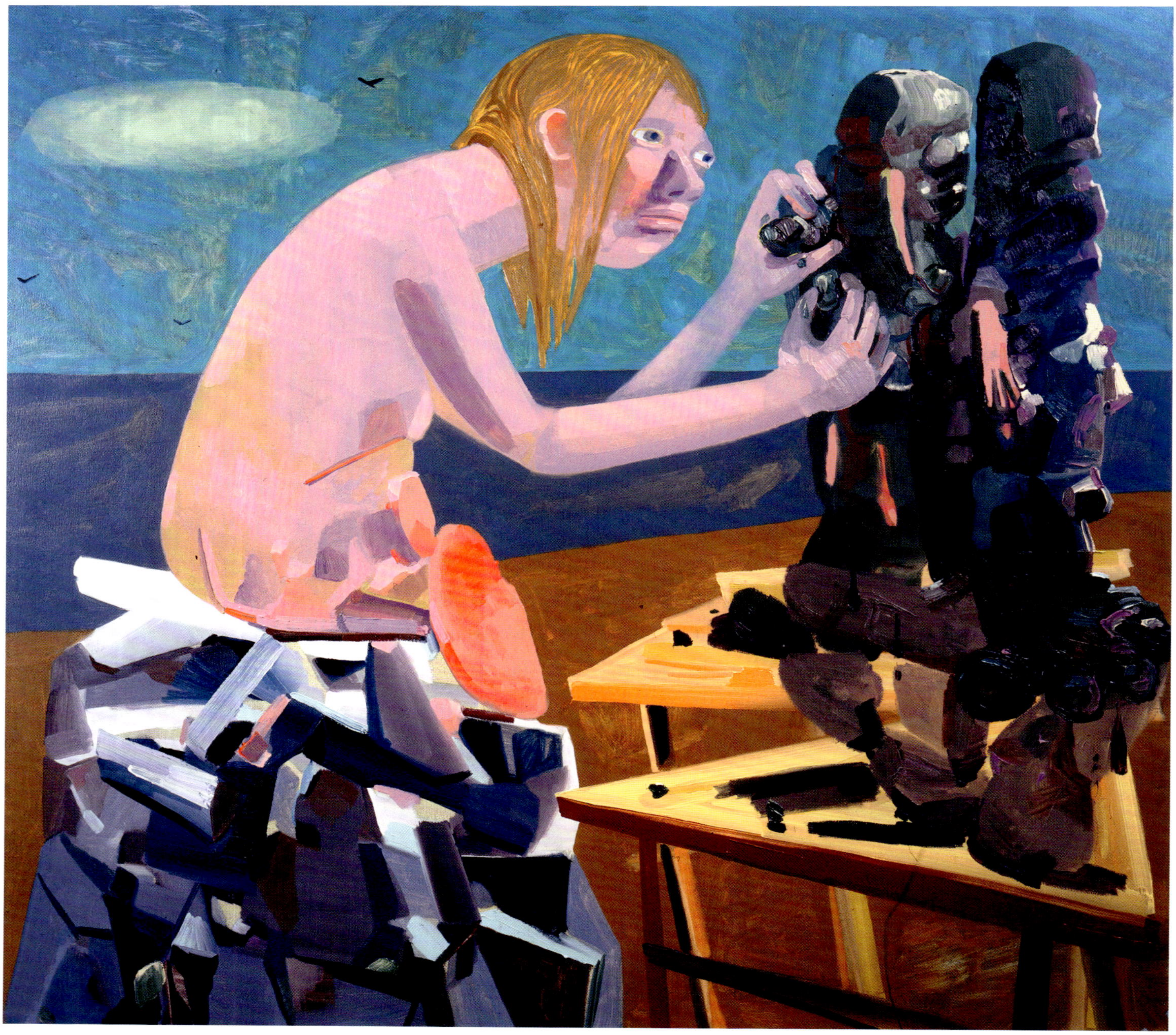

34

**Dana Schutz**

*Man Eating His Chest*

2005

Oil on canvas

137.2 × 106.7 cm

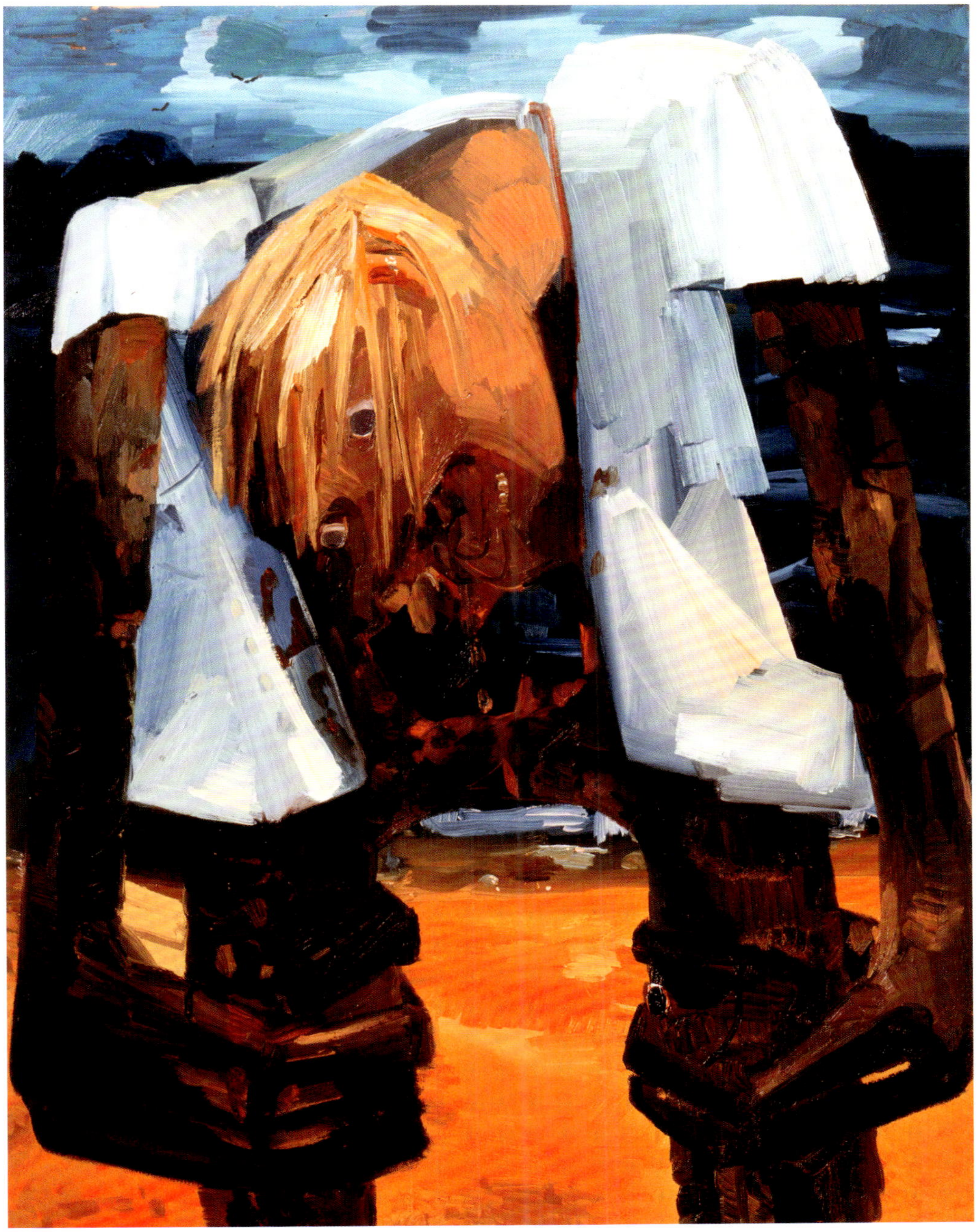

35

**Dana Schutz**

*Imagine You and Me*

2018

Oil on canvas

223.5 × 223.5 cm

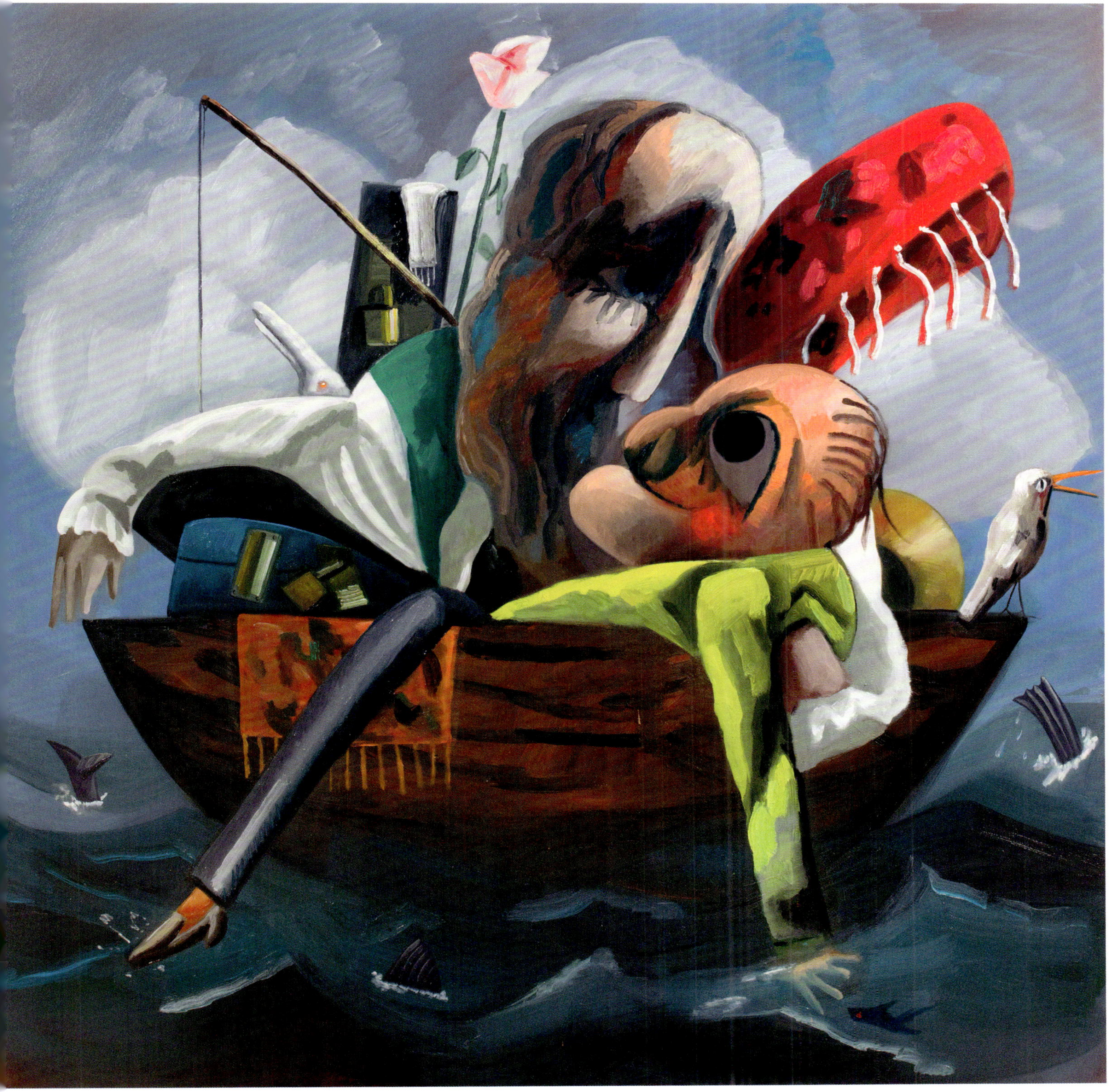

36
**Dana Schutz**
*Suspicious Minds*
2019
Oil on canvas
228.6 × 243.8 cm

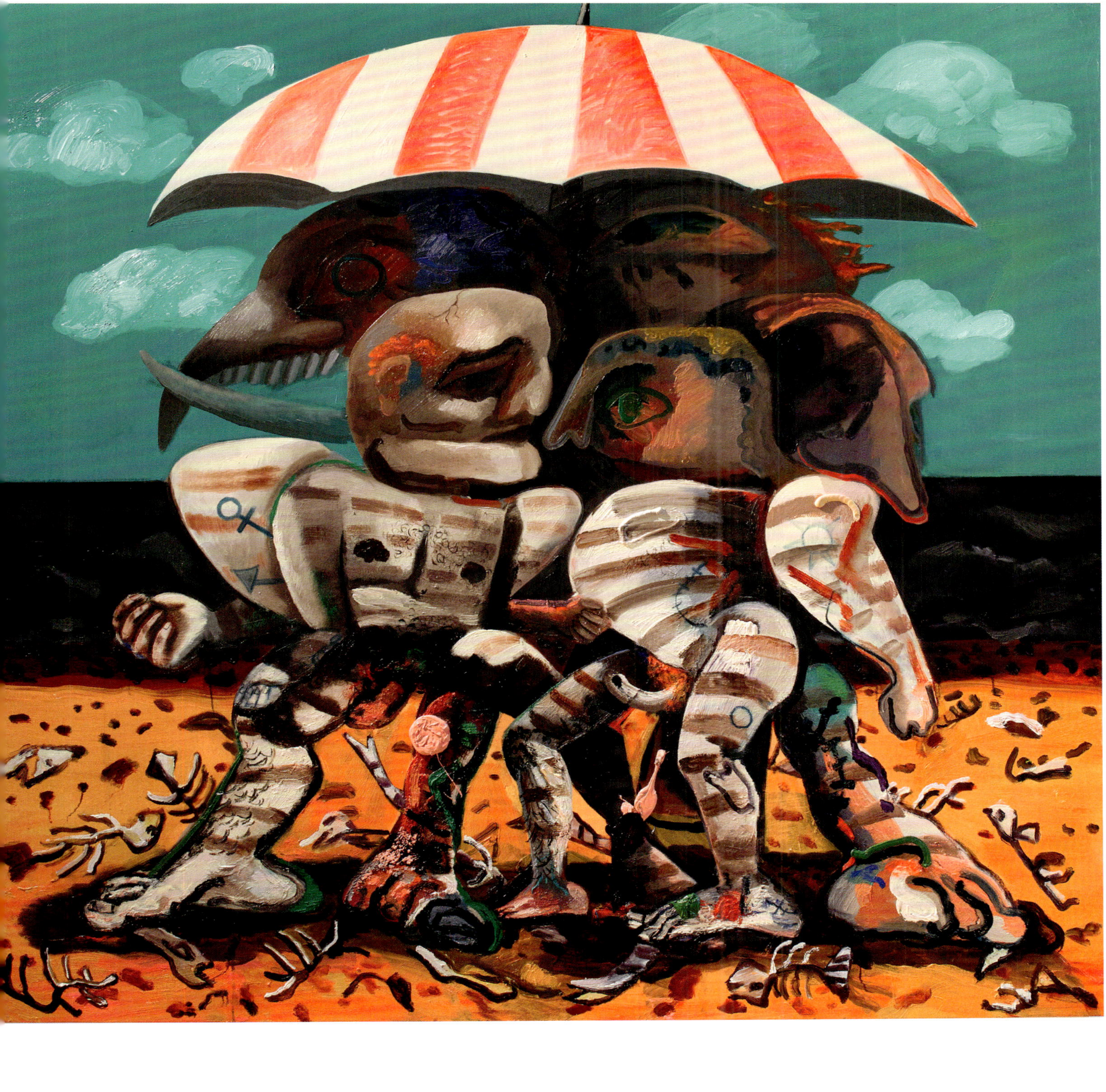

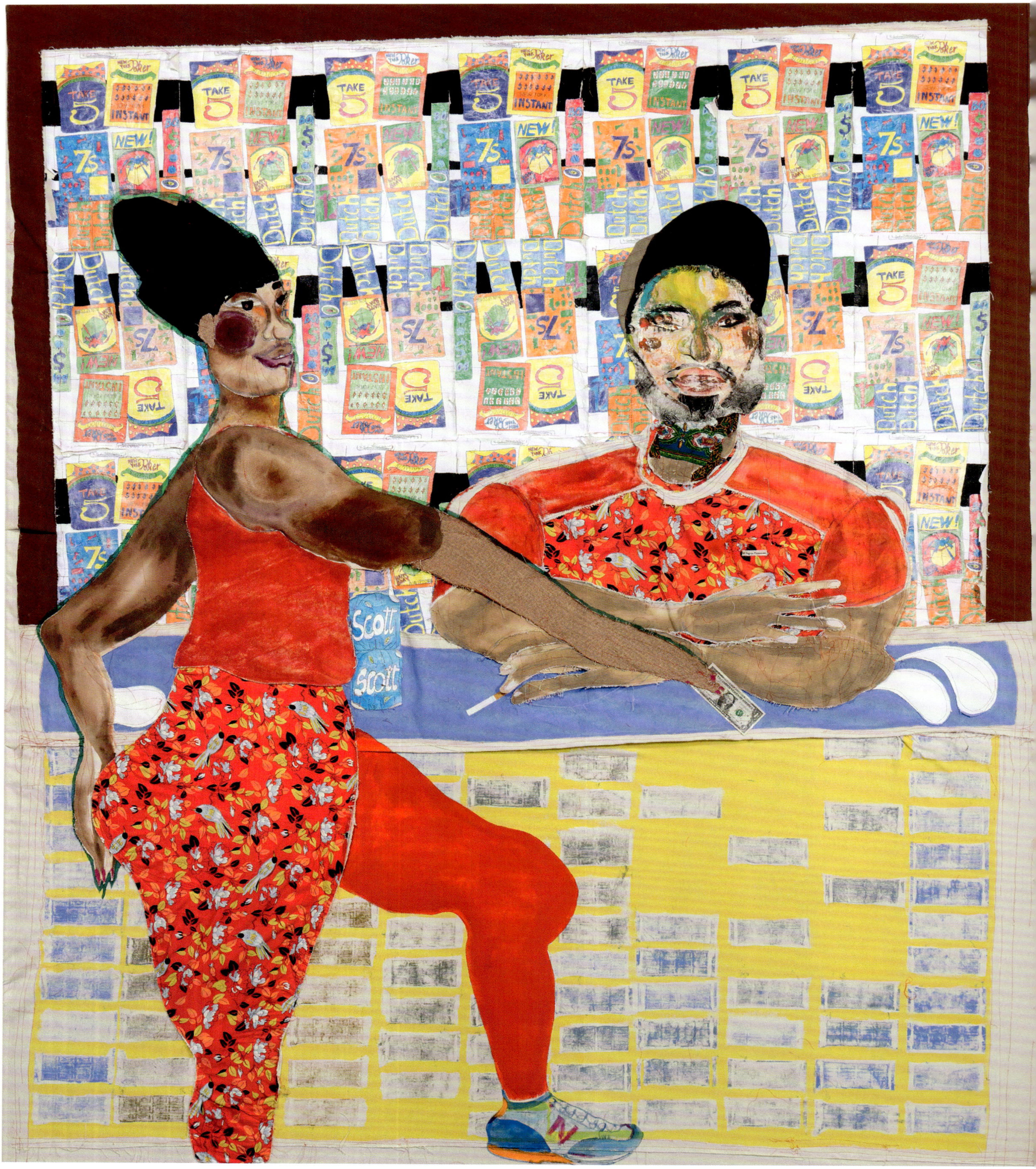
TAKE 5
7s
NEW!
INSTANT
Dutch
Scott

37
**Tschabalala Self**
*Koco at the Bodega*
2017
Coloured pencil, photocopies of hand-coloured drawings, acrylic, Flashe, fabric and painted canvas on canvas
243.8 × 213.4 cm

38
**Tschabalala Self**
*Lenox*
2017
Fabric, ribbon, painted canvas,
Flashe and acrylic on canvas
172.7 × 127 cm

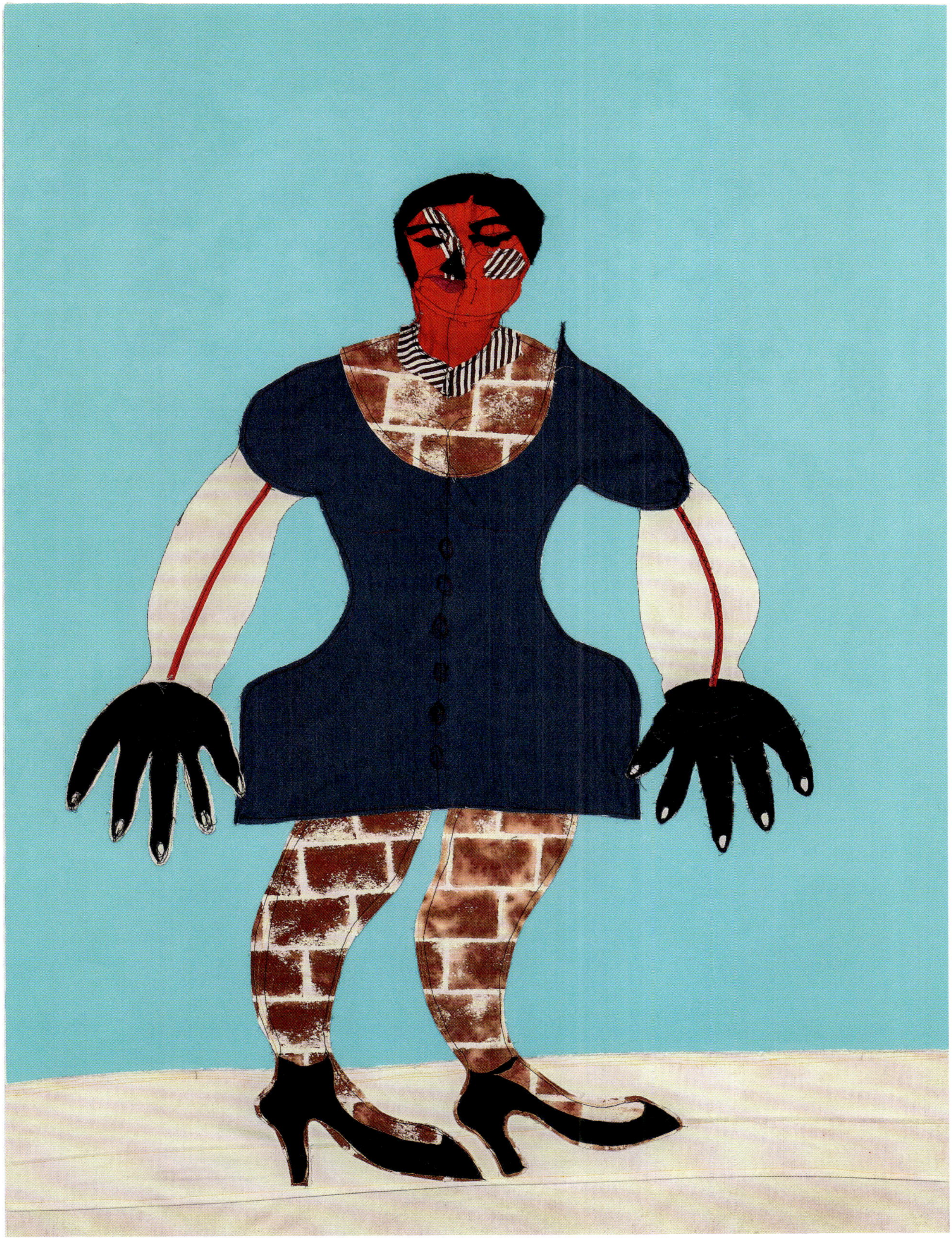

39
**Tschabalala Self**
*NYPD*
2019
Painted canvas, fabric, Flashe
and gouache on canvas
213.4 × 182.9 cm

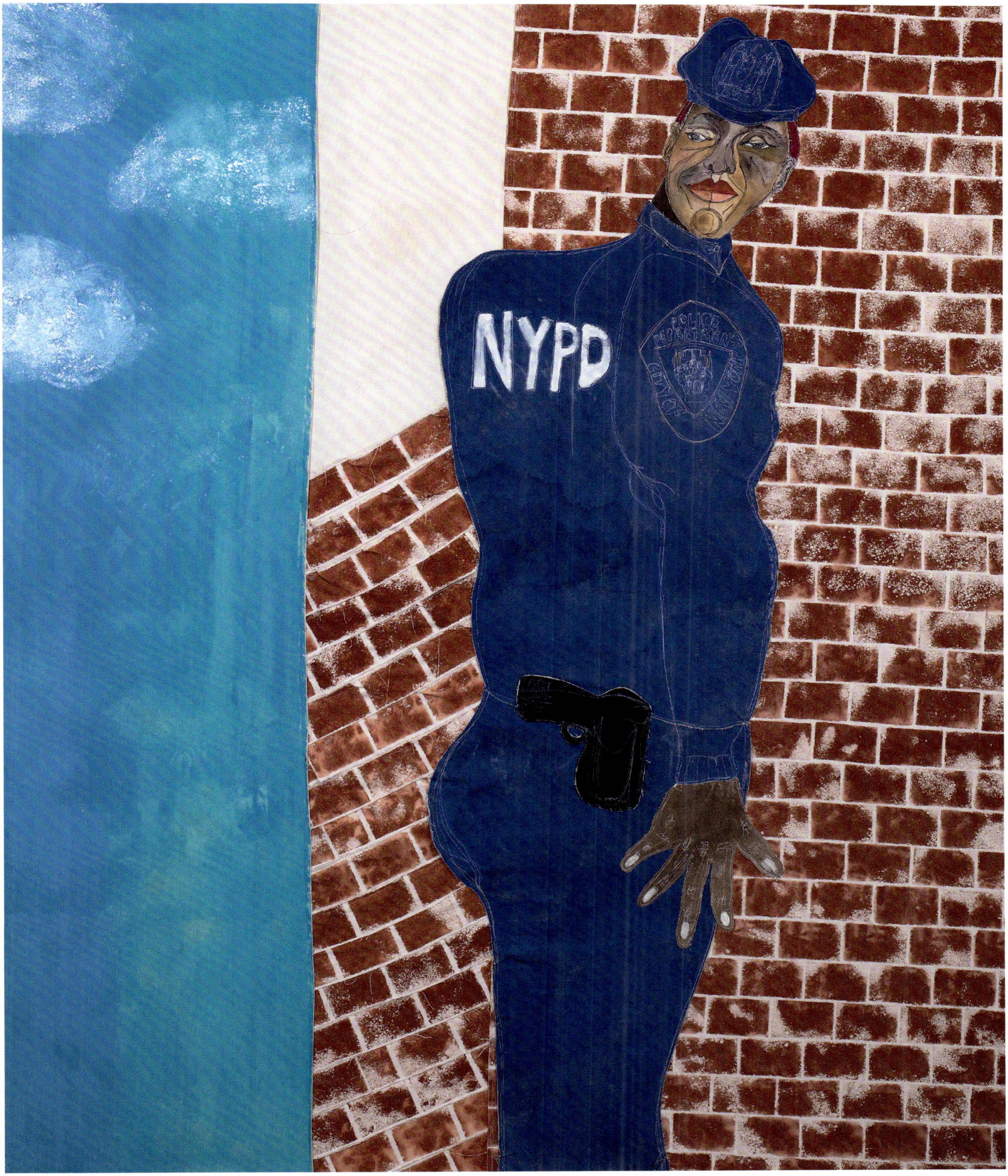
NYPD

40
**Tschabalala Self**
*Fade*
2019
Acrylic, fabric, Flashe,
digital print, painted canvas and
hand painted wall stencil
172.7 × 127 cm

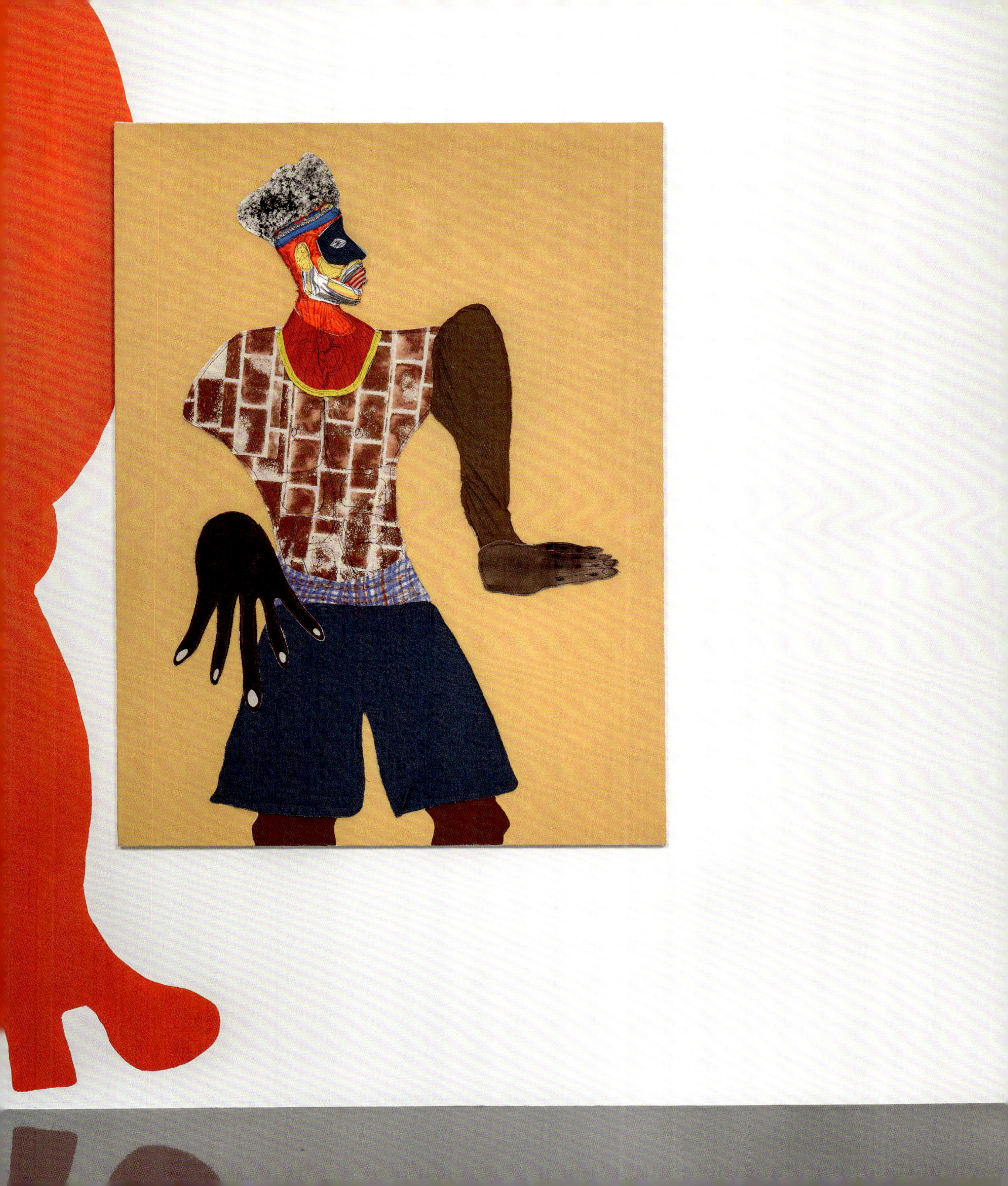

# Michael Armitage in Conversation with Lydia Yee

**Lydia Yee** Can you first tell us about your training? Where did you study and why did you choose painting?

**Michael Armitage** I did my Foundation at Byam Shaw School of Art, a Bachelor's at the Slade School of Fine Art and then a Postgraduate at the Royal Academy Schools. I've been painting since I was about six, so I never really felt it was a question of whether or not I would paint. My question throughout art school was more about how to use paint. I've tried other media, but painting has always been where I've thought things through.

**Yee** Is drawing related to this process?

**Armitage** Yes, I find it quite difficult to untangle the practices, apart from the fact that drawings are largely preliminary to the paintings. They feel very much like fragments of a sentence or ideas in service of what's to come.

**Yee** What kind of education came out of your relationship with your tutors and fellow art students?

**Armitage** The Foundation course was quite academic and set up for those who didn't know what they wanted to do. You had to do a little bit of anatomy drawing, a little bit of sculpture, a little bit of print, etc. When I finally got to the Slade, I really liked the freedom. We were given the space to make whatever we wanted. My contemporaries and tutors were rigorous in questioning everything I did. I felt I learnt a huge amount about concepts and materials, but it was also clear to me that the art-historical context I came from was different from what I was studying.

The Postgraduate course at the Royal Academy had a little bit too much deconstruction for me, which actually became quite crippling. It was too much to actually make the paintings. But having said that, it was exactly what I needed to develop the conceptual foundations of my practice.

**Yee** You were questioning the medium of painting?

**Armitage** Exactly. You had to think about all the reasons why you would make a particular mark. For me, this became really important because I kept finding that what I was making wasn't what I was talking about and interested in. Trying to rethink painting literally from the ground of the painting up took me a long while. It was very difficult and I didn't enjoy it at all. But I'm grateful for having gone through it.

**Yee** It sounds like there was a gap between your experience growing up in Kenya and the subjects that were discussed in your art education in London. Did you paint things that you feel disconnected from today?

**Armitage** Yes. Fortunately, my postgraduate degree show was eaten by mice, so I don't have to live with it. There were all sorts of things that I made that were just embarrassing, but necessary. One of the phases I went through, important to my development, involved thinking about Jacob Lawrence's *Migration Series*, in which he painted an existing culture into art history. I also made abstract paintings, which led me to question the importance of the figure in my work. After a while, I determined that I wanted to make something to which, if I showed it at home in Kenya, anyone who walked in off the street could directly relate.

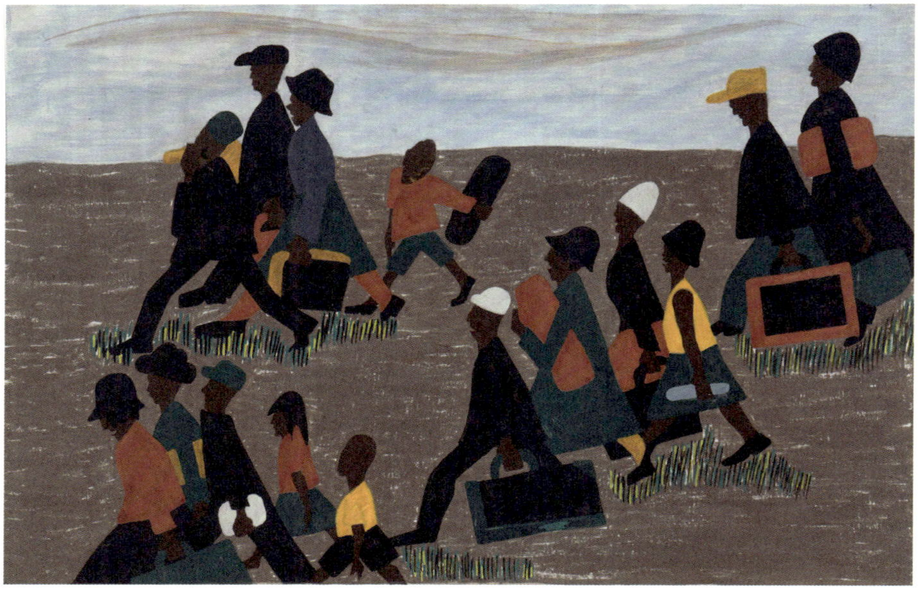

Jacob Lawrence, *The migrants arrived in great numbers*, panel 40 from *The Migration Series*, 1940–41, tempera on gesso on composition board, 30.5 × 45.7 cm

**Yee** How do you approach painting the figure? Do you draw or paint from life? How do you work out the composition?

**Armitage** To make a painting, I'll use anything that helps: I use photographs, I draw from life, some bits I make up and I also draw from other people's paintings. Anything that gives me a way forward, I'll use. With the preliminary work, I much prefer to draw from video stills rather than photographs.

**Yee** Really?

**Armitage** Yes. There's much more distortion and room for your own interpretation in them. But I do use still photographs as well. Pretty much all the landscapes that I use were life studies in the beginning before growing into something different. This is important when I want to convey a sense of a specific place.

**Yee** By videos, do you mean documentary and news footage?

**Armitage** Yes. I also find a lot on the internet. For example, I made a series of paintings about this Tanzanian bongo flava artist called Diamond Platnumz, whose music I love. I found his film *Nasema Nawe*, which has a dance in it called Baikoko. I made drawings from frozen points in the video. When I looked at the figures on the white paper, it looked like they were floating in the air in these really quite sexual and strange poses. They began to look a bit like Goya's witches. Baikoko and other overtly sexual dances were outlawed by the Tanzanian government. This meant they were pushed to cultural peripheries outside of public view, taking place in night clubs or wedding ceremonies, where Baikoko originated. I saw a parallel to how witchcraft was treated by authorities in Goya's time. I researched Baikoko in more detail

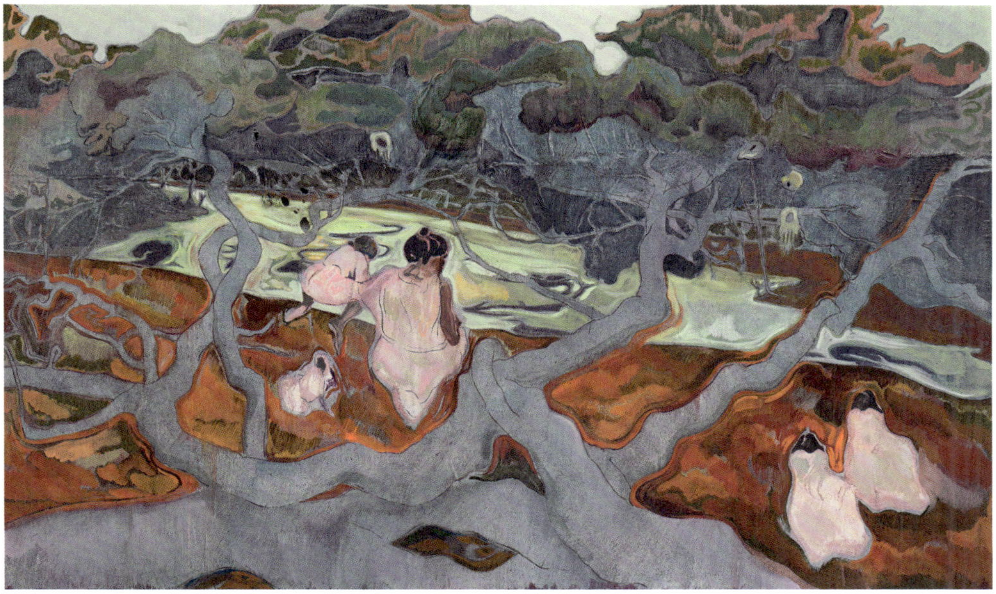

Michael Armitage, *Baikoko at the Mouth of the Mwachema River*, 2016, oil on lugubo bark cloth, 220 × 330 cm

and worked with an editor friend in Dar es Salaam to create some short videos, which I used as the basis for some more drawings. They ended up as figures in paintings like *Baikoko at the Mouth of the Mwachema River* [2016], where a Goya painting called *Atropos* [1819–23] was a reference for the composition.

**Yee** Can tell us a little bit about your technique and working methods? In particular, I'm interested in your use of bark cloth. How did you come to incorporate it into your work?

**Armitage** I came across the cloth about ten years ago. It took me about three years of trial and error to figure out how to use it. At first, I went through lots of different surfaces, including kanga cloth, woven palm leaf matting and other materials, but I found these surfaces always dominated the paintings I was trying to make. When I started to treat lubugo much like a normal canvas, by stretching and priming it, the material began to operate in a much more subtle way. It seemed very similar to a normal canvas in some ways, but it also located the origins of the work in East Africa. The uneven points and areas that were difficult to paint on, gave a resistance that I liked.

**Yee** What are the particular characteristics of this surface?

**Armitage** The surface is very irregular. Sometimes it has quite significant holes in it as well as stitching and wrinkles. I sometimes incorporate these features into planning the composition, adding my own cuts in the surface, which are then stitched up again. Beneath the skin of the painting, there are compositional elements, some inherent and some planned.

**Yee** Once you've prepared the surface, how do you approach the painting itself?

**Armitage** Usually, I'll start with flat areas of colour. Sometimes, I'll sketch out different parts of the composition or indicate characters, depending on the atmosphere that I want. After this, I'll start going back in and building up the characters or shifting the composition if it's not working. That's where all the pain and the joy of trying to make a painting really begins.

**Yee** Do you mix your own colours or do you use commercially available paints?

**Armitage** I use pre-mixed, commercially available paint. Usually I thin it down quite a lot before building up the paintings. The wood grain and surface irregularities of the lubugo cloth interrupt the brush, meaning that the marks are quite staccato and it's hard to get a smooth continuous line. I thin down the paint to allow me to make more fluid marks and I use thicker paint too. The whole process is a bit of a give and take with the surface, and every surface is unique.

**Yee** It's interesting that the material helps form the image and the composition. I can see in some of the larger works that you can't have one whole piece, so you have to piece the bark cloth together.

**Armitage** Yes, although the pieces of cloth can get quite big. The trees can grow up to forty years old and they're quite thin and tall. This means the cloth is irregular as the tree narrows at the top. The biggest piece I have is maybe 4.5 by 1.6 metres at its narrowest and by up to 2 metres at its widest. When they're that big, there are often really rough parts of cloth and also very slick parts. The slick parts are smooth and offer less resistance, so I always try and incorporate rougher sections of cloth, and particularly on larger paintings.

**Yee** How is this cloth normally used?

**Armitage** The lubugo cloth is used by the Buganda tribe. The majority of the cloths they make will be for burial shrouds – the word lubugo translates into English as 'funeral'. The Buganda sometimes wear them for major ceremonies, but most of the time they're used for burying the dead.

**Yee** Which current or historical painters have been important to the development of the paintings in the exhibition?

**Armitage** *#mydressmychoice* [2015] [pl. 3] is based on a Velázquez painting, *The Rokeby Venus* [1647–51], which is in the National Gallery. Gauguin has been a key artist for me in dealing with the fact that I'm making paintings based on subjects that are from a country that's considered to be exotic. He's also a damn good painter. Goya is one of the most important painters for me. His subjects and how and why he paints them have been fundamental to my own approach. Cézanne is important in terms of colour and mark, and Seurat for understanding the way colours work together.

Among contemporary work, Chris Ofili's Blue Paintings, for me, are extraordinary. There's also a Kenyan painter called Meek Gichugu who had one outrageous show at Gallery Watatu in Nairobi in the 1990s, which had a massive impact on me.

**Yee** I want to go back to Gauguin because he's often seen as quite a problematic figure in relationship to his subjects, particularly the Tahitian paintings. How do you sit alongside that history? Obviously, your relationship to your subjects is very different from his.

**Armitage** I think I wanted Gauguin in my paintings for some of the problems that he brings. I'm interested in the problems around tourism, how cultures interact, the geopolitics and the imbalance of economic and political power. All of these reflect aspects of looking at 'the other'. There's a point at which a genuine form of either ritual or cultural expression becomes a parody of itself when it's re-enacted for tourism or nostalgia. I'm interested in the effect of this on people and cultures.

**Yee** Are you talking about the tourism industry in particular?

**Armitage** No, I'm thinking about people who want to bring back some of the old rituals of tribal life, as a way of reclaiming some sort of Africanness, or Kenyanness, or whatever tribe you're from. I feel this is integral to the issues of Gauguin, who consistently presented himself as a 'primitive'. He looked at the cultures of Tahiti but in a way that built a narrative about himself. He exoticises both the people that he's looking at and his own artistic persona. He edited out what he didn't want shown in order to create and preserve this myth. I feel this way of thinking relates to the sometimes subtle and sometimes very crude issues around cultural development in Kenya. This is how Gauguin became important to me.

**Yee** Which exhibitions have made an impact on you and why? You mentioned Meek Gichugu.

**Armitage** Yes, I saw an unbelievable exhibition of his work in Nairobi in the 1990s. To be honest, like most things that have an impact, I didn't like the work that much at the time. It was so crude and outrageous. I was maybe ten or eleven and I just remember thinking, 'I'm sure I can make a better painting than that'. But then I kept seeing his work because the father of a friend of mine was involved in the gallery that showed him. When I went around to their house, I would see these paintings again and again, and they slowly became so intriguing, partly because of how repulsive they were.

I didn't go to any Western museums until I was in education in the UK at eighteen. Then I remember seeing an El Greco show at the National Gallery. It was a bit of a revelation because he's just a weird painter. I found so much of his use of colour really repulsive: this sickly lemon-yellow with Prussian blue. I was also really interested in his distortion of figures, which results in a very expressive caricature. Maybe the biggest impact, which I'm still getting over, was seeing Goya's *Black Paintings* at the Prado. They're like nothing else.

**Yee** No abstract painter has done that for you?

**Armitage** They have, but they've come and gone. I love Arshile Gorky and I still look at him and think about his marks. But he's also figurative. Julie Mehretu has this ability to make almost symphonic paintings, building up marks, references, colours and movement so that the paintings never feel settled. The more you look at the paintings the more intriguing they are, and the more extraordinary they become. There are lots of other painters who've had an impact on me in different ways.

**Yee** I know you haven't been working for long, but has the way you paint evolved over time?

**Armitage** Yes, a lot. I feel like every single year I've learnt something from the experience of making paintings. When I first started making paintings at the age of six, I remember this nervous excitement of creating something. Whether it was good or terrible, the potential for both was there. This excitement and feeling of potential hasn't changed. The challenge of making a painting is that you have to be inventive and react to what's in front of you. The process and the thinking behind the painting are always evolving.

**Yee** I think I know what your answer to this will be, but do you feel figurative painting can have a social or political dimension to it?

**Armitage** There will always be prejudice in the making and reception of a representation of a person. Prejudice is a social construct and a political tool.

**Yee** Your titles also suggest some sort of narrative. I'm thinking particularly of *Kampala Suburb* [2014] [pl. 2]. Can you talk about that scene?

**Armitage** *Kampala Suburb* was made at the time when the Ugandan government was trying to pass some pretty draconian anti-LGBTQ+ laws. It was already illegal to be LGBTQ+, but if you knew somebody who was from the LGBTQ+ community, they wanted to make it illegal not to report them to the authorities. For this, you'd go to jail for up to fifteen years. So I wanted the painting to be located in Kampala and I thought about the suburbs because that's where most people are. It was also important to make a tender painting that was about an ordinary scene of a couple of people in love, having a kiss before bedtime. I made the painting thinking that it would be shown in Nairobi, where we also have draconian attitudes and laws towards LGBTQ+ people, but the show fell through.

**Yee** The other painting in the exhibition, *Peace Coma* [2012] [pl. 1], features snakes. What function do animals serve in your work? Are they stand-ins for other kinds of figures or do they function as part of the landscape and setting?

**Armitage** Sometimes they're just animals. I like monkeys as they're a little bit too close to humans, which I find interesting. A lot of the artists I grew up looking at used animals as stand-ins for people as a way of talking through quite difficult social issues without having to paint a person at a time where government censorship was rampant.

**Yee** So in *Peace Coma*, are they snakes or do they represent something else?

**Armitage** They're just snakes doing their thing.

**Yee** Is there a biblical association?

**Armitage** Snakes are of course always biblical. But these ones weren't biblical. I think if you asked my mother, she'd find it biblical, but for me the painting is more the embodiment of an idea, as opposed to the depiction of something itself.

**Yee** Why do you think there's been a renewed interest in figurative painting in recent years? Did it ever go away?

**Armitage** Figurative painting has always been there. While I was studying, some of the most talked-about artists made figurative paintings: Martin Kippenberger, Sigmar Polke, Peter Doig, Chris Ofili, etc., not to mention pretty much all the painters that I grew up looking at in Kenya. If there is something that's changed, it is perhaps the use of irony in Western figurative painting. Previously, for something to be critically legitimate it had to be ironic. Now there are more diverse considerations for something to be seen as critically legitimate, but this is also problematic.

# Cecily Brown in Conversation with Jason Rosenfeld

**Jason Rosenfeld** I'm interested in your working process. When do you know that a painting is finished? You always say that you can't see what it's going to look like in the beginning. A lot of artists would say 'Oh, I had it in my head the whole time.'

**Cecily Brown** For me, there's a sort of notion that you're chasing something – that you don't know what it is until you see it. It's a bit like Mr Right, you know? You do have some vague notion of what this person is going to be, or this creature, or this thing that's going to be right. I think that's overly romantic, but …

**Rosenfeld** He's out there somewhere! [Laughter]

**Brown** That, for me, is the thrill, the chase of the imagery and of not knowing what it's going to be. In a way, the whole thing is about discovering the image, disrupting it, and almost deliberately losing it and pushing it around. So it's not the moment of recognition – it's really a question of living with it over time. I never decide then and there that it's done. I have a whole gestation area in the studio; I've got one wall painted a different colour. I'll often hang things over there. So there's a lot of, 'It's close, it's close, it's close', and often I decide it's done, or decide to stop, and then live with it, and three weeks later I say 'It's not done'. So there's always this time that has to be built into it.

**Rosenfeld** Would you say that the wall in the gestation area is olive?

**Brown** Sort of a drab olive, yes.

**Rosenfeld** How does that assist you in making the decision – the wall colour?

**Brown** It feels separate from the rest of the studio. So it sort of has a life outside the room. I never work on things on that wall.

**Rosenfeld** But you walk past them, and you might notice them and say …

**Brown** I walk past them, or I sit here, and I'll be noticing things about them. There's always this one little part of your mind that's percolating. I very much believe in peripheral vision, where you're working on something without paying close attention. So a huge part of it is just time and putting things away and bringing them back and seeing them afresh. I trust the fresh eyes. If you haven't looked at something for a couple of weeks – and you weren't sure – then when you flip it back round, you usually know straight away. When you've just worked on something, your relationship to it is too hot, overheated and emotional and neurotic, and you *so* want it to work. And sometimes you really want something to be done, just because it's gone on so long, and maybe the paint's getting more built up than you want it to be.

**Rosenfeld** Paintings are like relationships.

**Brown** Somewhat. I think they have their own inner lives as well. I am sounding so romantic!

**Rosenfeld** You don't control them totally.

**Brown** No. And you don't want to – I mean, it really is a back and forth. For me, the push and pull is between the painting, what it demands, and me imposing on it, but going back and forth.

**Rosenfeld** And the source material, the references – to me – are so remote by that point. In the *Paradise* pictures [2014–15], it was so concise, and these works at Paula Cooper Gallery [the venue for Cecily Brown's solo exhibition in 2017] and their references to Géricault or Delacroix, it's there, but it's not so evident, so obvious, and I think it has something to do with this process that you're engaged in.

**Brown** Delacroix is more-or-less my favourite. The oil sketches and small works are a bit like Rubens' oil sketches. I don't really like finished salon-y paintings that much. Manet is about as finished as I can go. But Delacroix's oil sketches ...

**Rosenfeld** Lots of animals.

**Brown** Lots of animals. The colour. I don't feel there's a particularly original way to talk about him. I think it's all just so obvious. It's like trapped energy, the way the fighting animals all become one thing. The compositions are so tight and held together, but at the same time there's this loose energy.

**Rosenfeld** When I look at your work, and I hear you talk about how you don't want to get rid of the figure or the figural, that seems to be the whole point. To get rid of it entirely is to put the viewer at sea. To retain a vestige is to give the viewer something to hang on to without making it necessarily narrative.

**Brown** I think it's the hardest thing in the world to do. I feel like I'm trying to do it. I would love to be able to make clear figuration. I just don't know how you do it. I think Dana Schutz does it brilliantly, John Currin – not in all his subjects, but... I think some people can do it, but I just can't. Someone just reminded me that Gerhard Richter used to call his abstractions 'realism'. I like the artifice of painting and the fact that it's this very fake world. But in a way, a strict representation is the most fake of all.

**Rosenfeld** Over your career, you've been exploring elements of past art. I think you're on the leading edge in that sense, and that stories are coming back. But it's interesting that you're talking about how you can't do the present: the idea that it's hard to tell stories about now.

**Brown** I think you can, I just think you don't want to do it very directly.

**Rosenfeld** How can an artist navigate that?

**Brown** Well, I'm doing it a bit by using Géricault and Delacroix rather than a news photograph to talk about people dying on a boat.

**Rosenfeld** It's operating on a level of metaphor. It grabs you on the inside. Did you see the Thomas Hirschhorn show next door?

**Brown** Yes, it's amazing.

**Rosenfeld** It's interesting, because what he's doing is not so far removed.

**Brown** I know! I thought it was such a great combination with mine.

**Rosenfeld** That pixelation, the obfuscation, and then forcing you to look at the horror. I thought it was a really powerful exhibition. It just shows you the level of the political that's possible in art. We're not in a space of remove. He's doing it. You're doing it.

**Brown** It would be ironic if this horrible period in our history was producing really good art for a change. I'm uncomfortable talking about something too specific to my time, because obviously one of the pleasures of painting – or why painting lasts – is because it's not too much stuck in its own time. The funny thing about painting is, I don't think it dates as much as other art. It might not feel as up to the minute, but it also doesn't look old as quickly. Hopefully, a good painting looks just as good in thirty years. A lot of people have mentioned the word 'time' to do with the big triptych [*A Day! Help! Help! Another Day!* (2016)], which I'm really pleased by. I haven't really thought of it like that, but you could get a sense of the time it took, of time passing, because it's so immersive. The layers work as meaning and paint, and you can see the way it was made maybe more than other works in the past. Having that much raw space to work on perhaps made me – in a good way – spread myself more thinly. It's

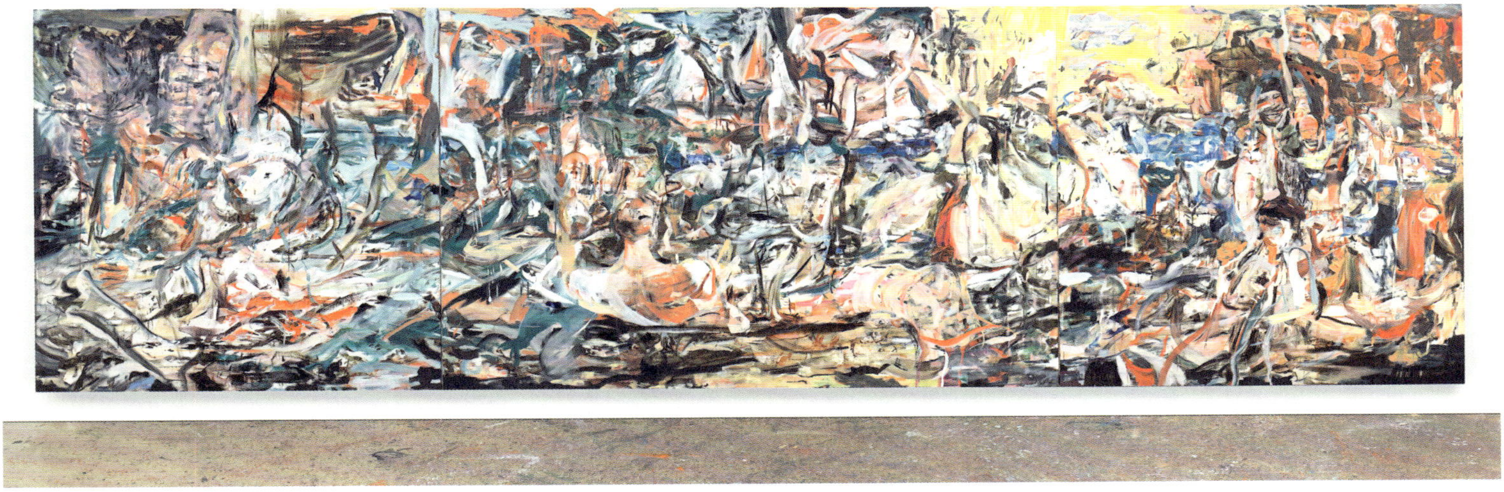

Cecily Brown, *A Day! Help! Help! Another Day!*, 2016, oil on linen, 276.8 × 1008.4 cm

funny how some of the little ones are the most worked and gnarly. On a small scale, it gets more intense.

**Rosenfeld** That durational element is really key. I was struck by the time that people were spending with the pictures. People were sticking with it. I love art that's aerobic, so you go up to it, you move back. We'll talk about your process, but I think that's probably how you work, too. I hadn't seen people giving work their full attention like that since the PACE show of Rothko's dark paintings a year ago, where people were connecting to the works, and then they'd sit down, then get up and go back into it.[1] People were spending much more time in the gallery than they ordinarily would.

**Brown** Well, that's basically all I ever want to hear – you know, 'My work here is done' – because I always wanted to make people look slowly, and to spend time, which partly comes from starting painting at a time when I felt like nobody was really caring. So it's using painting as a way to force people to really look at things. I just feel like one of painting's great strengths is that it can unfold slowly.

**Rosenfeld** And intricately. The brushwork seems to have a kind of energy that would imply freneticism, but in fact, there's a quietude related to looking at it, which I think people find surprising. The skeins all kind of work together.

**Brown** It's about time passing in a way. Especially the two big blue ones [*Madrepora (Shipwreck)*, 2016, and *Sirens and Shipwrecks and Bathers and the Band*, 2016]. And memory …

**Rosenfeld** Those two have a centrality that's lacking in the big one, where it's all dispersed. Your work strikes me as a kind of corrective against the culture of immediacy, and the pulverising amount of images that we're subjected to minute by minute. You talk about time and you talk about experience and you talk about the sheer labour that's involved in it, but I wonder if that's something that you consciously think about? Because when you look back over your career,

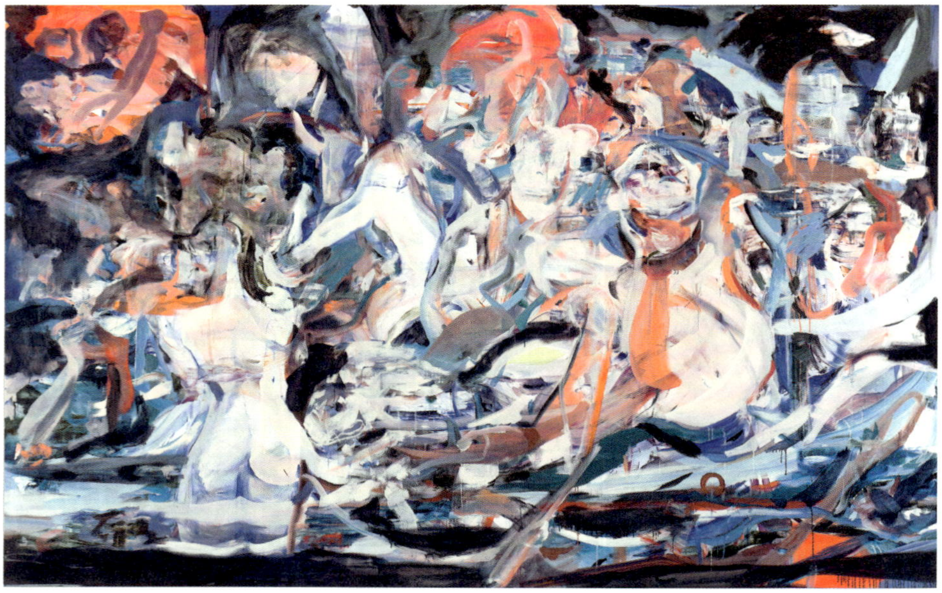

Cecily Brown, *Madrepora (Shipwreck)*, 2016, oil on linen, 246.4 × 283.5 cm

subjects change, the style changes, the colours change, the materiality and the size changes.

**Brown** I'm glad you think that. I always worry that it's all too much the same.

**Rosenfeld** No, I don't think so. I think it's pretty resonant, and there are sharp divisions. It's not just because there were rabbits in your early work and now there's paradise. It's a larger sense – when it's a conscious decision and when it just strikes you that you need to do something different.

**Brown** No, my worry isn't that things don't organically move into the next thing. The thing that worries me is, will I know what to do after this? Even when I'm really involved in a body of work.

**Rosenfeld** The abyss.

**Brown** There's always this panic at the edge. Like with the shipwrecks. I love this as a subject. It works in so many ways for me, but I'm always conscious that I can't keep doing it forever. It was like that with the *Electric Ladyland* women. In a way, I would have just loved to keep on painting those for the rest of my life, because I found it interesting enough, but I do say, 'No more. Don't do any more black paintings.' But then five years later, I think, 'I'm going to paint myself a black painting. Revisit an old subject.'

**Rosenfeld** How does large-scale printmaking relate to what you've been up to lately?

**Brown** I've done quite a few monotype shipwrecks. There'll be a moment in the middle of a painting where I feel like I really want to go and make prints of it, because it can be a way of getting to the image more directly or finding out what it is about the image that you're drawn to, because it's so immediate and you don't get bogged down in materials. Sometimes, I don't do watercolours for a year, or sometimes,

I won't print for nearly a year, and then suddenly, I say, 'Oh, this really needs to be a monotype'. I try to feel out which medium is most appropriate for the subject. Like with these [works for 'Cecily Brown: Shipwreck Drawings', Whitworth Art Gallery, Manchester, 12 November 2017–15 April 2018], it was the first time I'd used charcoal, I think, almost since art school. I wanted to do the image, and I started with water-colour and gouache like I normally do, and it just wasn't fast enough, so I was like, 'Fuck this!' I got so into the charcoal. It's so fast compared to watercolour or ink. They're definitely much slower. And the charcoal is just like chh chh chh chh chh. And I think you get the feeling of getting the information down quickly. Urgency is quite a good quality for a shipwreck painting to have.

**Rosenfeld** So the medium somehow corresponds to the themes that you're working on?

**Brown** Definitely.

**Rosenfeld** And the big prints that you've done, some of them were the *Paradise* series?

**Brown** Yes.

**Rosenfeld** Sort of utopian, Edenic works.

**Brown** Those were watercolour monotypes, which is very ethereal, and there's something poignant about the colour. Everything feels kind of faded and suggestive and like something's getting away.

**Rosenfeld** And it fit with the theme. You couldn't do that for shipwrecks.

**Brown** I don't think so.

**Rosenfeld** No, because they're too sort of visceral and unsparing.

**Brown** Brutal, yes.

**Rosenfeld** How do you interact with your large oil pictures when you're working?

**Brown** Well, these really big ones are completely different from other works, just because you do have to address it much more physically, and it becomes almost performance. Those first marks you put down do almost feel like a trace of a dance, because it really is larger than body scale. But you can be quite reckless because you can do a huge mark, and it's still not that big on the canvas, so you can sort of do whoop-dee-doo, like up the ladder and down, do one big, whoosh. It's like the whole length of your body almost – it's not like you do on an easel-sized painting. There's great liberation in it, physically. But if I'm exhausted I'll sit down and work on small paintings because they're basically done with the wrist and a much more intimate range. I love to move very fluidly between large and small. And as you see, I always have lots of different sizes going on at once and I go from charcoal to ink to watercolour all in a day.

**Rosenfeld** So anything that's up there is in play?

**Brown** Right. Exactly. I walk back and forth quite a lot in here. I can't get back and see it all at once, so I use my phone. I take photographs of it, and I'll often then sit down and instead of looking at the actual thing, I'll stare at it on my phone. And sometimes I think that's so sad. Like, look at the bloody painting! But it's really helpful to go back and forth. You just don't see the composition when you're next to it, and then looking at it on the phone you'll say, 'Oh, whoa!' And sometimes there's an absolutely massive head there that you didn't see. I played on that a lot in the first triptych. The phone would capture things that I wouldn't see with my bare eyes.

**Rosenfeld** So you have lots of pictures of it in progress? And then things might appear, and you'll just run with that. And they really are subconscious – the way that they just emerge?

**Brown** Well, the subject is in my head the whole time I'm working. So a huge head might be an accident. Of course, I don't really know what an accident is, because there's no knowing at this point, but I'm thinking about the head, and I'm thinking about changing the scale. The shipwreck – I always dread that moment when you don't know what to paint next, but this, I just sort of grasped on. There's that great combination of subject and formal quality – you know, it was that sweet spot where what it is and what it looks like meet.

**Rosenfeld** And what was percolating.

**Brown** I feel like, how come I've never done shipwrecks before? It's got everything I love in a painting. There's a crowd of figures, movement, drama, action, romance and contorted limbs.

**Rosenfeld** And a different kind of light. An aqueous sort of light.

**Brown** Yes, so I'd started drawing these, and I had the two lighter blue paintings, and I thought, 'Oh, they could be shipwreck paintings', so I went back into them thinking more of this as a subject, and it really was that combination of the formal device of the edge of the boat and the way that the boat contains the figures. I feel like I'm always trying to paint a crowd, and since those *Electric Ladyland* women, I'd been wanting to find a male crowd. One of the reasons why I love Hogarth is those figures all cram together. You know – that condensed, pushed-together energy.

**Rosenfeld** It's interesting, too, that you work from reproduction instead of the painting itself, because it seems like that allows you to do what you do on the surface in your own brushwork and not let Delacroix have a say in that.

**Brown** Yes. In fact, these were all drawn from a small reproduction. That's the first one I came across – a few inches – but a week before, I printed it out bigger so I could really see what was going on. It's really the composition that's so exciting to copy.

**Rosenfeld** It's interesting also that you seem to have an ability to look at things on a small scale and then look at them on a larger scale. So there's the idea of working from your phone and taking a photograph of a large painting like this and then being able to visualise it from that postage-stamp size.

**Brown** Well, I think that must be a recent thing, because we're so used to seeing things on our phone that it's very easy to translate. It's funny – I've got this massive great mirror to look at things. So when I'm physically working, rather than walk across the room, it's right here. It's like a dancer's mirror. Everything in the studio is on wheels. So when you're up on the ladder, especially when you're working on something big, it's so much easier to look over your shoulder at the mirror. And again, I like that. I feel like you get a slight remove, but it's also just a physical thing. By the time you get down the ladder, put the ladder away, walk across the room, you're like, 'What the fuck was I looking at?' And there's a certain speed and urgency while I'm physically painting. If I'm up the ladder, the paint does something – it's going to have changed by the time I get back. Whether you're going to catch a drip, let it drip or not: you really want to make those decisions quite quickly.

**Rosenfeld** Is there also an element of seeing yourself in the work when you're looking at the mirror? Artists have always used mirrors for self-portraits.

**Brown** It's a Renaissance thing, I think, to look at a painting in the mirror.

**Rosenfeld** That's how Brunelleschi rediscovered perspective. He used a mirror by the Baptistery in Florence, and it organised the world for him.

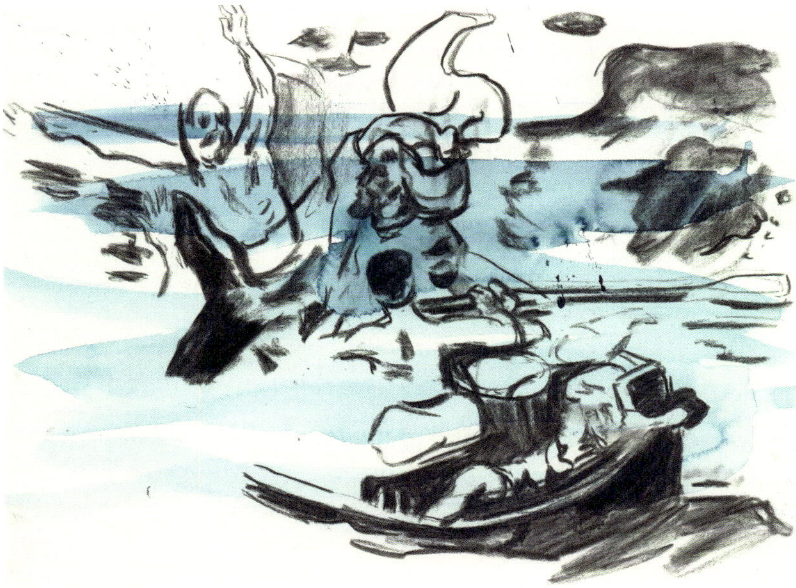

Cecily Brown, *Untitled (Shipwreck)*, 2016, watercolour, charcoal on paper, 30.5 × 40.6 cm

**Brown** Exactly. I love that. That's what a mirror does for the painting.

**Rosenfeld** But you can never see the whole of it.

**Brown** No, you can't. I don't look at myself. I think, again, it's just the remove, and also, the painting has many subplots, as I like to call them. I noticed that in the first triptych, I was ultra-right-handed. If I didn't watch it, I always found myself working down here on the right, and I had to really make myself go to the left side. But I decided to exploit that and kept the left panel very much more open. I realised, well, that's part of the rhythm of it – that it was less worked and more open on that side. And then it kind of gets more busy, and the right is very congested.

**Rosenfeld** You talk about being right-handed, and that's still a factor even at thirty-three feet. Because landscape painters who are right-handed, when they're painting, they're reaching out to their right. They're not reaching across to their left. They want to orient you on the left side of the painting, and you see the landscape spread out to your right. And you're still having to deal with that at 33 feet wide. It's fascinating, because it's not about your wingspan – your arms. It's about how you move around with your body and where you're orienting yourself. That's where I think the mirror helps. Because it flips it. It moves it around.

**Brown** Yes, the flip really helps. And I don't register the flip at all.

**Rosenfeld** No, it's just a corrective in a way. It's a fascinating process. Do you think about space in a very formal sense?

**Brown** Well, I like my space to be very aggressive. I play a lot with it: just as you think something is a long way away, it comes right up in your face again. So I think about space a lot, and I like really messing with space. I started that really early, realising that changing scale did weird things for the space. I'd often have one great big figure, and then smaller figures, a bit like Victorian fairy paintings. They weren't fairies, though. I like the illogical thing of just sort of fucking with space all the time. It does get me in a mess sometimes. You just get too bogged down. But I like space.

**Rosenfeld** Like a Poussin, where it pulls you in through serpentine lines and diminishing forms.

**Brown** Yes.

**Rosenfeld** The thing that you see in these, is that there's the boat, the horizontality at the bottom, which reads as a kind of foreground, but then when you come up, it doesn't anymore. There's maelstrom, which just comes out at you – in both of these pictures – and it denies your ability to get into it, because the person is moving. So it's the inverse of the whole Salon tradition of stability. I think there's a kind of connection between the figure, all the vestiges, the abstraction and the painting – that that's part of what you do – but it's never settled. And that lack of resolution is what gives it its power and its interest.

**Brown** That goes back to when to stop. Arguably, they can be finished on the first day. Often, they look best on the first day. I mean, they have a charm that they never have again.

**1** 'Mark Rothko: Dark Palette', PACE New York, 4 November 2016–7 January 2017.

Extract from an interview first published in *The Brooklyn Rail,* December 2017–January 2018 on the occasion of Cecily Brown's solo exhibition at Paula Cooper Gallery, 27 October–2 December, 2017.

## Nicole Eisenman in Conversation with Lynne Tillman

**Lynne Tillman** What were you looking for when you decided to be an artist?

**Nicole Eisenman** I recognised early on that creating other worlds was transporting and magical. I remember finger-painting in nursery school and accidentally making a shape that looked exactly like a mountain with a road wrapping around it, like in the *Road Runner* cartoons. It's one of my oldest memories; I was so excited to have used my hand to make something that looked so real. I continue trying to recapture that feeling, the 'AH-HA moment' in painting, when you create something that convincingly takes you into another world. As I got older, I found I could still escape from reality through drawing and painting.

**Tillman** You went to Rhode Island School of Design. What helped you most in art school? What hindered you?

**Eisenman** I learned how to design a picture in a formalist way. I guess that helped. I spent a year abroad in Italy and was turned on to Italian Renaissance art and Italian Gothic art, which was hugely influential, but it was also a hindrance. I had to unlearn the classical stuff to push forward with my work. The best aspect of college was that I got into the hard-core punk scene. I was a champion of violence; it was a real male-dominated scene in the 1980s and I loved it. I put my frustration, my energy there, and also started looking at and making comics.

**Tillman** You're such a modern character, with a contemporary take on the world. It's fascinating that you decided to be a painter, not a photographer, filmmaker or installation artist.

**Eisenman** I don't think of myself as a painter. In the morning, I go paint, and when I get tired of that, I draw. Some days I work on sculptures or play with the video camera or go to a bookstore or museum to seek out inspiration. There's no hierarchy among these activities.

**Tillman** What was it about the Italian Renaissance and Gothic art that compelled you?

**Eisenman** In Italian Gothic painting, particularly, the paint is crisp, and there's a theatricality that was appealing. It's linear and flat, and often there are tableaux of characters acting out a narrative, similar to the comics I was into. But there's more going on than just a story being told. Every detail, like a leaf or hair, has agency, and the painting becomes animated in surreal ways. I'm thinking of Matthias Grünewald – every aspect of it is emotionally dark and mysterious.

**Tillman** In a catalogue essay, painter Amy Sillman wrote about your relationship to earlier painting: 'Maybe part of Nicole Eisenman's fascination with old painting is exactly its collapse.' You moved into an area that excited you because it had been evacuated.

**Eisenman** Like a ruin.

**Tillman** You could, with your imagination, take that ruin and reanimate it.

**Eisenman** I'm like a developer building twelve-storey high-rise condos on the ruins of art history. [Laughter] I take painting lessons from history, but also I enjoy using familiar tropes to make ironic breaks from tradition so as to destroy expectations. The techniques various artists have used over the past 800 years are memos to self that there are many ways to handle the material, but ultimately it's about making a picture that reflects my life, my unconscious or conscious desires.

**Tillman** Your work refers to kitsch, porn, comics, Marsden Hartley, German Expressionism. Your world – your art – is an image bank.

**Eisenman** It's all of that stuff. Art history pulls me around in different directions. I feel the Impressionists tugging on my arm and Francis Picabia nipping at my ankle. There's so much compelling art. I look at a William Blake and think, that's the way to do it, but then I see Edvard Munch and that seems to trump all other styles. Looking at art is infectious. I'm won over easily, so for me, defining a single artistic style is difficult or impossible. It's like branding, a stylistic imperative that you follow through over and over again; it's a kind of trap when artists feel obliged to define themselves, especially for a market. I appreciate artists like Pablo Picasso and Dieter Roth, who both moved fluidly from one medium and style to another.

**Tillman** In writing, everything you've ever read goes into what you write; it's part of the way you think. And for you as an artist, what you've looked at becomes the way you paint and adds more layers and levels of meaning.

**Eisenman** That's true. This cumulative experience becomes a memory helix with Gordian knots of art history braided into it.

**Tillman** As a novelist, I like to work in different styles. Different stories need different voices.

**Eisenman** That reminds me of the original fantasy game. When you're a child, you're the Barbie doll, the GI Joe, and the horse they ride off on. You can be three characters at once. Painting is like this game, but messier. When Winslow Homer painted *Undertow* [1886], he had to understand the struggle of the man saving the women, the power of the woman clutching at the other woman and the force of the wave working against them all. He inhabited every force in the painting.

**Tillman** You give your characters an ability to be all sexes and genders, which is similar to your not limiting yourself to one style.

**Eisenman** I'd rather be no gender than all genders. I grew up with brothers and hung out with them. I didn't want to feel different. I was disappointed in the 1990s, when, as an artist having shows for the first time, I was forced to talk about issues of gender. To have to define yourself like that was miserable, like somebody putting a pile of shit on you that shouldn't be there.

**Tillman** You're turned into a 'woman artist', 'woman writer'.

**Eisenman** It's that loss of innocence when you go from being who you are, little Lynne the person, to being the 'woman' Lynne Tillman, who has to deal with sexualised representations of herself and stereotypes. I've made some sexually explicit works that invert stereotypes about gender, but I was also just making pictures, not necessarily interested in what they meant. I was reactive and unconsciously shooting from the hip. My intention now is to deal with a range of issues from social utopias to the visual similarity between bundt cakes and sphincters. But it's the writers and critics who frame the discourse, even if that's not what I want to talk about.

**Tillman** In your work, I see movement from freedom to constraint. A female figure who's bound, a male tied up. In portraits, pathetic-looking characters seem ruled by their emotions and their circumstances. Sometimes there's a riot of dancing forms, an explosion of eroticism.

**Eisenman** The power of the crowd is the offer to let individuals dissolve into it. Elias Canetti talked about the moment when the individual gets rid of his difference and then joins the crowd. It sounds wonderful, or like a nightmare. In drawings with a lot of people, the crowd becomes a block, a world unto itself. They might be pictures of humanity coexisting in a kind of sexualised tumult. On the other hand,

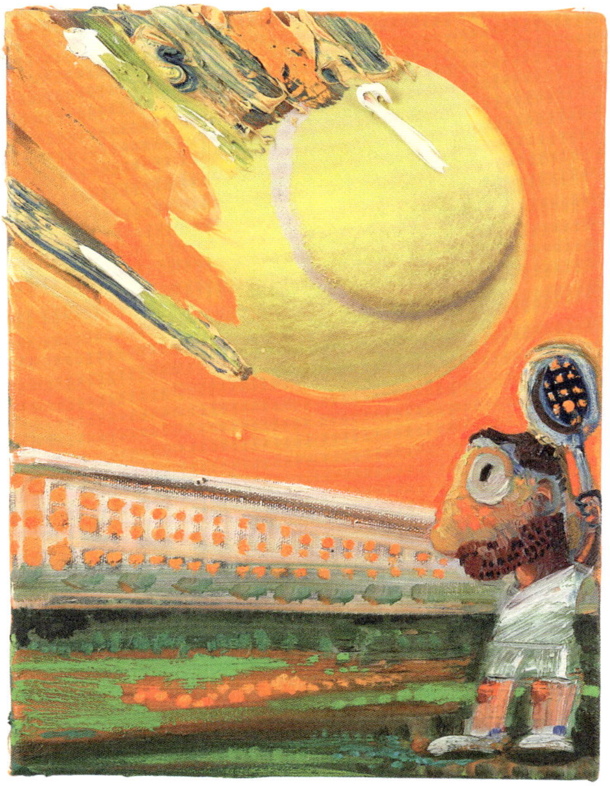

Nicole Eisenman, *Tennis Ball*, 2006, oil on canvas, 30.5 × 23 cm

binding individuals is visual shorthand for power relations, as in *Commerce Feeds Creativity* [2004].

**Tillman** In *Swimmers in the Lap Lane* [1996], a number of figures are in sexual poses.

**Eisenman** It's an orgy in a pool.

**Tillman** You painted the lanes in red. The motion of the painting is quite vertical, it's on a diagonal.

**Eisenman** In formal terms, there's no real space created; there's only a signifier of deep space. Whenever you have a diagonal in a picture, it creates space, but actually it's very upright. The figures are almost standing up.

**Tillman** I could see this on the ceiling of the Sistine Chapel: one of the figures, lying supine, as if a dying Christ, and, at the same time, because of the colours, there's a cartoon-like quality.

**Eisenman** The figures in the pool defy gravity. It's kind of a sexy painting, isn't it? I used to be a lifeguard at a pool, when I was a closeted teenager; it was a site of much fantasising. *Swimmers in the Lap Lane* was an important painting for me. It took me a while to figure out what I did right with it. Basically, it was about making a painting with the same attitude as drawing, namely being loose and keeping the line intact and the colour strong.

**Tillman** Your colours – oranges, reds, blues – belie the anxiety in your paintings, like *Tennis Ball* [2006]. A big orange tennis ball, thickly painted, is about to land on a face.

**Eisenman** Orange is the colour of high alert, of danger.

**Tillman** Tennis isn't violent or dangerous.

**Eisenman** Tennis isn't relaxing for me. I get tense watching it and competitive playing it. It's also another site of fantasy. When I play, I'm centre court at Wimbledon, with thousands of people watching me – not to mention the TV cameras.

**Tillman** The orange ball coming is …

**Eisenman** Anxiety, of course.

**Tillman** You mostly have figures in your work. You mentioned 'characters' before. Are they characters in a movie?

**Eisenman** They're characters who are aspects of me. I inhabit them, they inhabit me, and they live inside my poor head, crowded together. Part of my process is the business of discovering them. Like in *From Success to Obscurity* [2004]: he's always right there, tailing me. From 2001 to 2003, I took time off from painting. I spent two years in the country gardening and shovelling snow mostly. I was thinking about ageing, leaving New York, about obscurity, about death. Those ideas were with me constantly. It was the beginning of a prolonged eight-year long midlife crisis. I had certain fears, but painting those fears as abject characters was a way of grappling with them, making fun of it all, because fear is a dumb thing. Eventually I reapproached painting with new feelings about what I wanted to do.

**Tillman** What changed?

**Eisenman** I wanted the paint to become more active and stop taking a back seat to the image. The paint needed to be activated and opened up, made more fluid and sensuous. I didn't want to be in such tight control of it.

**Tillman** Abjection hovers in some of your portraits and paintings of small groups, like *Dysfunctional Family* [2000]. The father holds a phallus-like bong in his mouth; the mother is sexualised, her legs spread open.

**Eisenman** She's knitting, doing her lady work. The baby's got a meat tenderiser; he just finished pounding himself out. It's the family romance, but all the twisted, hidden sexual and emotional material has bubbled to the surface. Whenever there's repressed trauma on any level – basic Freudian stuff – it emerges somewhere else. In this, it's not bubbling up somewhere else; it's just there. They're actually not dysfunctional; they're at peace with each other's neurotic behaviour.

**Tillman** The painting mixes fantasy with a sort of naturalism. The bloody genitals obscure whether it's a boy or a girl.

**Eisenman** It's a boy who's pounded his dick with a cleaver.

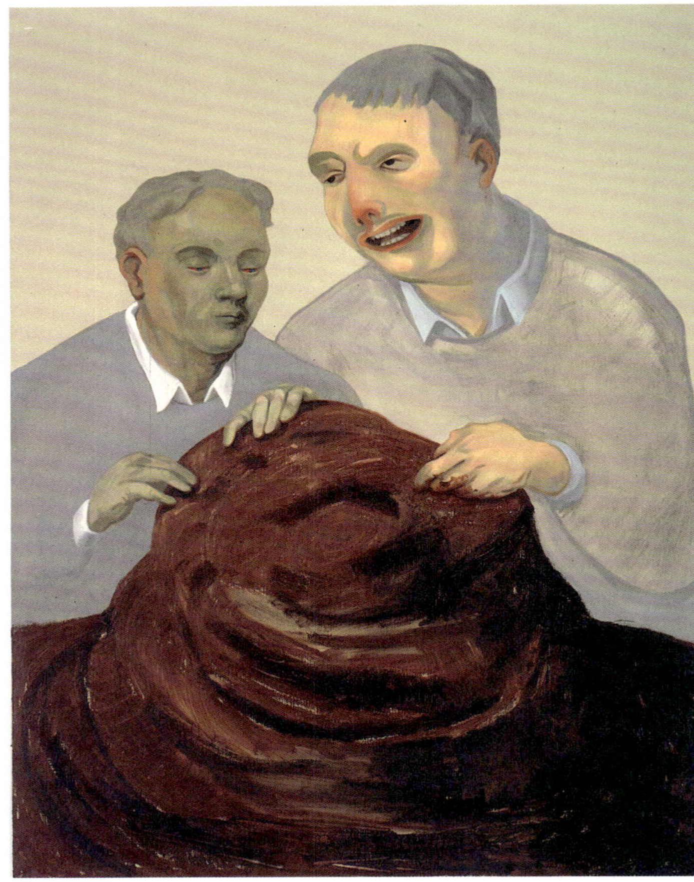

Nicole Eisenman, *The Work of Labor and Care*, 2004, oil on canvas, 129.5 × 100.4 cm

**Tillman** In *The Work of Labor and Care* [2004], two men in grey are looking down at a mound of shit.

**Eisenman** They're forming it, plying it with their hands. If you could have institutional critique as a painting, that one would be mine. I was thinking about when you don't have inspiration, all you have left is labour and care. I was once in a class at a graduate school and heard a teacher tell a student, 'If you just keep doing it, keep insisting on it, eventually, it'll be good.' The notion that you don't need an idea, but just have to keep pounding away, working, and eventually it might become something, is suspect. So, you could have labour and care, but without inspiration, a concept or an image, all you end up with is a pile of shit – or worse, something purely aesthetic.

**Tillman** Do you always have stories in mind when you make a painting?

**Eisenman** More or less, but I like to let go of that, too.

**Tillman** Ten years ago, you were working much more with narrative, weren't you?

**Eisenman** Yes, but narrative can become a closed system. I've loosened its reins, because I've felt constricted by it. Still, there always has to be an image, a symbol of something real or imagined, otherwise art consumes itself in a self-referential orgy and becomes too obtuse and disconnected from life. I love conceptualist painting, but formalism in and of itself is a bore.

**Tillman** Depicting aggressive females entails a new approach to painting the female form.

**Eisenman** Those images are also mostly ironic inversions of the relationships we're used to seeing in painting: dominant men, submissive women.

**Tillman** I wanted to ask you about *Hanging Birth* [1994], about representing the mother.

**Eisenman** A woman is giving birth while she's hanging.

**Tillman** Presumably dying.

**Eisenman** I'm amazed now that I was able to make that painting in 1994. I must have had a sense of the sacrifice of motherhood. She's hanging, giving birth, everyone is watching. It's a tough painting.

**Tillman** Do you think everyone is complicit in a mother's sacrifice?

**Eisenman** Maybe it's out with the old and in with the new. Society's complicit, because babies are so damn cute. The mother gives up almost everything for the child, at least initially. It's astounding to witness this happening.

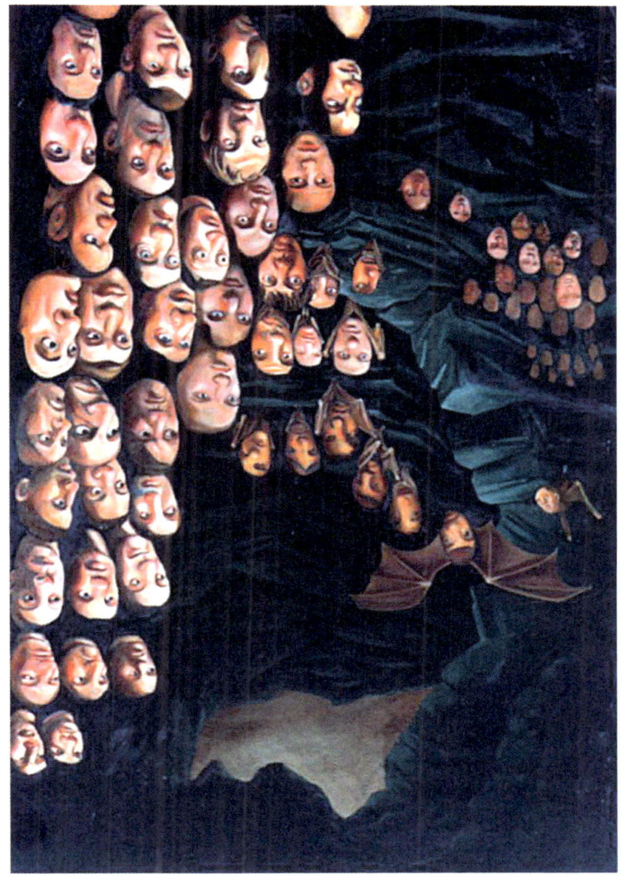

Nicole Eisenman, *Batcave*, 2000, oil on canvas, 185.6 × 116.8 cm

**Tillman** Because now you're a parent.

**Eisenman** Yes, a father of sorts. There's no name for what I am. [Laughter] I have a very sweet but needy six-week-old child, who needs absolute attention all the time. The baby is literally sucking the energy from my partner, who's breast-feeding her. It's a sacrifice.

**Tillman** In *Batcave* [2000], there's a profusion of faces upside-down, with a horrifying effect. It throws the viewer off.

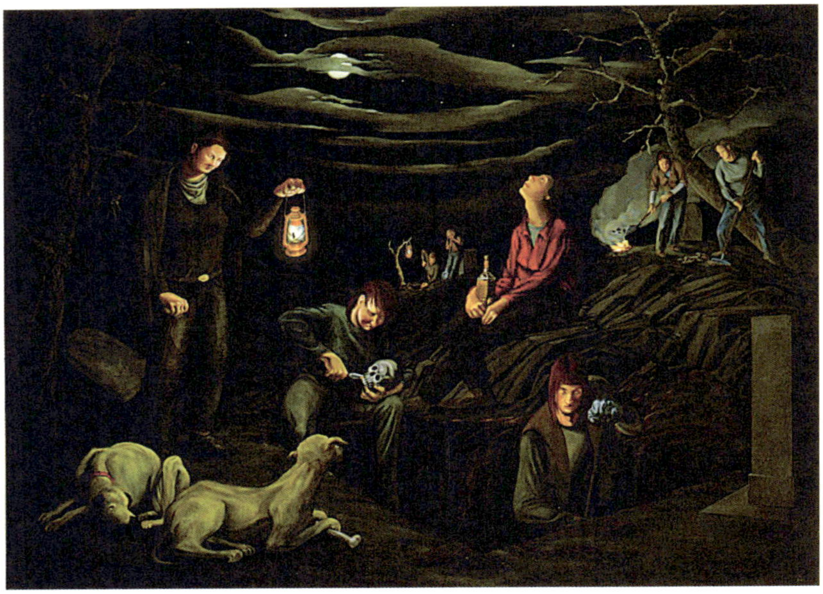

Nicole Eisenman, *Golddiggers*, 2002, oil on canvas, 97.2 × 130.2 cm

**Eisenman** Upside-down faces seem to lose their identity. They become stamps of colour.

**Tillman** People give so much importance to the face.

**Eisenman** We see them everywhere, even where they don't exist. It's a function of the primitive brain: we're wired to see faces for protection.

**Tillman** You de-familiarised them, also by hanging the faces in the dark, like a bat cave.

**Eisenman** They're the faces of bats. The painting is a bit surreal. Those guys are sinister yet a bit dopey.

**Tillman** In *Golddiggers* [2002], you applied the paint differently again. It's so different from *Tennis Ball*.

**Eisenman** *Tennis Ball* is different from every painting I've made. It works collage into the painting, which relates the painting back to my drawing. I tend to use collage in drawings a lot. These days, I'm thinking all the time about using the same strategies in painting that I do in drawing. Applying paint is like any language; communication in life varies. We talk in colloquialisms, we talk formally, we talk and act appropriately or inappropriately. This should be true in painting as well. Not every picture is a haiku; some paintings are big, messy tone poems, with an accompanying interpretive dance. In 2001, I was getting frustrated with how I was approaching painting. Around the same time, I made *Kickboxers* [2002], which was very difficult to do. Pretty much all the painting I'd been doing up until then was becoming un-fun, too constricted, and I felt it needed to open up.

**Tillman** Why was it constricted?

**Eisenman** I was paying attention to certain painting conventions, basically using the Italian model I learned as a student. The paintings became tighter and tighter, my brushes smaller and softer; my process was becoming too repetitive. That was around 2001, when

I stopped painting. When I returned to it, I looked at other models, the Expressionists and Dada. That opened things up.

**Tillman** In *Mountain Man* [2006] the forms look freer, looser.

**Eisenman** The paint means something; it's not simply representing something.

**Tillman** *Mountain Man* has a big, thick, red nose.

**Eisenman** It's not really a nose: it's an unruly glop of paint where something that should be painted to look like a nose might be.

**Tillman** What about your recent portrait, *Hamlet* [2007]? Why him?

**Eisenman** Hamlet is a great role model, a superhero for 2007, and a literary character who's thoughtfully incarnated.

**Tillman** He's not an action figure.

**Eisenman** But I like the idea of making him an action figure. It's part of a series of role models. In *Ketchup-Mustard War* [2005], there's a referee for a battle of colours. Given the scale of this painting, he'd be a giant 85-foot-tall referee walking around the world saying 'Time out' to everyone. That would be helpful.

**Tillman** What about painting women as heroes?

**Eisenman** I've probably done that already. In any case, *Hamlet* goes back to my ideal of a genderless state. In the painting, he's wearing a skirt; he's feminised because he's thoughtful.

**Tillman** What you're saying makes me think about the peculiar position we women artists and writers are in.

**Eisenman** It's a complicated or maybe just a crap position, since we have the 'burden' of the female body. We have to deal with representing ourselves

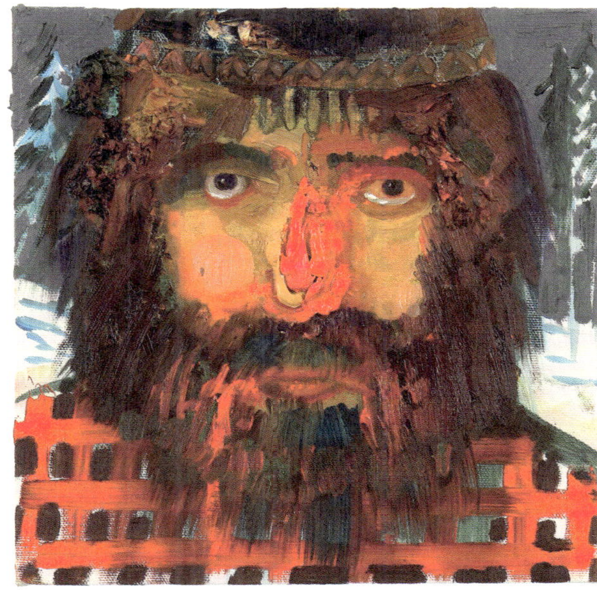

Nicole Eisenman, *Mountain Man*, 2006, oil on canvas, 25.4 × 24.4 cm

within the matrix of traditional narratives. So we need to have an ironic and critical view of the body, because of this history of objectification.

**Tillman** Your irony and candour shake things up, and you make all kinds of bodies. They challenge a viewer's perceptions and limits.

**Eisenman** Determining what constitutes a body is different in art; it's much more open than it is in actual life. Art doesn't eat and excrete and isn't restricted by needs like a glandular system or kidneys. In art, a mattress with two melons is a perfectly acceptable body. But unlike the human body, which is a container for an idea, a spirit, the art body is the idea incarnate. There is no separation. Form is substance.

First published in Nicole Eisenman, Beatrix Ruff, Lynne Tillman, and Laurie Weeks, *Nicole Eisenman* (Zurich: JRP Ringier, 2011), pp. 14–18.

# Sanya Kantarovsky in Conversation with Allison Katz

**Allison Katz** Do you think about empathy in the creation of a figure?

**Sanya Kantarovsky** I do, but I'm more interested in our capacity to identify with the pathetic over the sympathetic. I often think about books and films in which the audience is drawn into sympathising with someone who's gone deeply astray. Raskolnikov in *Crime and Punishment* [1866] comes to mind, or Erika Kohut in *The Piano Teacher* [2001]. These characters force us to inhabit their abject isolation, throwing our own empirical aloneness into relief. The figures in my paintings are often steeped in a sort of acute embarrassment and, in the best examples, the embarrassment doesn't spare any onlookers, myself included. At the same time, I tend to think of my figures in relation to the *teep* [ТИП], a Russian word which means type, but also means something else: a kind of unsavouriness. It's a way of referring to an unpleasant type of individual, as in: 'Who's that type lurking around the corner?' The specific characteristics that make a type aren't important. There's a deliberate negation of identity in labelling someone a type, a refusal to delve into details, as in a stereotype. I look at many of my subjects as types. The term implies that the type is someone to avoid. There's not enough there to consider them characters – they're bystanders, once-overs, *teeps*.

**Katz** The unsavoury is therefore a sort of release from the elegance of your own hand? A way to paint against facility and encounter abjection? I have an attraction to inverting my own lyricism, but not in any way that's random or forced. When I found a set of life drawings my younger sister had made in high school, I knew I had to use them: they were aggressive and restless marks, as she had no interest in the subject and couldn't wait to get out of there. All the same, she managed to unwittingly cruise through art history with her angst, and I could see traces of so many canonical paintings, by accident. I'm also fascinated by our family proximity: we share DNA, and our handwriting is similar, but her marks have a completely different origin and focus.

**Kantarovsky** I'm often drawn to this particular kind of authenticity – the sort that's unfettered by self-judgment, or any kind of burdensome sense of purpose. Painting about facility is usually boring. If there isn't a worthwhile idea at stake, facility can only go as far as novelty.

**Katz** I'm also interested in the collapse of narrative, or when it becomes a condition of transformation that doesn't necessarily have a moral, just moves forward from change to change, impossible to ascertain and explain and sum up, sort of like the impurity of Ovid.

**Kantarovsky** I think that a lot of Renaissance painting, with its grand narratives, chased after an ideal similar to that which Abstract Expressionism chased later on. They both shared a rigid moral structure, with their eyes set on reaching the unreachable – divinity, the sublime, transcendence. I've always been interested in artists who've compromised that narrative in one way or another. In his rebuke of AbEx, Guston said it best: 'I got sick and tired of all that Purity! [...] Painting is impure. It is the adjustment of impurities which forces painting's continuity.'

**Katz** That's a perfect summation. It also relates to the idea of nonsense, or how humour or inversions work like glitches in the operating system of language and communication. A way of showing the mind is on.

**Kantarovsky** Like the brilliant title of your most recent show: 'All Is On'. Exposing and embracing doubt is

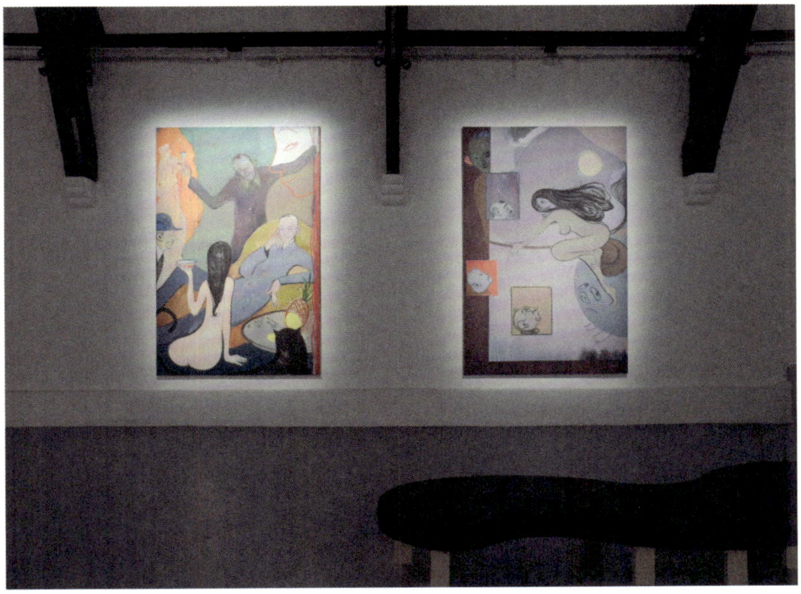

Sanya Kantarovsky with Ieva Misevičiūtė, *Apricot Juice*, 17 April–7 June 2015, installation view: Studio Voltaire, London

another way of showing the mind is on. I'm thinking about *pentimenti*, or previous iterations of a painting made visible, as one register of this doubt. The word literally means repentances. We paint over our sins! I often leave traces of past decisions on my surfaces, and I see it a lot in your work as well: in *Noses (2)* [2014] the window shapes are concealed by a thin veil of orange paint and some of the noses are erased, their residue deliberately left behind. These moments are so important – the sound of the box's own making. Do you also see *pentimenti* as having to do with this notion of the painter's 'search'?

**Katz** Yes and no. I see those traces more as simultaneity than searching. It's more about doubt and belief sharing the same plane. Refusing hierarchy. That's a form of perversion. I think the searching aspect of the painting process is overly romanticised. It's a private and not entirely interesting thing to me. I'm not into making a map. I want it all on at the same time. I'm happy to conceal the actual labour of a work. Some of my paintings take over two years, while others will take just a couple of hours. I'm into them hanging side by side, each emitting a different energy but, ideally, not because of how long it took for me to make a decision.

**Kantarovsky** I think we both tend to make the kind of paintings that could be finished at any moment. When they become cogent early on, it's a really satisfying feeling, and it doesn't happen very often. Arriving at that moment almost always involves doubt. When I was small, and I noticed a group of figures that had been painted over in Matisse's *The Dance* [1909–10], my grandfather told me that Matisse never made mistakes. A few years ago, I saw the Matisse show at the MoMA, *In Search of True Painting*, and thought about his questionable assertion again, as the show focused on paintings that had been incessantly readjusted.

**Katz** Right off the bat, the title of the Matisse show is feeding into this idea that painting equals truth! I reject the idea that painting is only valuable as an act of looking for something to reveal, to confess. It's refreshing to think of it in the opposite way. I'm not trying to be cynical, but I think one should question the assumption that a painting gesture must somehow be linked to a truth (the right answer), that it must somehow validate genius. What if we just saw all those readjustments as lies that got him closer to design, to the impersonal, to fiction?

**Kantarovsky** I agree that *In Search of True Painting* is a red herring of a title. The notion of true painting is as suspicious as the search that it supposedly necessitates. I'm reminded of David Foster Wallace's short essay 'Laughing with Kafka', which got me thinking about *No Joke*. In it, Wallace explains why he found it difficult to teach Kafka's humour to Americans: 'No wonder they cannot appreciate the really central Kafka joke – that the horrific struggle to establish a human self results in a self whose humanity is inseparable from that horrific struggle.' In that sense, the MoMA title is very American. America is built on the idea of the 'pursuit of happiness', an abstraction of the same variety as *In Search of True Painting*. I'm fascinated by your idea that Matisse's constant alterations could have been about moving in the opposite direction.

**Katz** Well, you just brought up something akin to this with the Guston quote about adjusting impurities ...

**Kantarovsky** It's the exact same thought really.

Extract from a conversation first published in Sanya Kantarovsky, Stuart Bertolotti-Bailey, Eli Diner, Allison Katz and Angie Keefer, *Sanya Kantarovsky: No Joke* (London: Koenig Books and Studio Voltaire, 2016), pp. 42–120.

## Tala Madani in Conversation with Lydia Yee

**Lydia Yee** I want to begin by asking you why you chose to paint, and why figurative painting in particular?

**Tala Madani** Painting for me wasn't necessarily a positive choice. It emerged out of the exclusion of other options. When I started drawing, I'd just come to the US and couldn't speak English, so I paid more attention to mathematics and painting.

**Yee** Language was more difficult.

**Madani** Exactly. I couldn't read any of the books in the library, so I just started drawing. It was a default choice.

**Yee** You were choosing to communicate in some way through figurative painting?

**Madani** Yes. I was never interested in painting from a design perspective. My interest was absolutely in representation and painting's capacity for communication. As a teenager without access to any porn, it was also a weird way of turning myself on. Seriously.

**Yee** [Laughter] You were creating your own porn?

**Madani** Yes, exactly. When I went to libraries, there were all these art books with naked figures in them. There was a funny little energy interaction when I saw them. I borrowed lots of books from the public library in Salem, Oregon, and just copied anything and everything from them. They had these massive survey books, particularly of early 1900s German drawing and painting. My interests were quite eclectic, so I wasn't just immersed in one artist. If I saw something that interested me, I copied it: a vase of flowers, some figures screaming, a group of Roman statues, a Rodin …

**Yee** Were you taking art classes at the time?

**Madani** No. I was just on my own, at home drawing whatever I could find. I also remember drawing pictures from *National Geographic* magazine.

**Yee** I'm curious about the way you go about painting. It seems quite rapid. The brushwork feels quite quick, deliberate and intentional. But I also know you map out a lot of your ideas in advance through drawing.

**Madani** I generate ideas in drawings, but I wouldn't suggest that I map them per se, because I'm not thinking about a spatial accuracy in the translation from a sketch to the canvas. Basically, I think you have to paint at the speed that excites you. So, if a slow speed gets you excited, that should be your approach; if you're thinking about all the minutiae of texture hitting that canvas and really following it, that's the speed you need. You just have to follow the speed of your thoughts with your brushstrokes.

**Yee** Do you work out the overall composition in advance?

**Madani** Sometimes. Sometimes not. Let's say I want to do some figures holding a piece of paper on their faces. I'll just start painting it. If it's interesting, I'll follow it. If not, I'll move on to the next canvas. I used to think that I had to know all of the painting in advance, but then I wasn't as present in the painting. That's also one of the reasons why I don't ever use any photographic references. It's because the minute I go this way to look at something and come back, the energy is disrupted.

**Yee** Flow is very important. You've said that the action or the performance is in the painting, but do you feel that you're performing as a painter?

**Madani** I'm not that conscious of myself. I think if I became too self-conscious, I'd lose focus on the painting. For me, it's really about the transfer of energy: mental energy, physical energy, whatever you can convey from a live being into an object. I'm not suggesting that you have to be animated. Not at all. But I think focus is important and that focus can't become self conscious.

**Yee** I also wonder how the process of painting relates to your animations. In your painting it seems like there's a background with figures on top. Do you plan these elements separately? Is the painting process faster or slower than animation? I imagine that animation has both slow and fast aspects to it.

**Madani** That's really interesting, because in both aspects of my work there's a total separation between background and foreground. To do a classical animation, you need to have the background on a different plane from what's being animated. I think that's a really interesting point you made about how the paintings are related.

**Yee** In your paintings, the backgrounds seem more worked or patterned in some ways. Whereas the figures seem as if they're animated and something is going on.

**Madani** The backgrounds are on the periphery of my thinking in a way.

**Yee** You sometimes have a patterned floor or focus on the light playing off the surroundings in a certain way.

**Madani** This is true. Generally, I try and convey a very ubiquitous idea of an interior, with the ground and some lines to represent the horizon. In the larger paintings, I try and create a 'no space' space with just some flat colour in the background.

**Yee** Without enough detail to suggest anything like perspective or depth.

**Madani** Exactly. I also make the figures more or less the same, to focus on the psychology of what's going on.

**Yee** When did you start introducing animation into your practice? Or has it always been there because of your drawing?

**Madani** I started animating during a residency in 2006 in Provincetown, Rhode Island. An artist, Ezra Johnson, who was doing animation taught me how to do it. He showed me how easy it was: you just take a picture with your camera, change it, take another picture, change it again, and then put all of your pictures in a row.

**Yee** You were already doing something like this on canvas.

**Madani** Yes. It just seemed to break the mystery of it. I did my first animation at the Rijksakademie in Amsterdam in 2007. I work very fast in painting. I have an idea, I paint it and it's done. With an animation, I have an idea, I paint it about 2,000 times, and then it's done. It was a way that enabled me to stay simply with one idea for a couple of months. I could simply pause while working and not have to generate new ideas.

**Yee** Do you work in series in your painting practice, rather than in animation?

**Madani** No, although I sometimes literally make the same painting multiple times. If a painting doesn't work out, I paint it again with a very slight change, eight or nine times, simply because I'm not ready to move away from the idea. It gives me an excuse simply to do it again. I can't really say it's working in series because nothing's changing. I just want to be involved with it longer. It's like you're meeting a friend and you just want to spend more time with them.

**Yee** In the end, do you edit your paintings or do you keep them all?

**Madani** If I'm having a show, I'll just show one of them and keep the rest. Sometimes I keep them in the studio and they could become something else, or else teach me something. Sometimes I realise much later that the one that I thought was the strongest, isn't the strongest.

**Yee** At the same time as you're making 'clones' of the same work, you do also have broader bodies of work, such as the *Shit Mom* paintings [pl. 21].

**Madani** Exactly. So, in the *Shit Moms*, I wanted to explore an idea in many different ways.

**Yee** In that particular series, how do you think the materiality of the paint relates to the subject? The shit is ultimately clumps of brown paint. Do you try to pick subjects that have an affinity with the material of paint?

**Madani** I think I do have a natural affinity to things that can feel very liberated within the material. As I say that, I've also become really interested in some things that are quite tough and rigid. In Lee Lozano's paintings, there are these really angular triangles that are painted super thickly. It's just so antithetical to the material. But she used the material to make almost metal-like sheaths.

**Yee** Why do the mothers in your *Shit Mom* paintings seem less formed than the children and male figures, which have more definition?

**Madani** I was thinking about how children seem more together alongside the complete fluidity of the mother. I was interested in their pristineness, and her shitness. I wanted to explore the moment they touch each other as a kind of contamination. When I was painting them, I also thought, where did the guys go in this series? Then, I had a ghostly character somewhere, which I thought could represent the guys.

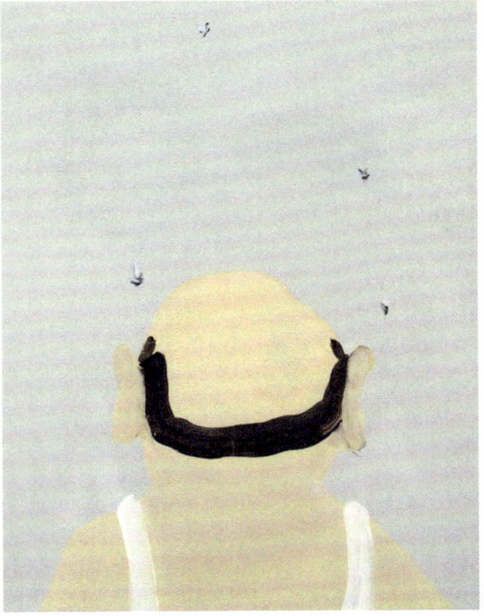

Tala Madani, Stills from *Headbug*, 2009
Single channel colour animation, 1:05 mins

**Yee** Like somebody's disappeared and shirked his responsibility?

**Madani** Yes, something like that. I thought, maybe the kids can still see these ghostly figures.

**Yee** Do the *Shit Moms* relate to feelings you experienced as an artist and a mother? Historically, women have had to balance motherhood with how much time they can devote to their practice.

**Madani** Totally. When I was pregnant with my first child, many people asked me how it would influence my work. I was very rigid and said it wasn't going to influence me in any way. I was very defensive about the suggestion that motherhood was going to take over my practice. Then, when I actually had my first child, I realised that it brought some really interesting things. For example, kids don't see anything except for a blur when they're born. Then they only see black and white, then green comes, then red and finally

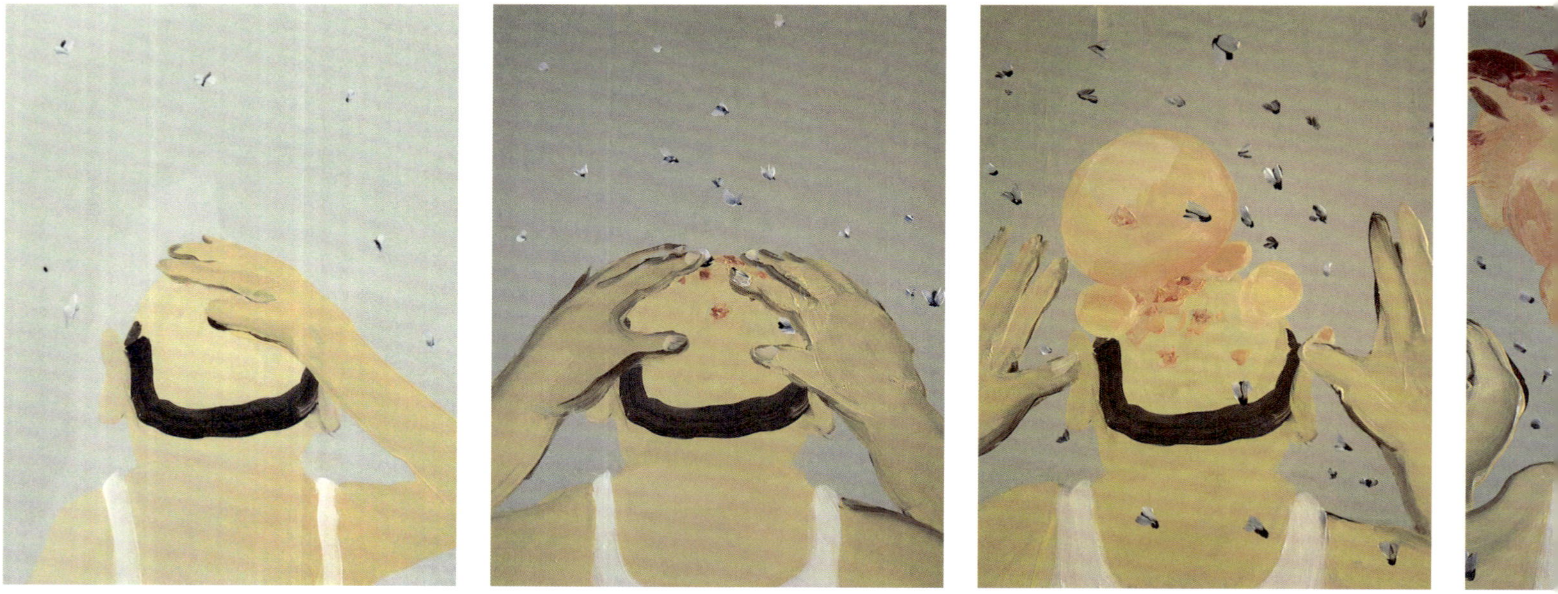

everything else. Because I'm very interested in the whole human experience, all of this became food for thought. I noticed my child's tactility developing as she experimented with the world. I became really interested in how I could experiment in a similar way with paint and brush. So I was really influenced by the birth of my first child in a way that I didn't expect.

At the same time, I was reading feminist texts that suggested that if you're an intelligent woman, mothering will bore you. Being with a child is boring. I just thought, if you have a chance to intellectualise the experience of it, and not just feel the weight of it on your shoulders, processing and sharing motherhood can be really valuable to your work.

**Yee** Were you also thinking about other female artists who include motherhood in their work?

**Madani** Yes, I realised that there are many painters or sculptors who bring their mothering experience into the studio. There's Louise Bourgeois, of course, and the French filmmaker Agnes Varda, who included her children in her films in the 1970s. Most mother and child paintings, of course, show virgin mothers, which is ridiculous.

**Yee** I don't think very many women painted those.

**Madani** No. The idealisation, symmetry, balance and everything the virgin mother stands for is so tedious. But the mother and child is perhaps one of the most painted motifs in the history of Western art, which is so funny. I just realised this was an area I really wanted to engage with.

**Yee** This is perhaps why Mary Kelly made *Post-Partum Document* [1973–79] – because she needed to respond to this history.

**Madani** Exactly. It's about bringing the material experience into the fore.

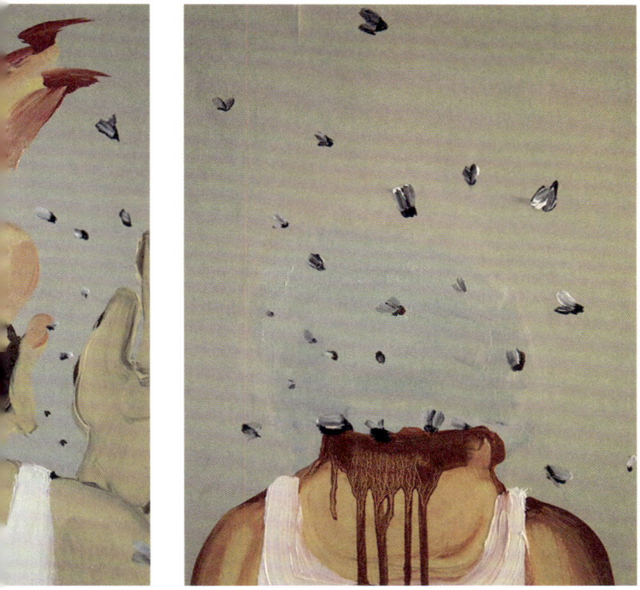

These two tracks have been a constant, as well as post-revolutionary Iranian pop songs of the 1980s.

**Yee** You reflect this in your choice of subject, of course, but also the tactile experience and physicality of motherhood in the way you put the paint on the surface of the canvas. You also mentioned that you don't typically paint from either photographs or life. What are some of the sources of inspiration for your work? I know you sometimes look at comics and children's story books.

**Madani** Yes. I think now, after fifteen years, painting has become a way of processing for me. Whatever I'm experiencing or thinking, whether socially or politically, comes into the paintings. It's really my brain that's the source and it could be anything that sparks an idea. I always return to music. There's one French born Monégasque pop singer Léo Ferré whom I've listened to since at least 2003. Every time I feel like my brain is too busy, I put one of his songs on and it focuses me. I also listen to Keith Jarrett's Köln Concert.

**Yee** I wonder about the dynamics among your figures. Sometimes you have singular figures that seem quite absorbed in their own world, but in other paintings, the figures appear to be participating in some group activity. What's going on in your painting *Dirty Stars* [2008] [pl. 17], for example?

**Madani** In this painting, there are three men bending down. They're all wearing the same thing and you can see the top of their bums. The other figure is showing them all kinds of different stars, like he's giving an introduction to the stars.

**Yee** Where does the 'dirty' come into it?

**Madani** The suggestion is that your bum is a star. Maybe your bum's dirty. Maybe everybody is a dirty star. It also relates to the gold stars you get in school.

**Yee** And what's going on in *Campfire* [2011] [pl. 19]?

**Madani** In this one, I was interested in trying to paint something about fire under a table. The figures in the painting are man-babies.

**Yee** Infantile men?

**Madani** Yes, for me, that's where the liberation is. If you're behaving like a child, that's when you're most creative or most forgivable. These are limbs coming out of these sacks. So I think they're cooking somebody on the campfire.

**Yee** Campfires are a primal experience in some ways.

**Madani** It's so true. But there's also a table. Tables have a history in painting: tables are where something could happen or you can have a discussion. Here, they're having a campfire under a table.

**Yee** I wanted to ask you about your interest in the digital. In a painting like *Corner Projection (Panic)*

[2019], it looks as if you've taken material that could be on a screen. The way you've handled the paint looks like the grease marks we leave on our phones. Is that a deliberate way you're working with paint? Is some of the imagery meant to appear photographic? What's your process?

**Madani** *Corner Projection (Panic)* is one of my corner projection paintings. In these works, I use silk screens to break the register of what's printed and painted. This means that what's projected is a different quality from the light emitted from the projector. Through the different materials, it gives the suggestion of two different worlds colliding. I'm also very interested in staining as a way to interrupt light. Light isn't a material until there's something in front of it, like dust.

**Yee** In *Light Balance* [2012] [pl. 20] you see these middle-aged male figures that you're probably best known for. Why don't they have hair? Is it way to signal that they're both children and middle aged? Their bodies are also like overgrown children.

**Madani** Yes. These figures are quite central in my work, especially in relation to the corner projectors.

**Yee** You were born in Tehran, where women don't necessarily get access to groups of men on their own. Are these paintings a way of trying to imagine what they're doing together?

**Madani** Totally. It's a weird psychological thing. In the café where we're having this conversation I can see two tables in front of us with groups of men sitting around them. I'd love to know what the hell they're talking about. It's my weird curiosity. I don't know about their medical problems or what their heartbreaks are, or how they stare at themselves every morning in the mirror. Do they wash their socks? Are they ever disturbed by their own smell?

**Yee** So, in a way, it's harder to understand these groups of men because you experience your body in a different way?

**Madani** Yes, exactly. Of course, my time in Iran probably has a lot to do with it, but my thoughts really solidified when I was in Berlin. There are all these Turkish tea rooms in Kreuzberg, always with matte glass windows so you can't really see inside. I always wondered, what the hell these rather good-looking, youngish or not so youngish Turkish men were doing in there. I was living in Berlin during the Iraq war with Bush. This very particular experience in Germany led me to the cake series.

**Yee** A lot of people might see these works as a critique of men and their behaviour.

**Madani** They are.

**Yee** It's also interesting that you're trying to empathise and inhabit their space.

**Madani** Totally. I've made so many paintings, and while some of them are very critical, some of them are empathetic. I'm also very aware that I'm making work in relation to a US or European context. Who am I and how does my audience complete the sentence? The standing of the characters that I depict within the global socioeconomic system is also relevant. I'm not criticising any particular man that I paint, but the conditions under which he finds himself.

## Ryan Mosley in Conversation with Cameron Foote

**Cameron Foote** I'd like to start by talking about your time at the University of Huddersfield and later the Royal College of Art. What was your experience of art education and why did you choose to work in figurative painting?

**Ryan Mosley** I can't really remember the exact point when I chose to work in figurative painting. For as long as I can remember, I've always made attempts to paint the figure. Even as early as infant school, I was more interested in drawing and painting and making images than the more academic subjects. Art seemed like the place I gravitated towards. I failed all my GCSEs apart from art, which possibly ignited more of a desire to follow through with the subject, or just to cling onto it for dear life. As a result of academic failing, I spent three years at art college before going on to study for my degree in drawing and painting, largely making painting and sculpture. Some of the paintings I made at this time were more obviously abstract, but there always seemed to be a figurative leaning, or at least, I pushed the images back to a more representative figuration.

**Foote** You worked as an invigilator at The National Gallery for some years while starting out as an artist. Did the experience of spending time with this historic collection of European painting inform your own artistic interests?

**Mosley** When I arrived at the RCA, I didn't really have an idea of what the course would be like or how they'd teach painting. I was in awe of the legacy of previous generations of painters who'd studied or taught there. Surprisingly enough, painting wasn't really discussed as a medium and there wasn't a great deal of discourse around the possibilities of paint. I guess I got that side of my education at this time from working at The National Gallery. Depending on shift patterns and room closures, you might spend the whole day with Rubens or a week with Velázquez. I'd go home feeling awake to the possibilities of paint, but then I'd want to wave the white flag at the prospect of making a painting the following day, as there was no way of even attempting to compete. The time working at The National Gallery reintroduced me to stories as much as visual motifs: it made me think about narrative and character.

**Foote** Are there more recent painters who've been important to you?

**Mosley** While studying for my BA, there was no way of avoiding Peter Doig's influence. At the time, Doig and Chris Ofili were the 'go to' figures for contemporary British painting. In many ways, they were influential in figurative painting globally. I remember when Phaidon's book *Vitamin P* was released, as art students on a painting and drawing BA we were suddenly exposed to a whole generation of painters. To go and research a painter or a painting online around 2000 or 2002, I remember you'd have to go and book a time slot in the library on dial-up internet. So when the painting department got a few copies of *Vitamin P*, it was a really big event. It seemed every student who at that point hadn't really engaged with the programme suddenly had eyes on stalks looking through the book. Artists like Tal R, Daniel Richter, Neo Rauch, Manuel Ocampo, were the kind I gravitated to. I then found myself going backwards in time, looking at Philip Guston, R.B. Kitaj, David Hockney, Pierre Bonnard, James Ensor, René Magritte and Edouard Manet. The Guston exhibition at the Royal Academy in 2004 was a real milestone moment for me. I'd seen his work in reproduction and pixilated images online, but viewing that show and experiencing his dynamic

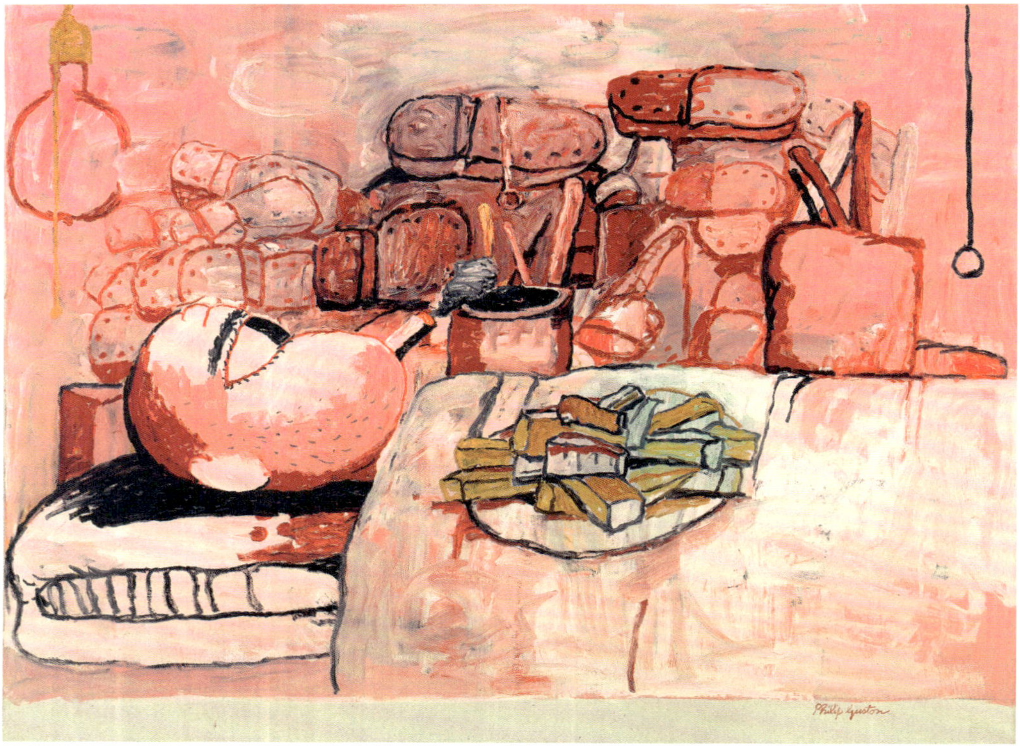

Philip Guston, *Painting, Smoking, Eating*, 1973, oil on canvas, 197 × 263 cm

visual language was the fuel I needed. I moved to London around this time, partly as contemporary painting seemed thin on the ground outside of London in the UK.

**Foote** The earliest of your works included in the exhibition is *Teaching Snakes to be Snakes* [2008] [pl. 22]. Could you talk about how the different elements, such as the falling bearded figure, the limb-like forms and the snakes, function together in the painting?

**Mosley** *Teaching Snakes to be Snakes* was one of the first times the character of the bearded figure appeared in my work. It was made pretty much straight after I graduated from the RCA. The residue of previous attempted paintings, ideas, failed motifs were very much on the surface of the painting. This approach almost became the backdrop to all the paintings I made at this time, partly by accident and partly because during my time at the RCA I decided to stop making drawings or preparatory images for paintings. Through this process, there was no set image I would hope to create, and there was a lot of room for the final painting to evolve.

**Foote** The different elements in the painting at some points seem to dissolve into each other. Is that the result of this process of evolution?

**Mosley** Yes, it's a dynamic process of failures and erasures becoming something else. A failed attempt at painting a leg, once erased, leaves the suggestion of the knee cap, which in turn reads to me like a head, a sceptre, a club, or even a new character I hadn't anticipated. Once scale shifts, then things don't need to adhere to anatomy or perspective anymore. I'm interested in these failed attempts because they suddenly offer the possibility of constructing figures through a kind of broken anatomy. The figure can be read on one level as a contortionist, with his only recognisable anatomy apparent from his torso up.

**Foote** How do these tumbling figures relate to the horizontal band along the lower edge?

**Mosley** I needed to ground the character in a physical point of contact to the floor, horizon line or stage. The hair of the monopod or limb-like characters acts like a ball-and-joint socket for both a hip and a knee. Then the rational thinking comes back. Even if he could stand up and walk, his feet would be the wrong way round. I wasn't pursuing something anatomically correct. I presumed if the central protagonist had to move, it would be by crawling. Maybe his legs wouldn't even carry his weight. This led me to think about the title. How would you teach a snake to be a snake? It's an impossible idea. My reading of the painting also shifts – maybe we're looking at serpents teaching the horizontal figure and maybe the fractured limbs are also doing the teaching.

**Foote** Was this the first time you used the motif of the snake?

**Mosley** The motif of the snake had come about in previous paintings, where I started painting a framework around the border of the canvas as a way of grounding the image. The border at one point looked like a pattern or snakeskin, so then that motif evolved and became both frame and simplified representation of a snake. The snake in *Teaching Snakes to be Snakes* is motif, subject, frame and an attempt at balancing the painting. The beard also becomes an extension of the figure. In the same way, the pipe and also the pipe smoke are extensions, a way of maximising the figure to balance the space.

**Foote** Many of your works place figures within constructions such as stages, platforms or thresholds that shorten the visible depth of field. What motivates your interest in these structural devices?

**Mosley** It's only the character or suggestion of the figure that I'm interested in. The geography, architecture or history is only really there to allow the figure to exist in that picture. By getting rid of everything and emptying the canvas, I was left with a simplified horizon line or a stage. As my paintings have evolved, the fore- and mid-ground and, to a certain extent, the background have all come to exist on the same flattened picture plane. The depth of field at some points has become so shallow that the paintings almost read to me like giant sketchbook pages. Over the years, the stage has become more obviously a stage. Now, the stage can be a wall or a pictorial device that supports the narrative or character in the paintings. A similar thing happens when I introduce a human presence into a work, and the internal reasoning of perspective and motif needs to be more tangible.

**Foote** Two of the works in the exhibition, *Duchess of Oils* [2014] [pl. 24] and *Wearing Another's Head on Your Jacket* [2014] [pl. 25] disrupt the tradition of the head-and-shoulders portrait. Could you explain how these compositions evolved?

**Mosley** I've always been interested in portraiture, and I got into painting through looking at portraits, postage stamps or silhouettes and by drawing cartoon faces. For many years, and even now to some degree, I skirted around the prospect of making portraits in my work. Twenty years ago, it seemed slightly naff or twee to want to make portraits. I made a series of miniature oval portraits while studying at the RCA as a way to avoid committing to the rectangular format. For a number of years, the oval became the perfect pictorial device to paint these portraits of masked performers from a fictitious *commedia del arte*. As well as avoiding the subject, I was avoiding the proportions of modernity and the 7 × 5 inch format of photography. Partly because, when making the portraits, I felt like they could only really ever be a portrait, there was no chance of the painting evolving through the process of making. It would only ever be read as a head-and-shoulders or three-quarter-length portrait.

*Duchess of Oils* exists because it seemed the right time to return to the rectangle format after these dialogues. I wanted to paint a character that was an actor inhabiting multiple characters, making visible the ghosts of previous speeches. It also became like a game of chicken in painting. How many faces is too many? If I'd painted three faces, I might as well continue until the image felt balanced to the point of failing again.

With *Wearing Another's Head on Your Jacket*, I'd long been interested in the anti-portrait, the idea of painting the back of someone's head. A lived experience filtered into the making of the painting: the frustration of viewing art in museums, where you have to look at the back of people's heads before being able to see the painting. More often, this happens with portraits, as they seem to command that gathering of people listening to the audio guide about the subject's life. It also reminded me of the theatre and the thing of being a spectator. The shared experience of the audience adds to the spectacle of the performance. I needed something to bring the figure back to the viewer.

**Foote** Can you talk about the idea of putting the image on the jacket in this work?

**Mosley** I've long thought how strange it is that fans or team supporters wear images of other people on T-shirts. It could be an icon – Elvis, Christ or Princess Diana – or even your favourite breed of pet – an Alsatian or a tabby-cat on a jumper. I grew up with band posters on my wall. They were always from the same music store. I went through a phase of buying Iron Maiden posters and merchandise, CDs, T-shirts. I wasn't massively into the music – it was the artwork I found fascinating. I guess a natural progression for anyone who was interested in motif and image was Che Guevara. It's that willingness to walk the streets wearing another's head or portrait emblazoned on the front or back. It felt like the perfect idea to be plundered. The central character wears a sports jacket; the double portrait crop allows the suggestion of foreground and background too.

**Foote** Could you talk about your technique and working methods?

**Mosley** Some of my paintings are started with a geometric pattern painted over the white of the canvas. *Cave Inn* [2011] [pl. 23] began in this way. The geometric forms served as a method to get far enough away from the bare canvas and also there was a desire to find form within the sections of the pattern underneath. I wanted at this time to allow access into the painted surface, to see how the painting was made, almost like the painting's DNA. The pattern also alluded to the Harlequin motif. Largely, though, within my practice the paintings are started without direct source material or preparatory drawing. The painting usually starts with an attempt to paint a figure and, through this process of editing and repainting, I hope to get somewhere near the initial idea or intuition. The way I've been making the paintings over the years means I have some idea of how things will appear on canvas. I welcome the mistakes and misjudging ideas. I work primarily with oil paint, which as a medium buys me time to reconsider previous passages of painting as the painting dries. I work on several canvases in a day, partly because of drying times and also because of restlessness with finding the image. This also allows for a cross-fertilising of ideas, which often reappear in subsequent paintings.

**Foote** Where do your titles come from? What do you hope they might convey to viewers?

**Mosley** Titles often come about through the process of making and the painting's evolution. Something will appear in the picture that might suggest the title's leaning, and then the painting might be guided towards the title or association to the title. With the portraits, this happens less frequently, as there's less room for the possibility of the subject or painting to be anything other than a portrait. I often write words and sentences down as a painting is being made, which relate to it at the time. These can start to form the catalyst for a painting, as can the lived experience or a misreading of a subject. I imagine an audience's reading of a finished painting would be different from when it was in its previous state of finding itself.

**Foote** Why do you think there's been a renewed interest in figurative painting in recent years?

**Mosley** I wonder if it's partly to do with the fact that most people now have the ability to take a photograph or a selfie on their phone camera, thus giving the medium of photography a greater spread and greater accessibility. It's hard to take a bad photograph of anything now, as you'd just delete the image and take another as you'd desire it to look. The age-old argument was prevalent when I was at college: why paint an image when you could take a photograph? But no-one really thinks about photography in that way anymore, because most people have access to the medium. Painting possibly presents itself as a harder-fought, less immediate way of making images. Maybe this instantaneous moment we're living in has given young artists and students time and access to look and think. Art and Design Foundation courses across the country are closing down, yet Fine Art has a greater number of applications for places than twenty years ago. Maybe younger students don't have the same hang-ups and arguments about subject and medium as before, and painting is being sought out. Maybe a creative career is seen as more valid now than twenty years ago, and then by that token, perhaps figuration is seen to have more validation. I also think there's an in-built desire for painters to paint what it is to be human.

## Christina Quarles in Conversation with Summer Bowie

**Summer Bowie** I thought I'd start by mentioning that you were pictured talking to Brad Pitt at the opening of your recent solo exhibition at Regen Projects ['But I Woke Jus' Tha Same', 6 April–9 May 2019], which became so much fodder for press and tabloids.

**Christina Quarles** [Laughs] That was so funny.

**Bowie** Does it feel strange when those random moments become very public?

**Quarles** I grew up in LA, so I'm used to being around people in film and television. My family all moved out here from the Midwest to work in film and television, so I'm not that fazed by celebrity. It was funny because you can really tell that the entire world is looking at you when you're talking to somebody like Brad Pitt. I've been having a few studio visits with people who make their living as actors. It's interesting, since so much of my work is about the normal experience of living in your body: having that experience of not really knowing what you look like. So then, talking to people whose profession is based on having people look at them, it's been an interesting thought experiment.

**Bowie** Speaking of Los Angeles, was this your first solo show in LA, over at Regen Projects? Have you been waiting for the right moment to present your paintings?

**Quarles** My first solo project here was at Skibum MacArthur, with Kibum Kim ['It's Gunna Be All Right, Cause Baby, There Ain't Nuthin' Left', 22 April–10 June 2017]. I reinstalled a piece that was my thesis work in graduate school. That work really informed and inspired the work that I did for *Made in LA* [3 June–2 September 2018, Hammer Museum, Los Angeles], but it was definitely the first time that I really presented a body of paintings in Los Angeles, so it was important to take my time with figuring out galleries to work with, and to make sure that it was a good fit.

**Bowie** Does it feel nice to be finally really thrusting your work out there, or is there a sense of unease?

**Quarles** I definitely am happy that I waited a while before putting the work out there, because I never really felt my work was in a place where I wanted it to be. I spent about seven years between undergrad and grad school trying out different jobs. I was a graphic designer for a while and I worked on *Sesame Street*.

**Bowie** What were you doing on *Sesame Street*?

**Quarles** I was an executive assistant in the international department. I was also a project coordinator for the productions in India and Northern Ireland, because they do completely unique *Sesame Streets* in different parts of the world.

**Bowie** Wow, I had no idea.

**Quarles** In Northern Ireland, they all live in a tree and it's called *Sesame Tree*. Big Bird is considered too American, so India has a Big Bear instead.

**Bowie** Did any of the work that you did on *Sesame Street*, or as a graphic designer, inform your practice?

**Quarles** I would say most of the experiences that have informed my practice are gender and sexuality, race, and things that really come from my own lived experiences. In undergrad, I got a philosophy degree and was very involved in a critical race theory dissertation. A lot of my practice was born out of my undergraduate research, as well as my ongoing daily experiences. But my work as a graphic designer has really informed the way that I make these paintings, because I use Adobe Illustrator a lot when making this work.

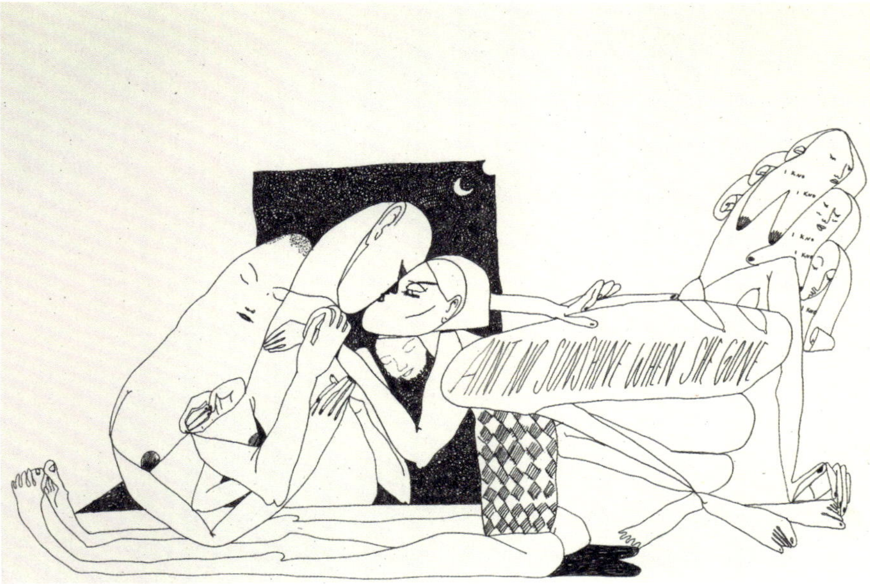


Christina Quarles, *I Kno, I Kno, I Kno, I Kno*, 2019, ink on paper, 33 × 48.3 cm

**Bowie** When assessing the figurative side of your work, there have been comparisons to Arshile Gorky and to Willem de Kooning. When it comes to your application of paint – this sort of courageous improvisation – there have been comparisons to Helen Frankenthaler and Lynda Benglis. Do you consider these people artistic influences?

**Quarles** When I was at Yale, Rob Storr gave this graduation speech, where he said something like, 'None of you will ever be folk artists again.' Basically, he was saying, 'You guys are all well-educated artists now because you went to a prestigious art school and got a master's degree.' So I definitely have had a lot of art-historical influence, but I also spent much of grad school feeling self-conscious about how limited my knowledge of art history was. It took me a while to really gain confidence in the references I did have, and the canon I was reaching into. I'm interested in referencing the advertisement that was lifted from historical reference – taking the reference that's about three iterations down; having that more mass-cultural influence. I do also have this art-historical knowledge, but I would say that the way I approach a canvas really comes from a more physical place.

**Bowie** You have a very particular approach to fragmentation. Do you look at the world through this fragmented lens?

**Quarles** I think a lot about fragmentation in representing the figures in my work. It's the sense of fragmentation that you feel when you look at your own body – it exists as these parts that you're more or less aware of – and the disadvantage you have of knowing yourself only in fragmentation. And of knowing all the different contradictions and idiosyncrasies of your own self. It's about seeing everybody else as these complete, fully formed people who make sense and look completely whole, and then seeing yourself as a fragmented kind of mess.

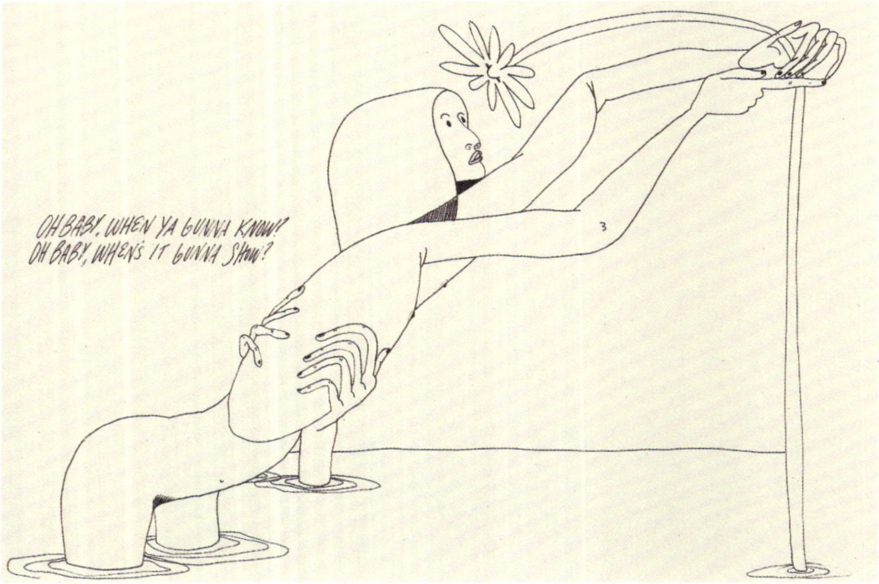


Christina Quarles, *Oh Baby*, 2019, ink on paper, 33 × 48.3 cm

**Bowie** There's also this interesting obfuscation between sex and sexuality that's constantly being represented, as well as notions of casual nudity versus romantic nudity.

**Quarles** Having moments of intimacy with other people, whether that's an intimate moment related to love, or even violence, hunger or sickness – these intimate moments are ways in which you can know somebody in their complications and fragmentations and compartmentalised selves. It comes from this idea that was drilled into me when I was in high school by a figure-drawing teacher. Basically, if you draw a line and it's not the correct line – maybe you realise that you've positioned the leg in the wrong place – if you erase that line, you're going to reinforce the mistake. So he taught you to draw the leg next to the leg that you did in error. It was a sort of moving forward from your mistakes, rather than fixating on them, because that would reinforce the muscle memory of the error. It's a nice poetic parallel to being in your body and living in the world; you're kind of working with what you've got.

**Bowie** Do you feel like there are these blurred lines between intimacy and casual nudity, or general vulnerability in your own life?

**Quarles** Yes, definitely. I always get a little annoyed when my work is framed as being overtly sexual. One of the things I like playing with, that can end up biting me in the ass later, is the way that the world will complete an image that isn't there. My worst-case scenario is that somebody is able to passively consume an image of a queer body, or of a female body. I want to encourage an active looking and questioning. It's a different thing when you acknowledge it as a queer relationship.

**Bowie** You did this group show at the New Museum called 'Trigger: Gender as a Tool or a Weapon.' Do you represent gender as a tool, or as a weapon in your work, and can you explain the difference?

**Quarles** When I think about that phrase, one of the quotes that I'll often repeat is this queer theory statement by Joshua Gamson that says, 'Fixed identity categories are both the basis for oppression and the basis for political power.' That was written in the early 1990s, so it was this moment of thinking about how inclusive queerness should be in order to still have a community that had enough in common to make advancements in policy change. I think of that a lot with identity positions, and with gender too: how it can be used as a tool, or as a platform from which to seek equality, or to advocate for how you see yourself, but also how that can be used as a weapon against you to restrict or limit the potential.

**Bowie** I want to talk about your use of slang and word play, and how that relates to the visual fragmentation. Are they analogues to one another, and how do they work together?

**Quarles** I used to use language directly in the paintings. Now, I'll write next to the paintings on pieces of paper, and then I'll usually incorporate it into the title. I've always been drawn to phonetic language. I'm interested in the utterance of language, and how there could be punning and double meaning in language. When I took the language out of the paintings, that was when I started really developing the patterns. I started looking for patterns that could have the same sort of visual punning and multiple locations, like a field of flowers that's a pattern on a bedspread, or a field of flowers in nature. In the titles, and the drawings, there's still certainly this use of slang and common expressions, or pop music lyrics. I find the idea of things that get stuck in your head, or repeated in your head, an interesting anchor for the work. And they kind of invoke a mood. I love the word 'morning', and how much that's used in pop music, but then misspelling it to be like grieving gives it this double location of language.

**Bowie** Speaking of dualities, making art always has this other side to it: the art market. How do you feel about that side of things?

**Quarles** I think it can be really challenging as an artist, because you want it to be a part of conversations with institutions and curators, but it can be easy to become seen as a market artist. I need to hire a studio manager who can deal with the market side of things. That said, it's something you should be aware of as an artist, because it is a reality of what you do. But it's important to not have it completely take over, because it's not what got me into making the work.

**Bowie** When somebody like Jeffrey Deitch says that you're 'The greatest artist in America right now', do you feel like it challenges your sense of self in any way?

**Quarles** I don't know. I have a lot of people in my world who are helpful in grounding me and reminding me that I'm just the same old person I always have been. You have to take it with a grain of salt because the art world is so fickle, and it has such a short-term memory. I've had enough experience to know that things go through cycles, and to not rely too heavily on any one thing at any one time. I don't think I could do this at all if I didn't really love making the paintings. I find that to be the most rewarding part of the process.

First published as 'Singing the Body Electric' in *Autre Magazine*, Los Angeles, California, Volume 2, Issue 8, Summer 2019, pp. 132–137.

# Daniel Richter in Conversation with Lydia Yee

**Lydia Yee** I'd like to ask about the relationship between the figure and abstraction in your most recent work, but first, could you speak about the more representational work you've been making?

**Daniel Richter** The last group of paintings I did in a more narrative or representational style was the romanticised, psychedelic, Taliban-meets-cowboy smoking a cigarette thing. One of the paintings you selected, *"HEY JOE"* [2011] [pl. 31], is titled after a Jimi Hendrix song about a man who's going to kill his girlfriend because he caught her messing around with another man – a horrendous idea. This group of works was about the romantic idea of manliness that has more or less vanished. Nobody looks at the smoking cowboy nowadays, whether straight or gay, and thinks, 'Oh that's hot'. Instead, they look at him and think, 'Poor guy, stuck in an idea of manliness that's ridiculous, he probably has lung cancer.'

**Yee** Yes and now you might imagine he's underpaid.

**Richter** An underpaid, hard-working guy. Actually, the original Marlboro man did die of cancer. I was looking for a way of painting without having to establish stages. Before, the paintings that I did were like constructed settings, rooms and spaces resembling theatre stages. And I was fed up with putting figures representing ideas of history and politics on a stage. I'd done it and didn't want to continue, because it was just turning into a bad habit. Instead, I started doing these loosely psychedelic paintings, into which I placed exoticised beauty clichés. I was thinking more about the mood created by looking at something that was once considered beautiful and worthy, and is now just a shabby remnant of popular culture. I didn't want to denounce it. I just thought it was fun, painting in a psychedelic style paranoid, smoking men in the mountains.

**Yee** Why did you choose to study at the University of Fine Arts in Hamburg and what sort of painting were your teachers doing?

**Richter** I went there to study with Werner Büttner. He, Martin Kippenberger and Albert Oehlen were a small group fighting against stupidity in painting, but also more generally in art. Their approach was a mix of hubris and irony, which had fragments of leftist radicalism. They called themselves 'the RAF of German painting', not after the British Royal Air Force, but after the far-left terror group Red Army Faction in West Germany. They said stuff that impressed the punk in me, and I liked the work because I could understand it and because it had a certain worldliness. But I didn't understand the criteria that made their work different from flyers or posters. I myself have this kind of squatter, DIY, hard-core background and did a lot of posters for demonstrations, advertisements for bands and other similar things and I wanted to understand what makes this kind of agitprop work different from 'real' art. It's kind of an anachronistic question nowadays, but I didn't know any better then. I applied and Büttner took me in his class. His paintings were like a run-down version of Expressionism with a strong, narrative content that wasn't easy to get, but I really liked a lot. He hooked me up with Albert Oehlen, whom I worked for as an assistant while I was a student. So everything I am now is rooted in this system. Oehlen and Büttner were both students of Sigmar Polke and Jörg Immendorff and were taught to stretch or attack certain formalistic and narrative habits. I'm kind of based in this way of reasoning.

When I started doing paintings in his class that were completely non-figurative, Büttner didn't oppose me, but he said, 'I believe that you know what you're doing, but I don't understand why you're doing it.'

It was kind of a dialectic way of teaching – you use a method and later try to transform it or do the opposite. When Oehlen stated that all paintings should be brown, since that's the result of mixing all colours, that sounded cool in some nerdy secret radical way, but the opposite could also be true. When you have 5,000 colours, why not use all 5,000, instead of just twelve? A kind of low-level debate, I admit!

**Yee** But you didn't want your paintings to turn into shit.

**Richter** Yes, exactly, I didn't. My approach at this time also had a certain, maybe slightly neurotic, idea that you had to constantly change and, if not, you're a sell-out. It wasn't about the market, but simply the thought that after achieving something, you learn and then you're obliged to do something new with your achievements.

**Yee** That's why you've continued to move on over time?

**Richter** Yes, but I thought everybody did. This was until I spent time in the US and was confronted with American painters, where the opposite was true – once they achieved something, they stayed with it. They called it coherency and continuity.

**Yee** Having a style that collectors would recognise …

**Richter** Maybe. Nowadays, I understand that the system favours a certain signature, but it meant repeating yourself endlessly, I thought. But I gradually had to understand that it was just German neuroticism that made me believe that I had to change. It would have been much easier for me to have established a style. But I just can't. I'm too easily bored. If you look at the most influential painters in Germany, it seems like a bad habit, passed over from generation to generation, torturing our wicked souls – mine at least.

**Yee** The shift away from your early, more abstract work took place at the beginning of the 2000s. What was the impetus for this?

**Richter** After five years of doing paintings based on the idea of trying to squeeze more information into a painting than anybody had ever done before, which I achieved at some point, I asked myself, where's it going to end? An overkill of gestures, invented, referenced, stolen, the dead-end street of too much. Around the turn of the millennium, the whole Leipzig school came around the corner, with its consumer-based, moody, conservative surrealism thing. I actually thought some of it was interesting. At least with Neo Rauch, there's a weird way of dealing with an idea of conservative Modernism, especially in the context of the former Socialist East. It was the tenth anniversary of German unification, of course, and embedded in zeitgeist debates of annoying identity issues etc, I felt the urge to leave my little optimistic free-jazz-techno tower. And to leave that ivory tower, you have to paint humans or buildings or cars – very simple. It was also a challenge, because for five years I'd told myself, it's wrong and reactionary to paint figuratively. Then, logically, I decided to paint figuratively, which was painful because the paintings all looked like shit. It was really disastrous.

During those days, I spent some time at the Musée d'Orsay in Paris. The Bonnard paintings seemingly related to debates that were common at the turn of the millennium circling around digitalism, chaos theory, how our way of perception is changing through the computer and new influences in popular culture. In Bonnard, you see the influence of Japanese culture, photography and an analytical method. Bonnard was transforming things not only subjectively, but also with a pseudo-scientific method. The work, even though not radical, but intimate and representing quite petit-bourgeois values, offered a challenge for me. I was wondering how his idylls would look after they'd been dragged through the past century, and I more or less used that as a starting point.

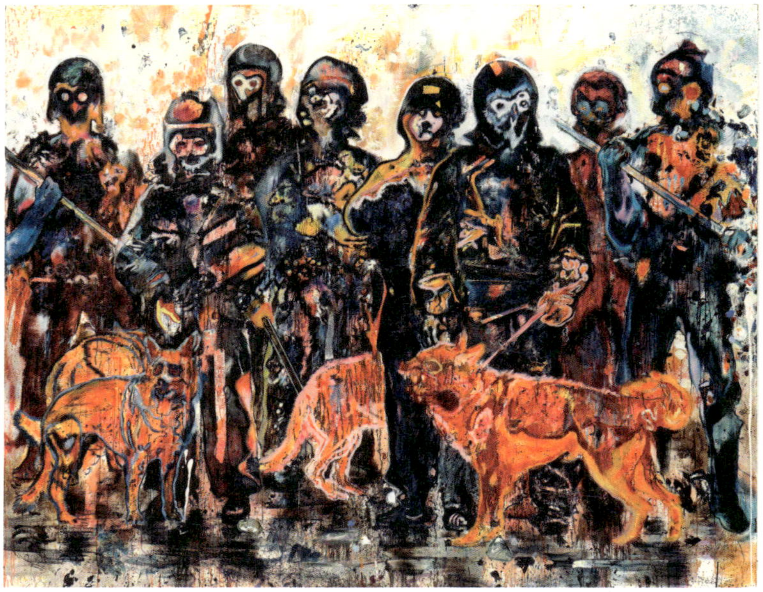

Daniel Richter, *Dog Planet*, 2002, oil on canvas, 280 × 351 cm

**Yee** Do you see your subjects from that period as being contemporary though? You were looking at photography and news items and so on.

**Richter** The aim was to do stuff that proved to myself that even if the world is a miserable place, painting – or better, art in general – may offer a counterpoint. I tried to do paintings that balanced an often serious topic and transformed it into something that was not one-dimensionally reproducing the found image, but transforming it into something more hysterical or paranoid.

Also, there were all kinds of influences. The night-vision camera, for example, was used in the first Gulf War to broadcast live footage of war for the first time, always with this greenish glow. The painting in this exhibition from 2001 [pl. 29] is based on an image of people trying to escape over to Tarifa in Spain, which was at that time a hot surfer spot. It hit the news when people started to find on the beach the dead bodies of migrants trying to enter Europe. And since I've always been politically active, I thought it would be important to do something with this topic.

**Yee** Were you also thinking about historical precedents, like Delacroix, for example?

**Richter** Yes, for sure. Around the same time, I did a painting called *Dog Planet* [2002], which has German shepherd dogs held by guys who could be hooligans or policemen, or just representatives of power or repression. The painting is done in a very shabby, expressionistic way because I liked that process of painting.

There were others from around this time that were more like historical speculations – I was also interested in R.B. Kitaj's 'bad' painting of three women called *The Rise of Fascism* [1975–79]. I made my own painting about the Hamburg uprising in 1923, a rather complicated story about mistakes the Communist Party had made while staging a German revolution,

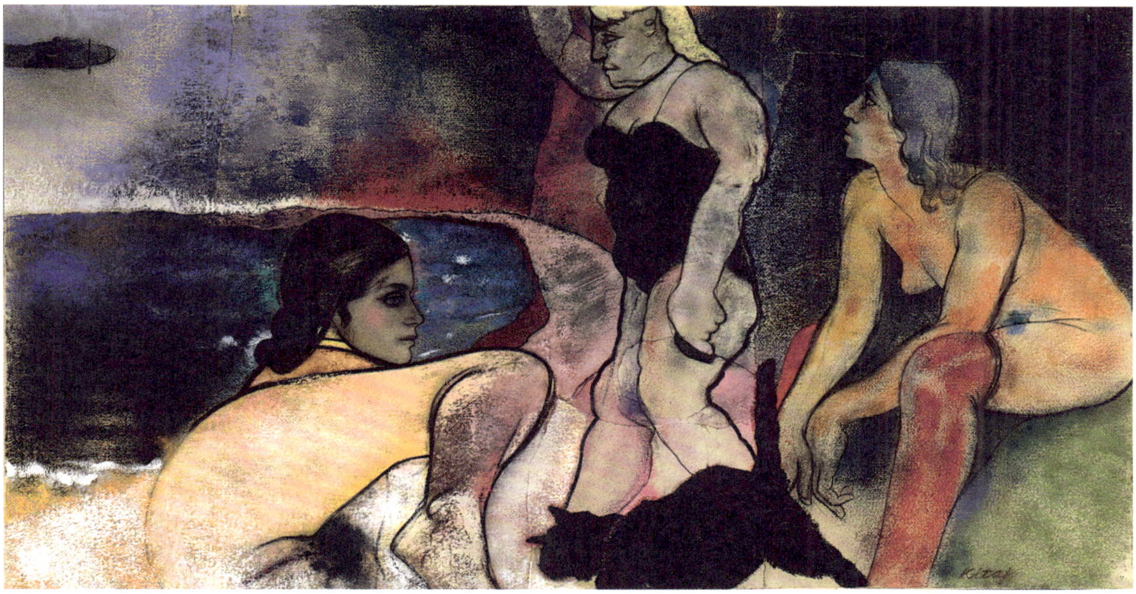

R.B. Kitaj, *The Rise of Fascism*, 1975–79, oil, charcoal and pastel on paper, 85.1 × 158.4 cm

and a real historical event, but the painting was speculation about whether it could have ended differently.

In the end, this line of work really became something that I wanted to avoid, because I felt as if painting was not able to shed light, but was establishing unnecessary mysteries and riddles that can't be solved. It's an aspect I don't like about a lot of modern painting. Is the artist just trying to be mysterious for its own sake? Or are they focusing on something that seems to be mysterious but that they want to solve via a painting?

**Yee** You mean, is it possible to solve a historical question with a painting?

**Richter** Yes. This is certainly impossible, but it was perhaps interesting to do and has rarely been done. Philip Guston tried something similar in his early work, as Kitaj and some German painters did. I actually don't really relate to the history of Social Realist paintings, because I think that work made sense only in its own time: mainly, it's just reproducing a dumb cliché. It's very self-righteous and very superficial – ugly representatives of the ruling class vs. upright socialist workers. Anyway, it was good because I was doing something in a field where not so many were, so that I felt free to occupy and mess with my own mistakes and failures.

**Yee** I think that's why a lot of people didn't take up painting in the 1990s, or in your generation: because they had fewer constraints doing performance or video.

**Richter** Absolutely right. That's the reason why I think all German female students who took a painting class went immediately afterwards to a performance or a video class. Socially, there's a cliché about dumb male painters. As a student, you had to listen to all this unreflective, superstitious blah, blah, blah about painting. Most students wanted to cut it out and leave class immediately.

**Yee** Because those voices were so strong in Germany?

**Richter** Supposedly. There must be a reason why, in relation to other parts of the world, there aren't a lot of female painters in Germany. Even when I was a student, it was fucking annoying. You didn't even have to be a feminist; you just had to believe in fair play.

**Yee** Can you tell me a little bit about the process of how you go about making a painting in your most recent body of work? Do you collect any visual reference material?

**Richter** With these more recent works, I didn't collect anything physical. It's all based on scribbles and sketches I do while using the internet or flipping through illustrated political atlases. The psychedelic paintings were all based on improvisations, mainly dropped colour. They have these kind of zigzag lines, which are like a heart-rate measurement or the DAX index. After the zigzag lines, the first formal choice was to consider whether I should make everything flat, with a monochromatic backdrop in yellow or red, or else to do horizontal lines.

**Yee** The painting from that body of work we're including, *Asger, Bill und Mark* [2015] [pl. 32], has bands in the background.

**Richter** Exactly. It's slow work, but I forced myself to do it. At the start, these works looked like minimalist paintings by the likes of Gerhard Richter, but with the effect of Rothko and Paul Klee.

**Yee** You put that down first, before any figures were added?

**Richter** Yes. At first, I had no idea what to do with them. Then there were two things that gave me ideas. I'd been reading a book about the history of mass forced migration. It was a book not just about Polish, Russian, Czech, German or Jewish people, but also about tribes that are long forgotten that were forced to migrate or got killed. The book was full of maps in multiple colours that illustrated these migratory routes. Because it was such a complex story, some of these illustrations weren't just in blue, red and yellow. These maps might have to show the history of 150 different counties. So, instead, they all had these weird colours, which shifted and pushed and pulled and squeezed. Somehow, while reading that book in combination with making these line paintings, I had this idea that the shapes I was seeing were similar to bodies. Bodies can have this quality of being everywhere. The pornographic and the violent body are a common low dominator in our society, depicting a cynical, capitalised representation and appearing everywhere. Somehow, this exploitative relation towards the masses and this approach to bodies mingled in my brain. And then I decided to try to paint these drifting elements on the canvas.

**Yee** Were you partly interested in creating a tension with the more rigid linear system underneath?

**Richter** Well, afterwards, it's easy to analyse. I have the first layer, which is controlled and slow, and it's translucent. Then I have the second, which is opaque and fat. Also, it doesn't really represent any order. It's just like dots.

**Yee** Amorphous.

**Richter** When you all look at these elements, it all looks like this stuff floating around. Then at the end, the fast decisive part is outlining. Here you can shift the painting into a completely narrative and banal direction, or else you can transform it so even you don't know what's going to happen. It's like making a stew – except it's only clear at the last minute whether it's going to be a lentil soup or a curry. For me, the last phase is the most exciting. Because I do things that I can't plan, I can look at a painting later and be surprised by it. I really have no idea how some of the paintings happened.

**Yee** What kinds of titles do you give the works, and what purpose do they serve?

**Richter** With this kind of painting, most of the titles are double layered. They often play with words, like the paintings themselves play with expectations, fragments or remnants.

**Yee** Do you give them titles as they're leaving the studio, when you're about to have a show?

**Richter** Yes. I never give them titles while I'm working on them. I did that when I was doing the narrative work, because I very often had specific ideas. It was a very different process, because I worked perhaps for half a year on one painting. Over that time, I had the events in my brain and I was thinking about the title. Here, there are no events to refer to, no hook; the only hook is the painting itself. I decide on the titles in the days after finishing a painting.

**Yee** It must be more difficult in this case.

**Richter** Depending on the painting. Some I take very seriously and others are perhaps more sardonic or sarcastic. Like the paintings themselves, maybe.

**Yee** Do your titles come from art or music or literature?

**Richter** All of that. It depends on what I read or listen to. It can be a phrase from a song that I turn around, or it can be based on a book or certain ideas that I'm interested in.

**Yee** Renaissance paintings often didn't have titles. They were typically commissioned for a specific situation and a title wasn't necessary. It's only when paintings started moving around and becoming part of a market system that they had to have titles in order to make it possible to inventory them. Later, titles became an important way to connect the work with a specific meaning or idea.

**Richter** For me, a good title often makes me laugh. Most titles are boring. Like you said, they can also represent a certain idea. Kitaj's already mentioned painting is a good example. If he'd called it 'Three Women', you wouldn't think about it too much, but because it's called *The Rise of Fascism*, you do.

**Yee** So your titles contribute to the content of the work?

**Richter** Yes. That's a little thing I envy about certain Conceptual artists. There are topics, observations and thoughts that definitely could be better phrased using other media. But I decided to stay with painting. It's very personal and intimate as a praxis. That's the main thing I don't like about the idea of doing Conceptual work – you depend on too many people.

**Yee** And do you feel that it's important to teach? You've been a professor at the Academy of Fine Arts, Vienna, since 2006.

**Richter** I like teaching. I'm very grateful that Werner Büttner took me on because my parents didn't have money, and I had no education. I got kicked out of school. I'd be working in a record store or bouncing at a nightclub otherwise. I would never have thought I could ever make a living from painting. It was a great thing, and it's also why I like teaching – part of a responsibility chain. You still have a lot of people from different backgrounds and who don't fit into bourgeois society. I don't know if they'll fit in after studying, but at least they have some years where they can find out.

**Yee** You're not a professor of painting, but have all kinds of art students, right?

**Richter** Yes. Very often, people start as painters because they think that's what artists are supposed to do. After a year, they decide to become

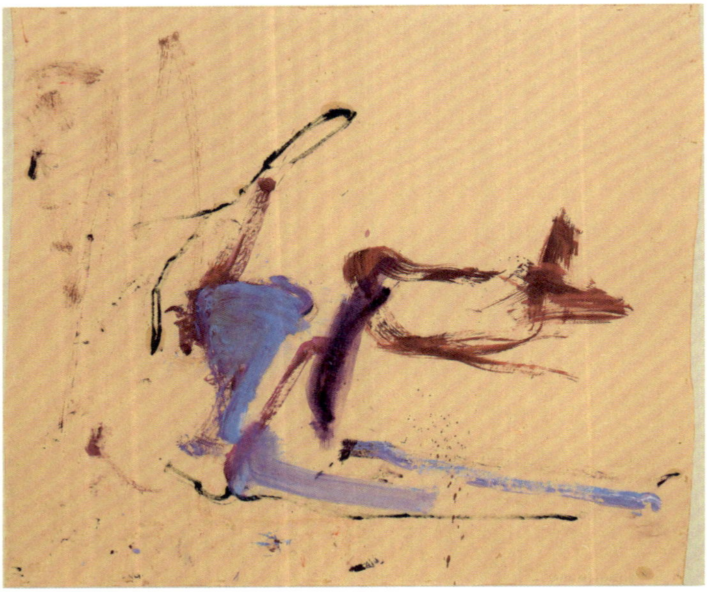

Martha Jungwirth, *Ich und Ricki*, 2018, oil on paper on canvas, 164 × 142 cm

photographers or something else. Some of my students who've got kind of well known, turned out to be musicians and writers, or performance artists. There are also one or two who are quite successful painters. In general, though, painting isn't all that popular, even though it's always mentioned in the news because of the auction record shit and all that.

As you know, there's actually not so much painting on show in institutions. It may have a comeback, especially in the US, because it's now a field that people who'd rarely touched it in the past are starting to use. And a lot of people are being 'rediscovered', especially older women painters. In Austria there's an artist, Martha Jungwirth, whose work I really like. She's now in her seventies, has been painting her whole life and rose to prominence just over the last five or six years. Rose Wylie in England I really like, too. And I knew her from exhibitions at 'off spaces', ten or fifteen years ago. For people who've been working their whole life and they've only been known inside the community, it's great to have an audience now.

**Yee** It's better to have recognition during one's lifetime than posthumously.

**Richter** That's also one of these fantasies that I often heard when younger. What kind of a justification for your own work is it to say that people will know about it in the future? I've had the weirdest conversations like this, mostly with older male painters.

**Yee** They're living for the sake of history.

**Richter** It's a bitter guy thing. They're saying, 'Yes, now it's all shit, but in the future they'll understand.' No. You have an opportunity now. Make some great paintings now!

## **The Truth of the Matter** Dana Schutz

What kind of art do you make? This question, often received while sitting in the backs of cabs or at social events, is never comfortable. No response ever feels right. 'I make figurative paintings that are kind of abstract – portraits and landscapes – and I guess they're pretty gloomy.' I've basically described the worst possible scenario for any art that I can imagine, and yet it's my own.

Sometimes, I try a different tack and describe a specific subject that I've painted or what I'm currently working on. I'll say, 'I've made paintings of people who eat themselves, and remake themselves with their digested material', or 'I'm working on a painting of a reader with a head injury', or 'a woman with a small bird-like mouth'. This approach is entirely too much information and can give the wrong impression. I might just as well say, 'Put the lotion in the basket.' There really is no good answer. The best I can manage is that I make figurative paintings of abstract situations; things that I find difficult to represent or are intangible.

Naming a subject without a painting can create all sorts of mental images. Yet a painting isn't an image – it's in the room; it has context and scale. Content can hover like a ghost between the actual thing and its viewer. Shifting and inhabiting, it comes and goes. And subject can often act as a cover for what the painting is truly about. This was made evident to me when, on a trip to the Prado Museum in Madrid, I encountered Goya's *Saturn* (1820–23) and Rubens' *Saturn Devouring a Son* (1636–38) – two paintings with very little to do with one another except their subject.

What the hell is going on in the Goya? Entering the room of his black paintings and seeing *Saturn* is startling. Saturn's wild eyes and silent scream, his body torqued half in and out of the picture, evoke a

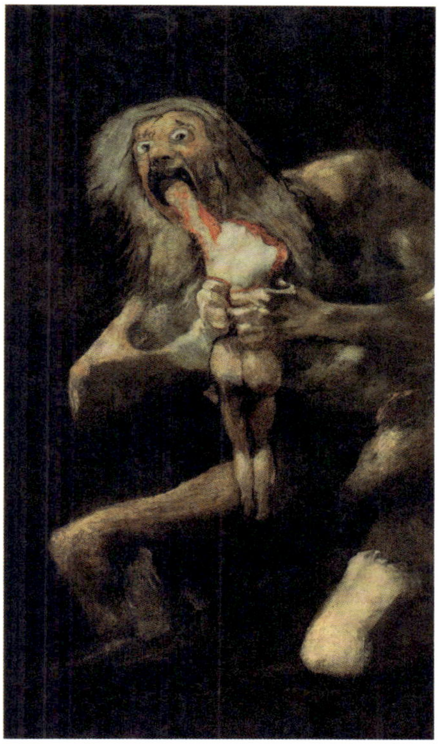

Francisco de Goya y Lucientes, *Saturn*, 1820–23, mixed media on mural transferred to canvas, 143.5 × 81.4 cm

fight-or-flight response. Nothing in this work is settled. The rangy body twists like driftwood, dissolving in shaggy shadowed mass and atmosphere. Alone, perhaps in a cave or imprisoned, he is half kneeling or squatting. His feet aren't visible. His popped eyes desperately peer out with an urgency to communicate, yet sound and utterance are gagged by the unusually large tongue-like arm of his strangely proportioned victim. Here, language – which pins the world down and illuminates, establishing order and hierarchy – is choked out. Even the identification of forms becomes unstable. Saturn's hands resemble paws, ratcheting sphincter-like around the pale bloodied body of … whom? It's hard to tell if this is the body of a child or an adult son or daughter, possibly not even of the

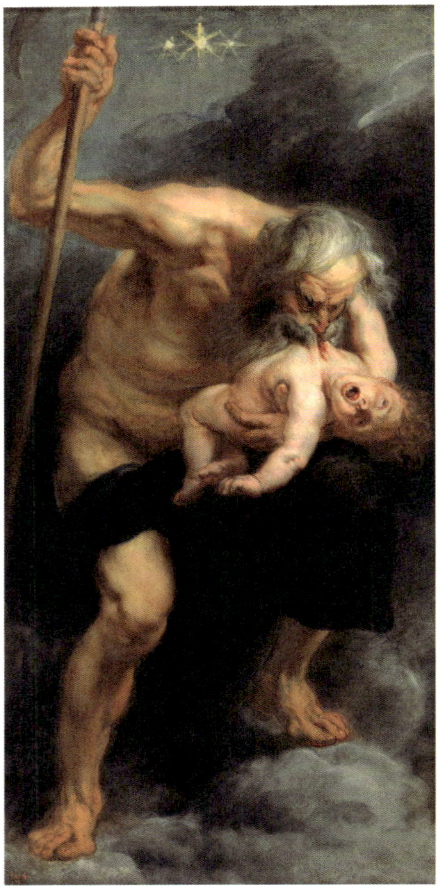

Peter Paul Rubens, *Saturn Devouring a Son*, 1636–38, oil on canvas, 182.5 × 87 cm

same species as Saturn. Sequence, too, feels up-ended as the figure's lower body dangles, unmarred, suspended halfway through what could be the process of consumption, digestion or regurgitation. What is certain is that this is a painting of total annihilation. There's no future or past or business as usual. There's no walking away after this.

The Rubens is not like that. His Saturn, feet firmly perched on velvety, weight-bearing clouds, seems as though he could carry on unscathed after his young lunch. His eyes are fixed on the task at hand; his teeth pull at the pearly translucent skin of his toddler son. It appears as if he is almost sucking the child up. This painting is so much about teeth on skin. Despite its luminous pools of color and soft gesture, it has the illustrative clarity of heavy-metal album art. Rubens' Saturn carries his signature scythe, which represents nature and the cycles of time. In the heavens, three stars dot the top of the painting – what the planet Saturn appeared like to Galileo at that time. In contrast to Goya's *Saturn*, which he frescoed to his walls in seclusion, and never titled, Rubens' version was a public painting. Commissioned in 1636 by Phillip IV of Spain for the Torre de la Parada, a hunting lodge outside of Madrid, this work aims to communicate.

A great painting can convey qualities of its subject that go beyond mimetic likeness. The Goya, in its malleable horror, is a rendering of chaos, the loss of power and language. Its true subject is, perhaps, fear. Rubens' is, more simply, Saturn – a man eating a baby. Goya's depiction is further from its nameable subject, yet closer to its truth. And like the best paintings, it describes something of the world, when words fail.

# Tschabalala Self in Conversation with Lydia Yee

**Lydia Yee** Your process combines painting, printing and sewing pieces of fabric on to the canvas. Do you define your work as painting?

**Tschabalala Self** Yes, despite that fact that I don't literally use paint on canvas in the traditional sense, I define my work as painting because of the substrate: stretched canvas over wooden bars. My canvases are relatively two-dimensional and are exhibited on the wall. Apart from this, painting is primarily concerned with the pictorial organisation of space and colour, ideas that my works employ.

**Yee** Can you tell us how you developed your particular way of working?

**Self** I developed this way of working incrementally, beginning with my printmaking practice. I once focused on making collographic monoprints using handmade matrices. The plates used to make these prints were modular and made up of many different materials. I had my first success with these works and felt excited about this development in my practice. However, at some point, I became frustrated with the limitations in scale I encountered on the press-bed, as well as the formal limitations of working on paper, given its delicate nature. So I wanted to find my own way back to painting and working on canvas. I started to unpack the most ambitious formal qualities of my monoprints and in doing so, I realised that the most interesting part of those works wasn't the impression that was being made on the paper, but rather the objects from which they came – my handmade collograpic matrices. I was most actively engaged with my works while making these plates. The paintings grew out of unpacking the formal and conceptual decisions I made during this time. Whereas previously I'd painted these objects and used them to produce a print, I now began focusing simply on the fashioning of these objects. The appliqué elements in my paintings, which compose the various figurative parts, are made in a similar way to how I once made my printing plates. My assemblaged figures arise through accumulation, varying texture and depth of plane.

**Yee** The collage element underscores the multi-dimensionality of your subjects, in that they're made out of many different things – fabric, print, paint and other materials. Do you purchase or find the materials for your works?

**Self** I always try to draw from the materials that already exist within my studio. I have so many materials. Some are purchased, some are found, some are from my family's home, some are just debris, scraps and bits of things that come in and out of my studio and life. I enjoy using materials that are of the world because they keep that energy from their original purpose. Even though they might not be immediately recognisable in the works, they feel familiar.

**Yee** How do you go about putting down a figure onto a surface? Is it planned in advance or do you improvise?

**Self** It differs from work to work. Sometimes I have a drawing that I recreate in a logical sequence. Other times, it's really just about playing with the materials and putting things together in a way that makes sense or nonsense through the use of abstracted forms. While some works start with a distinct plan and others from playing with material, they'll always result from the accumulation of scraps in my studio. I always work on the floor. In most works, I'll think about the foreground before the background, building out elements that I know will be sewn down onto a more consistent piece of canvas.

**Yee** Are some of the more detailed areas, such as the faces, applied at the end with paint, or does this happen more organically?

**Self** The facial details in the work are sometimes done with painting and sometimes detailed in stitches. The sewing in my work has two functions. It allows for the various elements of the painting to be held together, almost like a glue, and it's also a way for me to draw. The sewing allows me to further articulate different parts of the body and the features of my subjects. I can create depth, and a bulging kind of sculptural effect through stitching. The details in the figures are constantly evolving throughout the making of the piece, and aren't added at one particular point.

**Yee** So really, the stitching is kind of an extension of drawing, mark-making or creating a line?

**Self** Yes, it has a utilitarian function but also an aesthetic role.

**Yee** Is drawing something that's important to your practice? And does it precede painting or happen in parallel?

**Self** Yes, drawing is extremely important to my practice. 'Parallel' might imply that there's no intersection, so maybe 'simultaneously' would be a better description.

**Yee** I also wanted to ask you about other artists or painters who've been a source of inspiration for your work.

**Self** Recently, I've been thinking a lot about Howardena Pindell in regard to further developing an aesthetic language rooted in an economy of visual means and the significance of accumulation. Bill Traylor is a huge inspiration. I love his simplified silhouettes and identify with his narrative inspiration: black quotidian life. Faith Ringgold is my favourite artist. I'm encouraged by her use of textiles and her personal narratives. We're both from Harlem and I've been blessed to have the opportunity to meet her on multiple occasions. Romare Bearden and Jacob Lawrence have infinitely influenced my work. I've always been fascinated by William H. Johnson and his stylistic way of depicting a figure, allowing content to seamlessly integrate into form. I've also recently been thinking a lot about Martin Wong and the way he effectively and simply conveyed the idea of the urban space.

**Yee** You've described your work as about creating vignettes rather than creating portraits or specific characters. You generally focus on one or two figures without too much background detail. Do you see these works as part of a larger narrative, and if so, what kinds of stories are you telling?

**Self** Yes, I do see my work as potentially part of a larger narrative. I describe them as vignettes because I imagine each painting as capturing a moment. I guess the larger narrative is really about nothing in particular. In being about nothing, the paintings are about everything.

**Yee** When you put together a show, are you trying to group the figures in a certain way? Sometimes you seem to have exhibitions with more women or with more neighbourhood scenes, for example. Does an individual exhibition try to tell a story around a group of figures?

**Self** Each show has a different theme, which is sometimes irreverent. For example, the show I did in London recently [*Tschabalala Self: Thigh High*, Pilar Corrias, London, 2 October–9 November 2019], had only one theme, which was high heels. The show that I did many iterations of, *Bodega Run* [Hammer

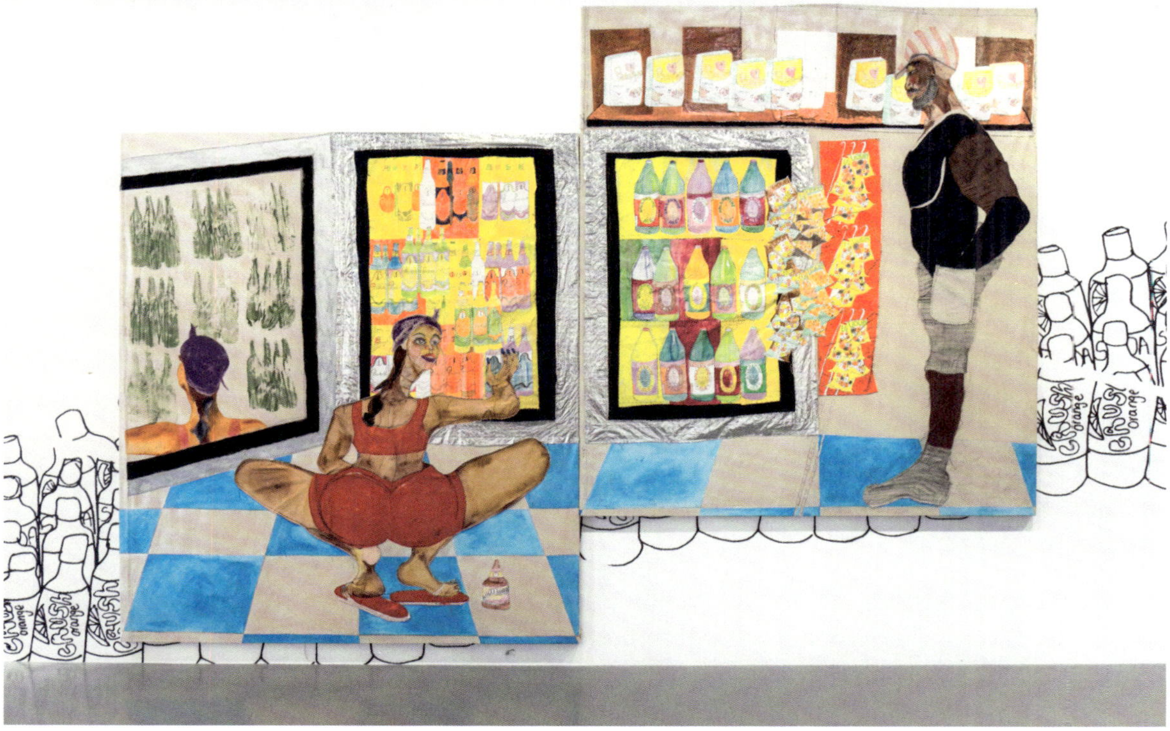

Tschabalala Self, *Bodega Run Diptych*, 2017, acrylic, watercolour, Flashe, gouache, coloured pencil, pencil, hand-coloured photocopy, hand-coloured canvas on canvas, 243.8 × 213.4 cm (each)

Museum, Los Angeles, 2 February–9 June 2017; Pilar Corrias, London, 7–27 September 2017; Yuz Museum, Shanghai, 22 September–9 December 2018], had a far more complex theme about understanding the cultural and social significance of New York City bodegas. It really just depends. I suppose I use some kind of thematic device in each show, but they vary in specificity.

When I'm able to spend more time with the work, I can start to organise shows in this way. Now that the opportunity for institutional exhibitions has come about, I'm able to pool together works from different periods and show them together, allowing me to create grander narratives. When I'm making new work, sometimes a larger narrative isn't immediately clear, but working on projects and looking at works in retrospect allows me to see some of the overarching themes.

**Yee** How do you go about finding your subjects? Is it mainly through observation, or do you do any research? Do you use any kind of source materials?

**Self** I don't really do research. I find my subjects through everyday interactions. I interact with lots of people by default, given work, travel and my social life. There are lots of opportunities to draw inspiration. I never really search for a subject or narrative. I often pull from my life, memories and fantasies.

Thinking of my upbringing, I was the youngest in a large family so I was always surrounded by lots of older siblings. They're much older than me, so when I was a child I use to spend lots of time alone painting, drawing or just playing. Perhaps that's why it's easy for me to project narratives or imaginary scenarios. I have a very good imagination.

**Yee** Can you tell us something about *Koco at the Bodega* [2017] [pl. 37]? The woman in the work is given a specific name, while other titles are more general – a street, hairstyle or occupation.

**Self** Koco is the nickname of one of my older sisters. Once I finished this work, I realised the woman looked a lot like my sister, so I named the work partially after her. Ironically, the woman in the painting is purchasing a loosie cigarette, but my sister doesn't smoke.

**Yee** I'm also fascinated by how the simple motif of the printed brick fabric operates in different works: as an exterior wall, as an article of clothing or as a woman's body.

**Self** The brick wall motif was developed simply to describe a metropolitan space. The brick wall later becomes part of the body of the woman in *Lenox* [2019] [pl. 38], which is an allusion to the colloquialism 'a brick house', referring to a curvaceous lady.

**Yee** You're known for your representation of female figures more than male ones. What's your approach to depicting women's bodies and how does your technique relate to the subject?

**Self** I try to depict women's bodies experientially rather than realistically. If I want to show a certain part of the body activated though movement, it'll be enlarged. I'll also distort and enlarge parts of the body that are charged with a kind of sexual energy. If you imagine that a person is the sum of many parts, composing the figure through a process of accumulation aestheticises this idea.

**Yee** In your recent exhibition at Pilar Corrias, you started to take the figures beyond the canvas, either by painting silhouettes on the wall or adding sculptural elements. Is this a natural extension of your painting practice? And where might you be taking this in the future?

**Self** I feel like the paintings have always had a sculptural dimension to them because of how they're made. For the figure to project even further out from the wall and into the exhibition space is really a continuation of that idea. After experimenting with sculptures and objects in installations, I wanted to activate other parts of the exhibition space. The wall presented itself as a location for activation. I'm concerned with foreground, background and the significance of the substrate. I'm trying to think about the space of the exhibition more holistically, rather than imaging each art object as discrete.

**Yee** You're also taking everyday materials such as fabric, thread and printed material from the external world and putting them onto the picture plane. I wonder if your collage technique and interest in coming out beyond the pictorial space connects to the social or political dimension of your work?

**Self** Yes, I think there's a social and political dimension to every art practice regardless of whether the artist admits to it or is even aware of it. I think it's impossible to avoid that conversation, especially when you deal with figuration. I want to make my figures as complex and multi-dimensional as possible. A lot of larger cultural dialogues that exist or are perpetuated around femaleness and blackness or black femaleness are two-dimensional. There are a lot of flat characters that don't have full emotional depth. By making my work increasingly complex, or even odd in some instances, I'm able to create alternative narratives.

## Selected Bibliography


Ammer, Manuela, Achim Hochdörfer, and David Joselit, *Painting 2.0* (Munich: Prestel, 2016)

Ardalan, Ziba, and Tom Morton, *Tschabalala Self* (London: Parasol Unit, 2017)

Armitage, Michael, Roger Malbert, Margot Heller, and Mukami Kuria, *Michael Armitage* (London: South London Gallery, 2017)

Ashton, Dore, *Cecily Brown* (New York: Rizzoli, 2008)

Brown, Cecily, Suzanne Cotter, and Caoimhín Mac Giolla Léith, *Cecily Brown: Paintings* (Oxford: Modern Art Oxford, 2005)

Brown, Cecily, Anders Kold, and Laerke Rydal Jorgensen, *Where, when, how often and with whom* (Humlebaek: Louisiana Museum of Modern Art, 2019)

Bryan-Wilson, Julia, Terry Castle, and Litia Perta, *Dear Nemesis: Nicole Eisenman 1993–2013* (Cologne: Buchhandlung Walther König, 2014)

Bullock, Natasha, Sean O'Toole, Yvonne A. Owuor, and Mukoma W. Ngugi, *Michael Armitage: The Promised Land* (Sydney: Museum of Contemporary Art Australia, 2019)

Byrt, Anthony, *Ryan Mosley* (London: Alison Jaques Gallery, 2011)

Christoffersen, Helga, Grace Dunham, Massimiliano Gioni, and Eileen Myles, *Nicole Eisenman: Al-Ugh-Ories* (New York: New Museum of Contemporary Art, 2016)

Cipriani, Cheryl, and Marcia Tucker, *'Bad' Painting* (New York: The New Museum of Contemporary Art, 1978)

Deitch, Jeffrey, Aria Dean, Johanna Fateman, and Alison M. Gingeras, *Unrealism: New Figurative Painting* (New York: Rizzoli, 2019)

Dinse, Lotte, Susanne Figner, Suzanne Perling Hudson, and Chrissie Iles, *Dana Schutz: Demo* (Cologne: Buchhandlung Walther König, 2015)

Dohm, Katharina, Eva Meyer-Hermann, and Max Hollein, *Daniel Richter: Hello, I Love You* (Cologne: Buchhandlung Walther König, 2015)

Eisenman, Nicole, Hannah Black, and Hendrik Bündge, *Nicole Eisenman: Baden Baden Baden* (Cologne: Buchhandlung Walther König, 2019)

Ferguson, Russell, and Jane Hyun, *The Undiscovered Country* (Los Angeles: UCLA Hammer Museum, 2004)

Fogle, Douglas, Michelle Piranio, Andrew Blauvelt, and Santiago Piedrafita, *Painting at the Edge of the World* (Minneapolis: Walker Art Center, 2001)

Folie, Sabine, Alison M. Gingeras, Michael Glasmeier, and Blazenka Perica, *'Dear Painter, Paint Me ...': Painting the Figure since Late Picabia* (Paris: Centre Pompidou, 2002)

Gisbourne, Mark, *Ryan Mosley* (Berlin and Leipzig: Galerie EIGEN + ART, 2012)

Godfrey, Tony, *Painting Today* (London and New York: Phaidon Press, 2009)

Graw, Isabelle, Niamh Dunphy, Brian Hanrahan, and Gerrit Jackson, *The Love of Painting: Genealogy of a Success Medium* (Berlin: Sternberg Press, 2018)

Heiser, Jorg, Raphaela Platow, and Katy Siegel, *Dana Schutz: Paintings 2002–2005* (New York: Distributed Art Publishers, 2006)

Heynen, Julian, and Fritz Kramer, *Daniel Richter, Grünspan* (Düsseldorf: Kunstsammlung Nordrhein-Westfalen, 2002)

Huldisch, Henriette, Kelly Shindler, and Philomena Mariani, *First Light: Tala Madani* (Munich, London and New York: DelMonico Books and Prestel, 2016)

Hyman, Timothy, *The World New Made: Figurative Painting in the Twentieth Century* (London: Thames & Hudson, 2016)

Joachimides, Christos M., Norman Rosenthal, and Nicolas Serota, *A New Spirit in Painting* (London: Royal Academy of Arts and George Weidenfeld and Nicholson Ltd., 1981)

Kantarovsky, Sanya, Stuart Bertolotti-Bailey, Eli Diner, Allison Katz, and Angie Keefer, *Sanya Kantarovsky: No Joke* (London: Koenig Books and Studio Voltaire, 2016)

Melick, Tom, Rebecca Morrill, Kathryn Rattee, and Barry Schwabsky, eds., *Vitamin P3* (London: Phaidon Press Limited, 2016)

Morrill, Rebecca, Karen Wright, and Louisa Elderton, eds., *Great Women Artists* (London: Phaidon Press Limited, 2019)

Mullins, Charlotte, *Painting People: The State of the Art* (London: Thames & Hudson, 2006)

Myers, Terry R., *Painting (Documents of Contemporary Art)* (London: Whitechapel Gallery, 2011)

Nesbitt, Judith, ed., *Examining Pictures: Exhibiting Paintings* (London: Whitechapel Gallery, 1999)

Quarles, Christina, Andrew Bonacina, and David J. Getsy, *Christina Quarles* (Wakefield: The Hepworth Wakefield, 2019)

Richter, Daniel, *Imitators be there* (Zürich: ProLitteris, 2010)

Richter, Daniel, Wayne Baerswandt, and Anne Denoon, *Daniel Richter: Pink Flag, White Horse* (Toronto: Power Plant, 2004)

Richter, Daniel, Holm M. Juul, and Poul E. Tøjner, *Daniel Richter: Lonely Old Slogans* (Humlebæk: Louisiana Museum of Modern Art, 2016)

Ruff, Beatrix, Lynne Tillman, and Laurie Weeks, *Nicole Eisenman* (Zürich: JRP Ringier 2011)

Schutz, Dana, Cary S. Levine, and Helaine Posner, *If the Face Had Wheels* (Munich: Prestel, 2011)

Schwabsky, Barry, *Dana Schutz* (New York: Rizzoli, 2010)

## List of Works

### Michael Armitage

1
*Peace Coma*
2012
Oil on lubugo bark cloth
110 × 75 cm
Private Collection

2
*Kampala Suburb*
2014
Oil on lubugo bark cloth
196 × 150 cm
Private Collection

3
*#mydressmychoice*
2015
Oil on lubugo bark cloth
149.9 × 195.6 cm
Private Collection

4
*Mangroves Dip*
2015
Oil on lubugo bark cloth
221 × 170.2 cm
Fondazione Sandretto Re Rebaudengo

### Cecily Brown

5
*Maid's Day Off*
2005
Oil on linen
200.7 × 198.1 cm
Hiscox Collection

6
*Oinops*
2016–17
Oil on linen
154.9 × 180.3 cm
Private Collection

7
*Lucky Beach*
2017
Oil on linen
210.8 × 170.2 cm
Collection of Laura and Barry Townsley, London

8
*The Last Shipwreck*
2018
Oil on linen
210.8 × 200.7 cm
Private Collection

### Nicole Eisenman

9–10
*Progress: Real and Imagined*
2006
Oil on canvas
2 parts:
left panel: 234.5 × 481 cm
right panel: 234.5 × 491 cm
Sammlung Ringier, Switzerland

11
*Brooklyn Biergarten II*
2008
Oil on canvas
165.1 × 208.3 cm
Valeria and Gregorio Napoleone Collection, London

12
*Sleeper*
2016
Oil on canvas
45.7 × 60.9 cm
Milk Collection, Portugal

### Sanya Kantarovsky

13
*Feeder*
2016
Oil and oil pastel on canvas
190.7 × 140 cm
Tate: Presented by Stuart Shave 2017

14
*Letdown*
2017
Oil, watercolour and pastel on canvas
215.9 × 165.1 cm
Fondazione Sandretto Re Rebaudengo

15
*Deprivation*
2018
Oil, watercolour and pastel on canvas
215.9 × 165.1 cm
Collection of Stuart Shave

16
*Друг [Friend]*
2018
Oil and watercolour on canvas
215.9 × 165.1 cm
Courtesy the artist and the ASOB Collection

### Tala Madani

17
*Dirty Stars*
2008
Oil on wood
30 × 40 cm
Hall Collection

18
*Sitting in White*
2008
Oil on linen
40 × 40 cm
ISelf Collection

19
*Campfire*
2011
Oil on linen
61 × 45.7 cm
Private Collection

20
*Light Balance*
2012
Oil on linen
50.8 × 40.6 cm
Collection of Alexander V. Petalas

21
*Shit Mom (Deluxe)*
2019
Oil on linen
50.8 × 61 cm
Collection of Alexander V. Petalas

**Ryan Mosley**

22
*Teaching Snakes to be Snakes*
2008
Oil on canvas on aluminium
170 × 190 cm
Private Collection UK

23
*Cave Inn*
2011
Oil on linen
214 × 180 cm
Private Collection

24
*Duchess of Oils*
2014
Oil on linen on board
65 × 55 cm
Collection of Marco Zanini, Milan

25
*Wearing Another's Head on Your Jacket*
2014
Oil on linen on board
65 × 55 cm
Private Collection UK

**Christina Quarles**

26
*Casually Cruel*
2018
Acrylic on canvas
196 × 244.3 cm
Tate: Presented by Peter Dubens 2019

27
*Sun Bleached*
2018
Acrylic on canvas
152.4 × 182.9 cm
Fondazione Sandretto Re Rebaudengo

28
*For Whom Tha Sunsets Free*
2019
Acrylic on canvas
142.2 × 152.4 cm
Christen Sveaas Art Collection

**Daniel Richter**

29
*Tarifa*
2001
Oil on canvas
350 × 280 cm
Ken and Helen Rowe

30
*Das erstaunliche Comeback des Dr. Freud*
2004
Oil on canvas
212 × 260 cm
Hall Collection

31
*"HEY JOE"*
2011
Oil on canvas
240 × 180 cm
Sammlung Lütjenburg

32
*Asger, Bill und Mark*
2015
Oil on canvas
200 × 270 cm
Sammlung Lütjenburg

**Dana Schutz**

33
*New Legs*
2003
Oil on canvas
152.4 × 167.6 cm
Private Collection

34
*Man Eating His Chest*
2005
Oil on canvas
137.2 × 106.7 cm
Sandra and Giancarlo Bonollo Collection

35
*Imagine You and Me*
2018
Oil on canvas
223.5 × 223.5 cm
Private Collection

36
*Suspicious Minds*
2019
Oil on canvas
228.6 × 243.8 cm
Private Collection

**Tschabalala Self**

37
*Koco at the Bodega*
2017
Coloured pencil, photocopies of hand-coloured drawings, acrylic, Flashe, fabric and painted canvas on canvas
243.8 × 213.4 cm
Valeria and Gregorio Napoleone Collection, London

38
*Lenox*
2019
Fabric, ribbon, painted canvas, Flashe and acrylic on canvas
172.7 × 127 cm
Private Collection

39
*NYPD*
2019
Painted canvas, fabric, Flashe and gouache on canvas
213.4 × 182.9 cm
Pilar Corrias Collection

40
*Fade*
2019
Acrylic, fabric, Flashe, digital print, painted canvas and hand painted wall stencil
172.7 × 127 cm
Private Collection

## Contributors

**Iwona Blazwick** is Director of Whitechapel Gallery, London and is a curator, critic and lecturer. She has written and published extensively on themes and movements in modern and contemporary art, exhibitions histories and art institutions.

**Summer Bowie** is managing editor of *Autre Magazine*, Los Angeles.

**Daniel Culpan** has written about art and literature for *Artforum*, *Frieze*, *The Times Literary Supplement* and elsewhere. He won the Frieze Writer's Prize in 2016.

**Cameron Foote** is assistant curator at Whitechapel Gallery, London.

**Allison Katz** is an artist based in London.

**Jason Rosenfeld**, Ph.D., is Distinguished Chair and Professor of Art History at Marymount Manhattan College, New York, and a Senior Writer and Editor-at-Large at *The Brooklyn Rail*.

**Lynne Tillman** is a novelist, story writer, and critic. Her novel *Men and Apparitions* is published by Peninsula Press, UK, in 2020.

**Lydia Yee** is chief curator at Whitechapel Gallery, London.

## Artists

**Michael Armitage**
(b. 1984, Kenya) lives and works in London. He received a BA in Fine Art from the Slade School of Art, London (2007) and a Postgraduate Diploma from the Royal Academy Schools, London (2010). Armitage paints in oil on a traditional Ugandan bark cloth called lubugo. Its course texture shows through the paint layers, rooting his practice within an East African context. His paintings have a dreamlike quality, with subjects drawn from Kenyan and East African folklore, popular culture, online news and his own memories of growing up in Kenya. Armitage has had solo exhibitions at South London Gallery (2018), the Museum of Modern Art, New York (2019) and the Museum of Contemporary Art Australia, Sydney (2019).

**Cecily Brown**
(b. 1969, UK) lives and works in New York. She received a BA in Fine Art from the Slade School of Art, London (1993). In her large-scale paintings, figures engage in lively physical activity within pastoral or bucolic settings. While inspired by the compositions of historic male painters such as Eugène Delacroix and the Expressionist techniques of Willem de Kooning, she presents a female-centred view of her subjects with sources ranging from pornography to High Renaissance painting. Recent solo exhibitions have been presented at the Whitworth Art Gallery, Manchester (2017) and the Louisiana Museum of Modern Art, Humlebæk, Denmark (2018).

**Nicole Eisenman**
(b. 1965, France) lives and works in New York. She received a BFA from Rhode Island School of Design, Providence, RI (1987). Eisenman uses allegory and satire to engage not only with contemporary social subjects, from gender and sexuality to inequalities of wealth and power, but also the tropes of Western figurative painting traditions. Her cartoon-like figures in often busily populated compositions explore human behaviour or consider the role of the artist. Eisenman's work in both painting and sculpture featured in the Venice Biennale (2019) and the Whitney

Biennale in New York (2019) and she has had solo exhibitions at the New Museum, New York (2016) and Secession, Vienna (2017).

**Sanya Kantarovsky**
(b. 1982, Russia) lives and works in New York. He studied painting at the Rhode Island School of Design, Providence, RI (2004) and received his MFA at the University of California, Los Angeles (2011). His references include early twentieth-century European and Russian figurative artists such as Matisse, Gauguin and Chagall, alongside folk art, children's illustrations and comic-book imagery. His paintings depict awkward and ungainly figures in darkly humorous, satirical or melancholic narratives, often suggesting male humiliation and discomfort. He has had solo exhibitions at Fondazione Sandretto Re Rebaudengo, Turin (2017–18) and Kunsthalle Basel (2018).

**Tala Madani**
(b. 1981, Iran) lives and works in Los Angeles. She received her MFA from Yale University School of Art, New Haven, CT (2006). Her psychologically charged works often feature bald, middle-aged men engaged in crude, sexual or slapstick activities. In the recent series entitled *Shit Mom*, the body becomes a medium for exploring artistic identity and the messiness of motherhood. Madani combines tactile and expressive brushwork with more precise techniques derived from animation. She has had recent solo exhibitions at MIT List Visual Art Centre, Cambridge, MA (2016) and the Contemporary Art Museum St Louis (2016), Secession, Vienna (2019–20) and the Museum of Contemporary Art, Los Angeles (2020).

**Ryan Mosley**
(b. 1980, UK) lives and works in Sheffield. He studied at the University of Huddersfield, UK, and received an MA from the Royal College of Art, London (2007). He assembles performative characters in antic carnivalesque scenarios where the figure seems to both emerge from and become one with the background. Recurring motifs such as top hats, beards or foliage are derived from sources as diverse as the paintings of Gauguin and Magritte or the visual clichés of Hollywood Westerns. Mosley's work has featured in institutional exhibitions including *One Day, Something Happens: Paintings of People*, Hayward Touring & Arts Council Collection exhibition, UK (2015) and *Walls Have Ears*, Aston Hall Museum, Birmingham, UK (2018).

**Christina Quarles**
(b. 1985, USA) lives and works in Los Angeles. She received a BA from Hampshire College, Amherst, MA (2007) and an MFA from the Yale School of Art, New Haven, CT (2016). Her vibrantly coloured paintings contain elements derived from computer programmes like Adobe Illustrator and feature entwined bodies in twisted or distended poses within abstracted environments. Quarles explores female, black and queer identity through the active agency of these contorted bodies, barely contained by the canvas and demanding direct engagement rather than passive consumption. Quarles had a solo exhibition at The Hepworth, Wakefield, UK (2019–20) and was included in *Made in LA* at the Hammer Museum, Los Angeles (2018).

**Daniel Richter**
(b. 1962, Germany) lives and works between Berlin and Hamburg. He attended Hochschule für bildende Künste Hamburg (1991–96), where he was taught by the German painter Werner Büttner. Since the early 2000s he has produced large-scale oil paintings concerned with socio-economic issues, which bring together contemporary mass-media images and closely observed figurative scenes. Shifting between abstraction and figuration, he often creates work in dialogue with nineteenth- and twentieth-century European painters like Casper David Friedrich, James Ensor and Francis Bacon. Richter has had solo exhibitions at Schirn Kunsthalle, Frankfurt (2014–15) and Camden Arts Centre, London (2017).

**Dana Schutz**
(b. 1976, USA) is based in New York. She received a BFA from the Cleveland Institute of Art (2000) and an MFA from Columbia University, New York (2002). Her paintings feature grotesque single or grouped figures engaged in absurd, humorous and sometimes abject activities. Referencing early twentieth-century German Expressionism and Cubism, Schutz often works in thick impasto, distorting and breaking up elements of the human body, sometimes depicted in the act of consuming itself. Schutz has had solo exhibitions at The Hepworth, Wakefield, UK (2013), Musée d'art contemporain de Montréal (2015) and the Institute of Contemporary Art, Boston (2017).

**Tschabalala Self**
(b. 1990, USA) lives and works in New York and New Haven. She received a BA from Bard College, Annandale-on-Hudson, NY (2012) and an MFA from Yale School of Art, New Haven, CT (2015). Self depicts black female figures in an exaggerated and bold style using a combination of sewn, printed and painted textures. Her work aims to navigate the stereotypical and sexualised representation of the black female and male body in contemporary culture through assemblage techniques that reveal how identity is made up of many different elements. Self has had solo exhibitions at Parasol Unit, London (2017), the Hammer Museum, Los Angeles (2019) and completed a residency at the Studio Museum, New York (2019).

## Exhibition Lenders

The ASOB Collection
Sandra and Giancarlo Bonollo Collection
Pilar Corrias Collection
Hall Collection
Hiscox Collection
ISelf Collection
Sammlung Lutjenburg
Milk Collection, Portugal
Valeria and Gregorio Napoleone Collection, London
Alexander V. Petalas
Fondazione Sandretto Re Rebaudengo
Sammlung Ringier, Switzerland
Ken and Helen Rowe
Stuart Shave
Christen Sveaas Art Collection
Tate
Laura and Barry Townsley, London
Marco Zanini, Milan
and those who wish to remain anonymous

## Image credits

pls. 1, 4 © Michael Armitage. Courtesy White Cube. Photo: Prudence Cuming Associates Ltd
pl. 2; front cover © Michael Armitage. Courtesy White Cube
pl. 3 © Michael Armitage. Courtesy White Cube. Photo: George Darrell
pls. 5–8; p. 103 © Cecily Brown. Courtesy the artist, Thomas Dane Gallery, and Paula Cooper Gallery, New York
pls. 9–10; inside flap © Nicole Eisenman. Courtesy Ringier AG / Sammlung Ringier, Switzerland
pls. 11–12; p. 15 © Nicole Eisenman. Courtesy the artist
pl. 13 © Sanya Kantarovsky. Courtesy the artist, Modern Art, London, and Luhring Augustine, New York. Photo: Robert Glowacki
pl. 14 © Sanya Kantarovsky. Courtesy the artist, Modern Art, London, and Luhring Augustine, New York. Photo: Sebastiano Pellion di Persano
pls. 15–16 © Sanya Kantarovsky. Courtesy the artist, Modern Art, London, and Luhring Augustine, New York. Photo: Adam Reich
pls. 17–19; p. 117 © Tala Madani. Courtesy the artist and Pilar Corrias, London
pl. 20 © Tala Madani. Courtesy the artist and Pilar Corrias, London. Photo: Joshua White
pl. 21 © Tala Madani. Courtesy the artist and David Kordansky Gallery, Los Angeles. Photo: Lee Thompson
pl. 22 © Ryan Mosley. Courtesy the artist, Galerie EIGEN + ART, Berlin and Leipzig, and Tim Van Laere Gallery, Antwerp. Photo: Julian Lister
pls. 23–25 © Ryan Mosley. Courtesy the artist, Galerie EIGEN + ART, Berlin and Leipzig, and Tim Van Laere Gallery, Antwerp. Photo: Dave Morgan
pls. 26–27 © Christina Quarles. Courtesy the artist, Pilar Corrias, London, and Regen Projects, Los Angeles. Photo: Damian Griffiths
pl. 28 © Christina Quarles. Courtesy the artist, Pilar Corrias, London, and Regen Projects, Los Angeles. Photo: Evan Bedford
pls. 29–31; p. 132 © Daniel Richter / DACS, London 2019. Courtesy Galerie Thaddaeus Ropac, London, Paris, Salzburg
pl. 32 © Daniel Richter / DACS, London 2019. Courtesy Galerie Thaddaeus Ropac, London, Paris, Salzburg. Photo: Jochen Littkemann
pls. 33–34 © Dana Schutz. Courtesy the artist and Petzel Gallery, New York
pls. 35–36 © Dana Schutz. Courtesy the artist, Petzel Gallery, New York, and Thomas Dane Gallery
pl. 37 © Tschabalala Self. Courtesy the artist and Pilar Corrias Gallery, London. Photo: Andrea Rossetti
pl. 38 © Tschabalala Self. Courtesy the artist and Pilar Corrias Gallery, London
pl. 39 © Tschabalala Self. Courtesy the artist and Pilar Corrias Gallery, London. Photo: Matthew Septimus
pl. 40; p. 141 © Tschabalala Self. Courtesy the artist and Pilar Corrias Gallery, London. Photo: Damian Griffiths
p. 6 © RMN-Grand Palais (musée du Louvre). Photo: Gérard Blot
p. 11 © Maria Lassnig Foundation/ Bildrecht Vienna, DACS London 2020
p. 92 Courtesy The Museum of Modern Art, New York. Gift of Mrs. David M. Levy. Photo: Scala, Florence
p. 93 © Michael Armitage. Courtesy White Cube. Photo: Ben Westoby
p. 99 © Cecily Brown. Courtesy the artist. Photo: Genevieve Hanson
pp. 107–111 © Nicole Eisenman. Courtesy the artist and Anton Kern Gallery
p. 113 © Sanya Kantarovsky. Courtesy the artist; Luhring Augustine, New York; and Stuart Shave/Modern Art, London. Photo: Studio Voltaire / Andy Keate
p. 122 © The Estate of Philip Guston. Collection of Stedelijk Museum Amsterdam
pp. 127–128 © Christina Quarles. Courtesy the artist, Pilar Corrias, London and Regen Projects, Los Angeles
p. 133 © The estate of R. B. Kitaj. Photo: © Tate
p. 136 © Martha Jungwirth. Courtesy Modern Art, London. Photo: Robert Glowacki
pp. 137–138 © Photographic Archive Museo Nacional del Prado

## Radical Figures: Painting in the New Millennium


### Supported by

The Radical Figures Exhibition Circle

Galerie EIGEN + ART

Luhring Augustine

Pilar Corrias Gallery

Galerie Thaddaeus Ropac

Thomas Dane Gallery

Laura and Barry Townsley

White Cube

CHRISTIE'S

BISTROTHEQUE

### Special thanks to

Louie Lane, Cecily Brown Studio; The Brooklyn Rail; Daniel Culpan; Astrid Hamm, Galerie EIGEN + ART; Sam Roeck, Nicole Eisenman Studio; Stephanie Biron and Maryse Brand, Hall Art Foundation; Whitney Hintz, Hiscox Collection; Melissa Larner; Vanessa Thill, Sanya Kantarovsky Studio; Allison Katz; Geneva Viralam, Luhring Augustine; Eleanor Crabtree, Modern Art; Rachel Lepley and Anatol Orient, The Perimeter; Jason Murison, Petzel Gallery; Charlotte Brooks, Pilar Corrias, Jana Suhani Soin, Alba Montano Spiers and Florian Weingruell, Pilar Corrias Gallery; Shaun Regen, Regen Projects; Christoph Selke, Daniel Richter Studio; Rahel Blättler, Sammlung Ringier; Jason Rosenfeld; Julia Benjamin, Dana Schutz Studio; Studio Voltaire; Henry Babbage, Tanya Leighton Gallery; Enrico Tassi; Hella Pohl, Galerie Thaddaeus Ropac; François Chantala and Lotte Hetherington, Thomas Dane Gallery; Lynne Tillman; Irene Bradbury and Romilly Phillips, White Cube Gallery



### Whitechapel Gallery Trustees

Chair: Alex Sainsbury
Erin Bell, Kevin Brady, Peter Carew, David Dibosa, Ann Gallagher, Anupam Ganguli Sam Hill, Jonny Kanagasooriam, Nicola Kerr, Melanie Manchot, Sarah Miller

### Whitechapel Gallery Staff

Director: Iwona Blazwick
Managing Director: Tony Stevenson
Christopher Aldgate, Daniel Allison, Molly Baro, Lea Barre, Connie Butler, Emily Butler, Janine Catalano, Valerija Cerovec, Miles Clemson, Elizabeth Clowes, Jenny Cooper, Erin Cork, Ines Costa, Sarah Crocker, Rosalind Dahlstrom, Lisa Darrer, Amina Darwish, Helen Davison, Asa Desouza-Jones, Jas Dhillon, Andre Emmanuel, Gareth Evans, Sue Evans, Jake Farrant, Alessia Filipponi, Trinidad Fombella, Cameron Foote, Siobhan Forshaw, Wells Fray-Smith, Natalia Gomolka, Tim Gosden, Luke Gregory-Jones, Samuel Hailey-Watts, Lucy Hawes, Jessica Heritage, Alexandra House, Smitha Islam, Samuel Jacobs, Ranbir Jhutty, Rosie Kennedy, Jennifer Lea, Ryszard Lewandowski, Marthe Lisson, Lauren Lockett, Sandra Louison, Kirsty Lowry, Megan Miller, Glen Moxon, Binita Naik, Renee Odjidja, Justine Pearsall, David Piriz, Jane Scarth, Antonia Seroff, Carolina Silva, Laura Smith, Vicky Steer, Candy Stobbs, Grace Storey, James Sutton, Beatrice Taylor Searle, Alice Thomson, Adam Vaudin, Sofia Victorino, Francesca Vinter, Sam Williams, Monica Yam, Lydia Yee, Nayia Yiakoumaki, Marianna Zicari



### Whitechapel Gallery Supporters

Whitechapel Gallery would like to thank its supporters, whose generosity enables the gallery to realise its pioneering programmes

### Exhibitions Programme

Acción Cultural Española (AC/E)
Ace Hotel London
Philippe and Antonie Bertherat
Lisa and Tom Blumenthal
Calouste Gulbenkian Foundation
Ravi Chidambaram and Yana Frey
Cockayne Grants for the Arts
Tiqui Atencio Demirdjian
The Dena Foundation
Darryl de Prez and Victoria Thomas
Nicoletta Fiorucci (Founder, Fiorucci Art Trust)
Jack and Sandra Guthman
Hauser & Wirth
Henry Moore Foundation
Rhona Hoffman Gallery
Marcelle Joseph
Elie Khouri
Jane Lombard Gallery
London Community Foundation
Collezione Maramotti
Max Mara
Paul McCartney
Mondriaan Fund
NEON
Catherine Petitgas
Q-International: Fondazione La Quadriennale di Roma
Russell Tovey
Evgeny Tugolukov and Natalya Pavchinskaya
V-A-C Foundation
Shelby White
Whitechapel Gallery Commissioning Council
and those who wish to remain anonymous

### Public Events Programme

The Aldgate Partnership
Brick Lane Regeneration Partnership
Derwent London
SAHA Asssociation
Stanley Picker Trust

### Education Programme

The Arts Society Westminster
Artworkers Retirement Society
Dorota and Olivier Audemars
The Bawden Fund
Capital Group
Paul Hamlyn Foundation
Paul Hedge and Paul Maslin, Hales Gallery
The Estate of Howard Hodgkin
Mayor of London
Newham Council Enrichment Programme
Phillips
ZVM Rangoonwala Foundation
Swarovski Foundation
The London Borough of Tower Hamlets

### Capital Renewal Programme

The Headley Trust
The Wolfson Foundation

### Artworks Insurance Partner

Hiscox

### Framing Partner

FRAME London

### Signage Partner

Omni Colour

**Whitechapel Gallery Corporate Patrons**
Bloomberg Philanthropies
Frasers Property UK
Gazelli Art House
Modern Art
Phillips
SPLIT Music
White Cube
David Zwirner

**Whitechapel Gallery Corporate Supporters**
Ace Hotel London
The Aldgate Partnership
Bistrotheque
Brick Lane Regeneration Partnership
Capital Group
Champagne Castelnau
Derwent London
Martinspeed
Max Mara
Collezione Maramotti
Pentagram
Phillips
Swarovski

**Future Fund Founding Partners**
Mahera and Mohammad Abu Ghazaleh
Sirine and Ahmad Abu Ghazaleh
Swantje Conrad
Mr Dimitris Daskalopoulos
NEON
Maryam and Edward Eisler
V-A-C Foundation
Sir Siegmund Warburg's Voluntary Settlement
Arts Council England Catalyst
Endowment Fund

**Future Fund Supporters**
John Smith and Vicky Hughes
Luigi Maramotti
Dominic Palfreyman
Catherine Petitgas

**Whitechapel Gallery Commissioning Council**
Dorota Audemars
Erin Bell
Heloisa Genish
Leili Huth
Irene Panagopoulos
Catherine Petitgas
Mariela Pissioti
Alex Sainsbury
and those who wish to remain anonymous

**Whitechapel Gallery Director's Circle**
Mohammed Al Baker
Nick and Caroline Clarry
Erin Bell and Michael Cohen
Pilar Corrias
Aud and Paolo Cuniberti
D. Daskalopoulos Collection Greece
Taymour Grahne
Peter and Maria Kellner
Yana and Stephen Peel
and those who wish to remain anonymous

**Whitechapel Gallery Curator's Circle**
Rob and Lesley Briggs
Laura and Peter Carew
Marcelle Joseph
Chris Kneale
Adrian and Jennifer O'Carroll
Dasha Shenkman
Audrey Wallrock
and those who wish to remain anonymous

**Whitechapel Gallery Patrons**
Farah Asemi
Beverley Buckingham
Matt Carey-Williams and Donnie Roark
Sadie Coles HQ
Beth and Michele Colocci
Swantje Conrad
Michael and Elizabeth Corley
Aud and Paolo Cuniberti
Dunnett Craven Ltd
Sarah Elson
James Freedman
Theresa Froehlich
Belinda de Gaudemar
Richard and Judith Greer
Sarah Griffin
Deborah Gundle
Jill Hackel
Mark Harris
Robert Hiscox
Frank Krikhaar
Yisi Li
Xi Liu and Yi Luo
George Loudon
Sarah Miller
Jon and Amanda Moore
Heike Moras
Farshid Moussavi
Bozena and William Nelhams
Maureen Paley
Dominic Palfreyman
Jasmin Pelham
Darryl de Prez and Victoria Thomas
Alice Rawsthorn
Bianca Roden
Alex Sainsbury and Elinor Jansz
Cherrill and Ian Scheer
Matthew Slotover and Emily King
Karen and Mark Smith
Bina and Philippe von Stauffenberg
Mr and Mrs Christoph Trestler
Samantha Wainstein
Yusi Xiong
Lian Zhang
Sharon Zhu
and those who wish to remain anonymous

**Whitechapel Gallery First Futures**
Cedric Bardawil
Crane Kalman Gallery
Isabel Elson
Olimpia Isidori
Marie Krauss
Dominika Kulczyk
Petra Kwan
Di Luo
Supriya Menon
Victoria Mikhelson
Indi Oliver
Katherine Proudlove
Maria-Cruz Rashidian
Eugenio Re Rebaudengo
Henrietta Shields
Tammy Smulders
Joe Start
Nayrouz Tatanaki
Elisabeth von Schwarzkopf
Vanessa Vainio
Olga van Vuuren
and those who wish to remain anonymous

We remain grateful for the ongoing support of Whitechapel Gallery Members.

Whitechapel Gallery is proud to be a National Portfolio Organisation of Arts Council England.

Supported using public funding by ARTS COUNCIL ENGLAND

Published on the occasion of the exhibition:

**Radical Figures:
Painting in the New Millennium**

Whitechapel Gallery, London
6 February–10 May 2020

**Exhibition**
Chief Curator: Lydia Yee
Assistant Curators: Cameron Foote and Candy Stobbs
Head of Exhibition Design and Production: Christopher Aldgate
Gallery Manager: Ryszard Lewandowski

**Publication**
Editors: Lydia Yee, Cameron Foote and Candy Stobbs
Head of Publications: Francesca Vinter
Copy Editor: Melissa Larner
Designer: Peter Willberg
Colour reproduction: DL Imaging, London
Printer: optimal media, Germany

ISBN 978-0-85488-283-0

First published 2020 by Whitechapel Gallery, London
© 2020 Whitechapel Gallery and the authors

All rights reserved. No part of this book may be reproduced or transmitted in any form or by any means, electronic or mechanical, including photocopying, recording or any other information storage or retrieval system, without prior permission in writing from the publisher.

The editor and publisher gratefully acknowledge the permission granted to reproduce the copyright material in this book. Every effort has been made to trace copyright holders and to obtain their permission for the use of copyright material. The publisher apologises for any errors or omissions and would be grateful if notified of any corrections that should be incorporated in future reprints or editions of this book.

A catalogue record for this book is available from the British Library

Whitechapel Gallery
77–82 Whitechapel High Street
London, E1 7QX
whitechapelgallery.org

Distributed outside the United States and Canada by
Thames & Hudson
181a High Holborn
London, WC1V 7QX
Tel: +44 (0) 20 7845 5000
sales@thameshudson.co.uk

Distributed in the United States and Canada by
ARTBOOK | D.A.P.
75 Broad Street, Suite 630
New York, N.Y. 10004
Tel: (212) 627-1999

Whitechapel Gallery